harlan ellison

edgeworks.2

stalking the nightmare

ACKNOWLEDGMENTS

The Author, besotted with humility, would like to take this opportunity to thank all the *little* people whose support and assistance made his climb to the top possible: Lemuel Gulliver; the girl in the Golden Atom; Billy Barty; General Tom Thumb; the Ty-D-Bol man; Barbie & Ken; Manners the Butler; Dr. Miguelito Loveless; Poppin' Fresh, the Pillsbury Dough Boy; the representatives of the Lollipop Guild; Speedy Alka-Seltzer; Henri de Toulouse-Lautrec; Snap, Crackle & Pop; Scott Carey, the Incredible Shrinking Man; Chip'n'Dale; Tattoo; and all the gang over at Dr. Cyclops's.

But seriously, folks.

I couldn't'a done it widdout'cha, friends:

Diana Adkins, Sid Altus, Isaac Asimov; Richard Fontaine, Dale Hardman, Bobbie J. Kroman and Willie Wilson of B. Dalton Bookstores; Greg Bear, Alex Berman, Arthur Bernhard, Ben Bova, Mayer Alan Brenner, Jeff Bridges, Edward W. Bryant, Jr.; Sharon Buck, Mark Carlton, Alan Chudnow, (Ms.) Marty Clark, Jon Clarke, Ed Coffey, Catherine Crowell; Arthur Byron Cover, Lydia Marano and Linda Mayfield of the *Dangerous Visions Bookstore* in Sherman Oaks, California; Buzz Dixon, Clint Eastwood, Audrey and Edward L. Ferman, Charles Garcia, Mel Gilden, Joanne Gutreimen, Burt Handelsman, C.E.; James Haralson, Joe L. Hensley, Walter Hill, Richard Hoagland, Michael Hodel, Nancy Hodel, Terry Hodel, Stephen King, Steve Kirk, T.E.D. Klein, Cele Goldsmith Lalli, Gil Lamont, Shelley Levinson, Barry R. Levin, Tim Lewis; Jane Mackenzie in a class by herself; Elinor Mavor, Jon R. McKenzie, Larry McMurtry, Joyce Muskat, Sharon O'Hara, Frank Olynyk, Jerry Pournelle, Eric Protter, John Ratner, Mary Riordon, Jeff Rubenstein, Bonnie Sue Russell, Jared Rutter; John Sack, W.W. Scott, Larry T. Shaw, Robert Silverberg, Judith Sims, Tad Stones, William Stout, Genadie Sverlow, Leslie Kay Swigart, the impossible-to-locate Mike Taylor; Emily Boxer and Tom Brokaw and the late Jessica Savitch of the *NBC Today Show*; Dan Turner, (Ms.) Randall Warner, and my former editor at *Future Life*, the long suffering Bob Woods.

For each and all of you, a blessing of the 18th Egyptian dynasty: "God be between you and harm in all the empty places you walk."

STALKING THE NIGHTMARE: CONTENTS

THIS BOOK IS FOR
(MS.) MARTY CLARK,
WHO DID THE
WORK, SMILING

I don't have much patience with the facts, and any writer is a congenital liar to begin with or he wouldn't take up writing…I write to say No to death…an artist is a creature driven by demons. He don't usually know why they chose him and he's usually too busy to wonder why…

—**WILLIAM FAULKNER**

FOREWORD
STEPHEN KING

It drives my wife crazy, and I'm sorry it does, but I can't really help it.

All the little sayings and homilies.

Such as: There's a heartbeat in every potato; you need that like a hen needs a flag; I'd trust him about as far as I could sling a piano; use it up, wear it out, do it in, or do without; you'll never be hung for your beauty; fools' names, and their faces, are often seen in public places.

I could go on and on. I got a million of 'em. I got them all from my mother, who got them all from *her* mother. Little kernels of wisdom. Cosmic fortune-cookies, if you like.

They drive my wife absolutely BUGFUCK.

"But honey," I'll say in my best placatory voice (I'm a very placatory fellow, when I'm not writing about vampires and psychotic killers), "there's a lot of truth in those sayings. There really is a heart-beat in every potato. The proof of the pudding really is in the eating. And handsome really is as —" But I can see that it would be foolish to continue. My wife, who can be extremely rude when it serves her purpose, is pretending to throw up. My four-year-old son walks in from the shower, naked, dripping water all over the floor and the bed (*my* side of the bed, of course), and also begins to make throwing-up noises.

She is obviously teaching him to hate me and revile me. It's probably all Oedipal and sexual and neo-Jungian and dirty as hell.

But I have the last laugh.

Two days later, while this self-same kid is debating which card to throw away in a hot game of Crazy Eights, my nine-year-old son tells him, "Let me look at your hand, Owen. I'll tell you which card to throw away."

Owen looks at him coldly. Calculatingly. Pulls his cards slowly against his chest. And with a humorless grin he says: "Joey, I'd trust you just about as far as I'd spring a piano."

My wife begins to scream and roll around on the floor, foaming, pulling her hair out in great clots, drumming her heels, crying out: "I

WANT A DIVORCE! THIS MAN HAS CORRUPTED MY CHIL-
DREN AND I WANT A FUCKING DIVORCE!"

My heart glows with the warmth of fulfillment (or maybe it's just
acid indigestion). My mother's homilies have slipped into the minds of
yet another generation, just as chemical waste has a way of seeping into
the water table. I think: *Ah-hah-hah-hah! Another triumph for us bog-
cutters! Long live the Irish!*

Another of this wonderful woman's wonderful sayings (I told you —
I got a million of 'em; don't make me prove it) was "Milk always takes
the flavor of what's next to it in the icebox." Not a very useful saying,
you might think, but I suspect it's not only the reason I'm writing this
introduction, but the reason I'm writing it the *way* I'm writing it.

Does it sound like Harlan wrote it?

It does?

That's because I just finished the admirable book which follows. For
the last four days I have been, so to speak, sitting next to Harlan in the
icebox. I am not copying his style; nothing as low as that. I have,
rather, taken a brief *impression* of his style, the way that, when we were
kids, we used to be able to take a brief impression of Beetle Bailey or
Blondie from the Sunday funnies with a piece of Silly Putty (headline
in the *New York Times Book Review:* KING OFFERS EERILY APT
METAPHOR FOR HIS OWN MIND!!).

How do I know this is what has happened? I know because I have
been writing hard for about twenty-five years now — which means (as
Harlan, or Ray Bradbury, or John Crowley, or any other writer worth
his or her salt will tell you) that I have also been *reading* hard. The two
go together. I am always chilled and astonished by the would-be writers
who ask me for advice and admit, quite blithely, that they "don't have
time to read." This is like a guy starting up Mount Everest saying that
he "didn't have time to buy any rope or pitons."

And part of the dues you pay while you're doing this hard reading,
particularly if you start your period of hard writing as a teen-ager (as
most of us did — God knows there are exceptions, but not many), is
that you find yourself writing like whoever you're reading that week.

If you're reading *Red Nails*, your current short story sounds like that old Hyborian Cowboy, Robert E. Howard. If you've been reading *Farewell, My Lovely*, your stuff sounds like Raymond Chandler. You're milk, and you taste like whatever was next to you in the refrigerator that week.

But this is where the metaphor breaks down...or where it ought to. If it doesn't, you're in serious trouble. Because a writer isn't a carton of milk — or at least he or she shouldn't be. Because a writer shouldn't continue to take the flavors of the people he or she is currently reading. Because a writer who doesn't start sounding like himself sooner or later really isn't much of a writer at all, he's a ventriloquist's dummy. But take heart — little by little, that voice usually comes out. It's not easy, and it's not quick (that's one of the reasons that so many people who talk about writing books never do), but there comes a day when you look back on the stuff you wrote when you were seventeen...or twenty-two...or twenty-eight...and say to yourself, *Good God! If I was this bad, how did I ever get any better?*

They don't call that stuff "juvenilia" for nothing, friends'n'neighbors.

The imitativeness shakes out, and we become ourselves again. *But.* One never seems to develop an immunity to some writers...or at least I never have. Their ranks are small, but their influence — at least on this here New England white boy — has been profound. When I go back to them, I can't *not* imitate them. My letters start sounding like them; my short stories; a chunk of whatever novel I'm working on, maybe; even grocery lists.

Lovecraft. Raymond Chandler (and, at second hand, Ross Macdonald and Robert Parker). Dorothy Sayers, who wrote the clearest, most lucid prose of our century. Peter Straub.

And Ellison.

That's really where it hews to the bone, I guess. When you take it right back down home, you come to this: the man is a ferociously talented writer, ferociously in love with the job of writing stories and essays, ferociously dedicated to the craft of it as well as its art — the latter being the part of the job with which writers who have been to college most frequently excuse laziness, sloppiness, cant, and promiscuous self-indulgence.

There are folks in the biz who don't like Harlan much. I don't think I'm telling you anything you don't know; if you know the imprint this book bears, then you probably know enough about speculative fiction to know that. These anti-Harlan folks offer any number of reasons for their dislike, but I believe that a lot of it has to do with that ferocity. Harlan is the sort of guy who makes an ordinary writer feel like a dilettante, and an ordinary liver (i.e., one who lives, not a bodily organ which will develop cirrhosis if you pour too much booze over it) feel like a spinster librarian who once got kissed on the Fourth of July.

Coupled with the ferocity of purpose is a crazed confidence — the confidence of a man who does not just walk wires but runs across them full-tilt-boogie. There are folks who find this trait equally unendearing. People who are afraid don't like people who are brave. People who eat pallidly and politely at the Great Banquet of Life (Chew that fish — there might be a bone in it! Skip the beef — if you eat enough of it, you get cancer of the bowel! No eggs — cholesterol! Heart attacks! Eat the carrots. Eat the carrots. They're safe. Boring, but safe.) resent people who dash wildly up and down, trying some of this, scarfing up some of that, swallowing something really *gruesome* and barfing it back up.

Put another way, Harlan knows now — and has, I would guess, since about 1965 — that if you're gonna talk that talk, you gotta be able to walk that walk; that if you got the flash you better have the cash, and that sooner or later you gotta put up or shut up. He rides the shockwave.

All of this comes through admirably in the man's fiction and essays (as it damn well should; otherwise his impact would die with him), and I think that's the reason I always end up writing like the guy after I've been reading the guy. It's the force of his personality, the sense of Harlan Ellison *as a living person* that's caught in the lines. There are people who don't like that; there are many people who are convinced that Harlan is some sort of trick, like that miniature guillotine that will slice a cigarette in two but leave your finger intact.

Others, who know that few tricksters and literary shysters can hang around for better than twenty-five years, publishing fiction which has steadily broadened its area of inquiry and which has never declined in its energy, know that Harlan is no trick. They may begrudge him that apparently inexhaustible energy, or resent his *chutzpah*, or fear his refusal to suffer fools (of some people it is said they will not suffer fools gladly; Harlan does not suffer them at all), but they know it isn't a trick.

The book which follows is a case in point. I'm not going to pre-chew it; if you want someone to chew your food for you, send this book back to the publisher, get a refund, and go buy a few volumes of Cliff's Notes, the mental babyfood of college students everywhere for the last forty years or so. You won't find one on Harlan, and I hope you never will (and speaking of wills, why not put it in yours, Harlan? *"NO FUCKING CLIFF'S NOTES! IF YOU WANT TO KNOW WHAT GOES ON IN DEATHBIRD STORIES, GO READ A COPY, YOU FUCKING MEN-TAL MIDGET!"* God, I sound like Harlan today — don't you think so?). Certainly you won't find a Harlan-Ellison-in-a-nutshell in this introduction.

But I will point out that these stories and essays range from almost Lovecraftian horror ("Final Trophy") to existentialist fantasy ("The Cheese Stands Alone," with its almost talismanic repetition of the phrase "My fine stock") to the riotously funny (take your pick; my own favorite — maybe because it's gifted with a title that even Fredric Brown would have admired — "Djinn, No Chaser") to good old nuts-and-bolts science fiction ("Invulnerable").

The essays have a similar range; Harlan's essay on the Saturn fly-by of the *Voyager* I bird could fit comfortably into an issue of *Atlantic Monthly*, while one can almost see "The 3 Most Important Things in Life" as a stand-up comedy routine (it's a job, by the way, that Harlan knows, having done it for a while in his flaming youth).

Harlan's wit, insight, and energy inform all of these stories and essays. Are they uneven? Yes, of course they are. While I haven't been given the "lawyer's page" — that is, the dates of copyright on each short story and essay, along with where each was previously published — just the Xerox offprints I've been sent suggest that there is also a wide range of time represented in *Stalking the Nightmare*. Different typefaces and different return addresses tell part of the tale: the evolution in style tells part of it; the growth of confidence and ambition tells much more of it.

But even the earliest stories bear the unmistakable mark of Ellison. Take, for example, "Invulnerable," one of my favorite stories in the present collection — in fact, I guess I'd go a step further (God hates a coward, right?) and say it's *the* favorite, mostly because of the original way Harlan handles a very old idea — here is Superman and Krypto the Wonder Dog for thinking adults. Exactly how old is the tale? Without the lawyer's page it's impossible to tell, but it's possible to don the old deerstalker hat and make a couple of Sherlock Holmes-type deductions just the same. First, "Invulnerable" was originally published in *Super-Science Fiction*, and the illustration (just a hasty pen-and-ink; you're not missing a thing) is by Emsh, whose work I haven't seen in years. So, still wearing the deerstalker hat, I'd guess...maybe 1957. How far off am I?

Take a look at the lawyer's page, if you want. If it's more than five years either way, you're welcome to a good horselaugh at my expense.*

So there's a certain amount of dating in the story; it doesn't just

---

* Readers of the above-entered praise, seeking in vain for the story "Invulnerable" (published in the April, 1957 issue of *Super-Science Fiction* — you get the Mad Hound of the Moors award for deductive logic, Steve), will be confused, bemused and even dismayed — as will Stephen King — to find the work absent from this book. I suppose some sort of explanation is in order. It goes like so: "Invulnerable" was one of the original selections included in the twenty tales slated for this collection. It was among the tearsheeted stories sent to Steve prior to final editing, so he could write his Foreword in a leisurely fashion. Subsequently, when I went back over the stories and read them more closely, I realized some of the older tales desperately needed extensive revision, updating, smoothing and rethinking. One of these stories was "Invulnerable." I had forgotten that Steve mentioned it so prominently in his essay. The qualities admired by Steve are definitely present in the story, but the quality embodied in Steve's remark that "there's a certain amount of dating" was too great to allow to pass untended. Yet to leach out that dated aspect would have meant virtually writing a new story. I decided not to do it. I started revising the original manuscript, written very early in my career, and realized after three pages that the job was akin to rebuilding an edifice that had been burned to the ground, from bottom up. Instead of doing that, I decided to include a recent story, "Grail," at twice or three times the length. So Stephen King has whetted your appetite for a "lost" story, one that I may some day rewrite and update completely. But search not for "Invulnerable" in these pages. It ain't here.

Harlan Ellison

happen to the *best* of us, it happens to *all* of us. And yet, even 'way back then, in those fabled Old Days when there was such an artist as Emsh and such an organ as *Super-Science Fiction*, we find Harlan Ellison's true voice — clear in tone, dark in consideration. This was the era when science fiction's really big guns — guys like Robert A. Heinlein, for instance — were touting space exploration as The Great Panacea for All Mankind, The Last Frontier, and The Solution to Just About Everything. There's a certain amount of that in "Invulnerable" (but then, why not? I suspect there's a certain amount of that wistful fairy-tale still in Harlan's soul…and mine…and maybe in yours, too — read "Saturn, November 11th," and see how you react), but Harlan also sounds the horn of the skeptic, loud and clear.

> Forstner was waiting. He was surrounded by the top brass. The place was acrawl with guards; guards on the guards; and guards to guard the guards' guards. The same old story. It wasn't as noble an endeavor as they would have had me believe.
> *It was an arms race, an attempt for superiority of space before someone else got there…*

Yeah, it was an arms race. We all know that…now. But to have said it back in the days when Good Old General Ike was still the top hand in the old Free World Corral (and let's not forget his chief ramrod, good old Tricky Dick Nixon — I know we'd like to, but maybe we'd better not), when Reddy Kilowatt was supposed to be our friend and nuclear power was going to solve all of our energy problems, back when the only two stated reasons we had for getting Up There were to beat the Russians and to study the sun's corona for the International Geophysical Year (which every subscriber to *My Weekly Reader* knew as IGY)…to have had such a dark thought back in those days — and about *us* as well as *them* — well, that was tantamount to treason. It's a little amazing that Harlan got into print…unless you know Harlan, of course. And it's *damn* fine to have it here, preserved between the boards of one of this admirable book.

But I promised not to chew your food for you, didn't I?

So I'll get out of here now. Harlan's going to come along very soon, grab you by the earlobe, and drag you off to a dozen different worlds. You're going to be glad you went, I promise you (and you may be a little bit surprised to find you've made it back alive).

Just one final comment, and then I promise to go quietly: there's no significant correlation between the quality of a writer's writing and the quality of that same writer's personality. When I tell you that reading Harlan is overwhelming enough to start me writing like the guy — taking his flavor as my mother said milk takes the flavor of whatever you put it next to in the icebox — I am speaking of ability, not personality.

Harlan Ellison's personality is every bit as striking as his prose style, and this makes the man a pleasure to dine with, to visit, or to enter-tain. But let's tell the gut-level, bottom-line truth. Most of you reading this are never going to eat a meal with Harlan, visit him in his home, or be visited by him. He gives of himself in a way that is profligate, almost dangerous — as does any writer worth his salt. He'll tell you the truth in a manner which is sometimes infuriating (see "The Hour That Stretches" or "!!!The!!Teddy!Crazy!!Show!!!" in this volume, or the classic short story "Croatoan," where Harlan managed to accomplish the mind-numbing feat of simultaneously pissing off the right-to-lifers and the women's liberationists) and always entertaining...but don't confuse these things with the man, do not assume that the work *is* the man. And ask yourself this: why in Christ's name would you want to make *any* assumption about the man on the basis of his work?

I for one am sick unto death with the cult of personality in America — with the assumption that I should eat Famous Amos cookies because the dude is black and the dude is cool, that I should buy an Andy Warhol print because *People* magazine says he only owns two shirts and two pairs of shoes, that I should go to this movie because *Us* says the director has given up cocaine or that one because Rona Barrett says the director has recently taken it up. I am sick of being told to buy books because their writers are great cocksmen or heroic gays or because Norman Mailer got them sprung from jail.

It doesn't last, friends'n'neighbors.

The cult of celebrity is cogitative shit running through the bowel of the intellect.

For whatever it's worth, Harlan Ellison is a great man: a fast friend, a supportive critic, a ferocious enemy of the false and the foolish, maniacally funny, perhaps insecure (I'm not sure what to make of a man who doesn't smoke or drink and who still has such crazed acid indigestion), but above all else, brave and true. If I knew I was going to be in a strange city without all the magical *gris-gris* of the late 20th century — Amex Card, MasterCard, Visa Card, Blue Cross card, driver's license, Avis Wizard Number, Social Security number — and if I further knew I was going to have a severe myocardial infarction, and if I could pick one person in all the world to be with me at the moment I felt the hacksaw blade run down my left arm and the sledgehammer hit me on the left tit, that person would be Harlan Ellison. Not my wife, not my agent, not my editor, my accountant, my lawyer. It would be Harlan, because if anyone would see to it that I was going to have a fighting chance, it would be Harlan. Harlan would go running through hospital corridors with my body in his arms, commandeering stretchers, I.C. support units, O.R.s, and of course, World Famous Cardiologists. And if some admitting nurse happened to ask him about my Blue Cross/Blue Shield number, Harlan would probably bite his or her head off with a single chomp.

And do you know what?

It doesn't matter a damn.

Because time flies, friends. *Tempus* just keeps *fugit*-ing right along. And as 1982 becomes 1992 becomes 2022 becomes 2222, no one is going to care that Ellison once wrote stories in bookshop windows, or drove an old Camaro with cheerful, adroit, scary, leadfooted abandon, or that Stephen King ("Who's that, Tonto?" "Me don't know for sure, *Kemo sabe*, but him write just like Harlan Ellison.") once nominated him The Man I Would Most Like to Have With Me in a Strange City When My Ventricles Go on Holiday. Because by 2222, the people reading fiction (always assuming there are any people *left* in 2222, ha-ha) aren't going to have a *hope* of taking dinner with Harlan, or shooting a rack of eight-ball with him, or listening to him hold forth on the subject of why Ronald Reagan would be a better President if he 1) lit a firecracker, 2) put the firecracker between his teeth, and 3) jammed his head up his ass. By 2222, Harlan will have put on his boogie shoes and shuffled off to whatever Something or Nothing awaits us beyond this Vale of Quarter Pounders.

If the cult of celebrity sucks (and take your Uncle Stevie's word for it; it does indeed suck that fabled Hairy Bird), it sucks because it's as disposable as a Handi-wipe or a Glad Bag or the latest record by the latest Group of the Moment. Andy Warhol ushered in the celebrity era by proclaiming that, in the future, everyone would be famous for fifteen minutes. But fifteen minutes isn't a very long time; while any number of you guys and gals out there may have read the science fiction of H.G. Wells or the mysteries of Wilkie Collins, how many of you have read such big bestsellers of thirty plus years ago as *Leave Her to Heaven, Forever Amber,* or *Peyton Place?*

You don't make it over the long haul on the basis of your personality. Fifteen years after the funny guys and the dynamic guys and the spellbinders croak, nobody remembers who the fuck they were.

Luckily, Harlan Ellison has got it both ways — but don't concern yourself with the personality. Instead, dig into the collection which follows. There's something better, more lasting, and *much* more important than personality going on here: you've got a good, informed writer working well over a span of years, learning, spinning tales, laying in the needle, doing handstands and splits and pratfalls...entertaining you goddammit! Everything else put aside, is *anything* better than that? I don't think so. And so I'll just close by saying it for you:

Thank you, Harlan. Thank you, man.

Stephen King
Bangor, Maine
1982

INTRODUCTION
Quiet Lies the Locust Tells

She thinks we were all killed when they made the Great Sweep, but I escaped in the mud.

I was there when the first dreams came off the assembly line. I was there when the corrupted visions that had congealed in the vats were pincered up and hosed off and carried down the line to be dropped onto the rolling belts. I was there when the first workmen dropped their faceplates and turned on their welding torches. I was there when they began welding the foul things into their armor, when they began soldering the antennae, bolting on the wheels, pouring in the eye-socket jelly. I was there when they turned the juice on them and I was there when the things began to twitch.

No wonder She wanted all of us dead. Witnesses to their birth, to their construction, to their release into the air — not good. The myrmidons were loosed on the Great Sweep.

I think I am the last one left alive. The last one who can create dreams and not nightmares. I am the locust.

The reversal is sweet. What we always knew to be nightmares — the empty lives, the twisted language, the squeezing of the soul — they now call dreams. What we looked high to see as dreams — silliness, castles in the sky, breathing deeply on windy afternoons — She has commanded be termed nightmares, lies. I am the locust. I tell quiet lies. Called nightmares. That are truly fine dreams.

I swam in the mud till I was the color of the land. And made my escape. Overhead I saw the corrupted things soaring off to spread their rigor of obedience and fear and hatred. For many days I lay there, hidden, turning on my back for the rain, trapping small fish and insects for my food. Finally, when the Great Sweep was done and all my brothers and sisters were dead or locked away in madhouses, I went to the forest.

But like the locust that the Middle Ages saw as the symbol of passion, I will live forever. I will tell my quiet lies and no matter how blindly the people follow their instructions, in every generation there will be a hundred, perhaps a thousand, if chance is with them even a hundred thousand, who will keep the quiet lies alive. To be told late at night to the children. With their bright eyes they will pay attention, and the dreams that have been outlawed, now called nightmares, will take root and spread.

And fifty years from now, a hundred years from now, when She thinks all courage has been drained out of the people, the children of the locust will be retelling the quiet lies. We will never be eradicated. Decimated, yes, but still we survive.

Because in us lives the noblest part of the human experiment. The ability to dream.

I've watched, since the Great Sweep. Oh, what wonders She has given them in place of what they had. They have no real freedom, they have no genuine control of their lives, their days and nights are set down for them though they don't even perceive it that way. But She has given them endless flickering images on screens: surrogate dreams (the real lies, the true nightmares) that make them laugh because they hear laughter behind the flickering images, and scenes of death and destruction that they think are representations of the real world that She commands be termed "news." She has given them more and greater sporting events, young men and women hurling themselves at each other in meaningless contests She tells them represent survival in microcosm. She has given them fashions that obsess them — though they do not understand that the fashions are one more way of making them facsimiles of each other. She has given them acts of government that unify them into hive groups, in the name of removing responsibility from their daily lives. She has taken control completely, and now they believe that the grandest role they can play is that of cog in the machine of Her design. In truth, what they have become are prisoners of their own lives.

All that stands between them and the shambling walk of the zombie are the quiet lies the locust tells.

Because I keep on the move, I have come to miss two aspects of human congress more than all the others combined. Love and friendship. Before the Great Sweep I never had the time or the perseverance to discover what raids love can make on the boredom of silent days spent alone. Nights are worse, of course.

I long to share confidences with a friend. But because I have placed myself outside the limits of their society, I fear striking up acquaintances. Who would be my friend, in any event? I live in the last of the forests and I sleep in caves. The countryside is best for me. The cities are like the surface of the sun: great flares blast off the concrete; there are no places to hide, no cool corners in which to wait. Geomagnetic storms, sunspot occurrences, enormous air masses. I am wary of the cities. She rules without mercy there. And the people do not touch each other. Like those who are terribly sunscorched they avoid each other, passing in silence but with their teeth bared.

A day's walk from the forest, there is a small town. I began going to the town innocently, making myself known by showing only that edge of myself that would not alarm anyone. And after a time I came to know a small group of young people who enjoyed hearing my stories.

Now they come to the small cave where I sit cross-legged. They do not tell their parents where they're going. I think they gather roots and herbs as a cover for the afternoons in which they sit around me and I tell them of transcending destiny, of the three most important things in life, of true love and of my travels. They lie about having gone on many picnics. And each time they bring one of their friends who can be trusted — one of the ones with that special sly, impish smile that tells me the flame burns steadily. Inside. Where She cannot snuff it out. Not yet. (I do not believe in Gods, but I ask God never to let Her discover a way of reading the inside of the people. If She ever finds a way to probe and drain the heart, or the head, then all hope will be lost.)

The young people surprised me. The last time they came, they brought a much older woman to the cave. She was in that stretch of life somewhere between seventy and the close of business. For an instant I cursed their enthusiasm. It had blurred their judgment. Now I would have to run again and find a far place to begin again.

But the sly smile was there on her wrinkled face as she stooped to enter the cave. Firelight caught my wary expression and as she entered, she drew a pinback button from the pocket of her padded jacket and clipped it on the left breast. It read: *Étonne-moi!*

She grinned at me as she sat down on the other side of the fire. "I read French imperfectly," I said.

"Diaghilev to Jean Cocteau in 1909," she answered. *"Astonish me!"*

I laughed, as the children settled down around us. How long had this woman kept her badge of defiance secret? Surely since the Great Sweep. Fear dissolved. The old woman was not one of Her subjects. This dear old woman, corpulent and cat-eyed, with pain in her joints, was determined to live every moment with sanctification until the end. So I spun spiderwebs about looking for true love, about transcending destiny, about the three most important things in life, about times before the Great Sweep, and about just desserts.

"You're a Calvinist," she said. "Irreducible morality." But she said it with humor, and I shrugged, feeling embarrassed. "I don't think you really like shouldering the burden, even if you do it."

"You're right," I answered. "I would gladly lay it down; if I knew others would carry it."

She sighed. "We do, friend. We do."

I learned later that She had sent myrmidons against the old woman and her brother; and they were killed. They had tried to lead a strike. No one joined them and they were caught out naked in the daylight. And were killed. The children told me. The terrible sight of it had not been wasted on them. They were angry when they told me.

I loved her, that old woman. She was the locust.

I heard the sound of the locust from the hills one night. It was a man with an alto saxophone playing all alone, long after midnight. He was playing the kind of music I haven't heard in years. It was jazz. But it was the kind of sky-piercing jazz that long ago I had resisted, wondering if it was jazz at all. It had been rooted in the old order of what "Negroes" were lauded for playing, but as intense as steel, passionately soaring, the breaker of the circle. It had manifested radical inclinations; and I had refused to hear it.

But hearing it now, a solitary corner of one man's loneliness, afloat in the night, I longed to hear more. To return in time to that place where the music had been new, and I swore if the miracle of transport could be done, I would listen without insisting memory be served. I would hear it without narrow judgments. The locust played "Green Dolphin Street" and "Since I Fell For You." I remembered the name of the man who had played those tunes, years before the Great Sweep. His name had been Eric Dolphy, and I wished he would come down out of the far hills and travel with me.

I miss friendship. I miss music. What She gives them now, what She has led them to believe they want to hear, is as empty of human concern or enrichment as the fury of a thunderstorm.

It made me so sad, hearing him up there against the sooty night sky in which no stars had shone for a time beyond my recollection; a sky through which Her myrmidons flew to find old women and their brothers; a sky that would soon enough drop on the man with the horn. So sad I packed my few belongings in the rucksack…and I went away from the forest; from the cave, from the hills, and from the children. They would either hoard the quiet lies the locust had told, against the day when such tales would be needed, or they would follow their parents into the mouth of the machine she had oiled and set running.

Even I grow tired.

I warned them not to follow me. I am not the Pied Piper. They said, "We'll go with you. We can trust you." And I said, "Where I go there is no following. Where I go there is no mother and no father; no safe days and no safe nights; where I go, I go alone, because I travel fast." But they followed. They hung back and I threw stones at them, then ran as fast as I could to lose them. But they kept coming. Three of them. Two boys and a girl. I wouldn't let them sit with me when I rested, and they stayed out of range and yelled through the forest to me.

"Our parents stood by and watched. They didn't lift a hand. When those things fell out of the sky and took the old woman and her brother, they didn't do a thing. When they set fire to them, no one tried to stop them. We can't live with people like that. You told us what that means."

I tried not to listen. I am not their leader. I am just the locust. I cannot even lead myself. I cannot do what they think must be done. All I can do is tell them quiet lies.

That isn't enough.

Some among them have to take the strength upon themselves. Some among them must rise up from their midst to lift the real burden. *Must I do all the work?*

I can tell them of the night of black glass, and of the hour that stretches, and of the visionary...but I am no one's hero.

I waited behind a tree and when they passed I stepped out and explained my limitations, the amount of burden I was prepared to carry. They smiled the impish smiles and said I was better than that; I could beat off myrmidons with my bare hands; I was their inspiration. I slapped one of the boys. He took it and looked hurt, but they wouldn't leave me.

A man hides in the far hills and plays slow soft melodies. Nothing more is asked of him. Until he goes to the final sleep. That is a peace greatly to be desired. Why can't they hear the message? Do any of them really listen?

I struck out again and let them fend for themselves.

And when She sensed our movement, because there were four of us, unauthorized, moving at random, She sent the nightmares on their night flight, like bats that see in the dark, and they fell upon us. And I did not stay to help them. In the chaos I escaped, went into the ground and hid. I tried not to think about the sounds the children made. And finally there was silence.

There are no leaders. There are only terrified souls trying to live till the day when She loses control and the machine turns on Her. Until that day, unless I find a distant hill where the final sleep will free me, I will tell my quiet lies. There is nothing more to it than that.

There are no heroes of my generation. That role has yet to be filled. For my part, I am just the locust.

I speak of dreams called nightmares. No more should be expected, at risk of driving the reflection so deep into the mirror it will never emerge again.

The ability to dream is all I have to give. That is my responsibility; that is my burden. And even I grow tired.

Harlan Ellison
Los Angeles
18 February 1982

| GRAIL

Years later, when he was well into young adulthood, Christopher Caperton wrote about it in the journal he had begun to keep when he turned twenty-one. The entry had everything to do with the incident, though he had totally forgotten it.

What he wrote was this: *The great tragedy of my life is that in my search for the Holy Grail everyone calls True Love, I see myself as Zorro, a romantic and mysterious highwayman — and the women I desire see me as Porky Pig.*

The incident lost to memory that informed his observation had taken place fourteen years earlier, in 1953 when he was thirteen years old.

During a Halloween party from which chaperoning adults had been banished, it was suggested that the boys and girls play a kissing game called "flashlight." All the lights were turned off, everyone paired up, and one couple held a flashlight. If you were caught kissing when the flashlight was turned on you, then it became your turn to hold and flash while the others had free rein to neck and fondle in the dark.

Because he was shy, Christopher volunteered to be the first holder of the light. Because he was shy, and because he had, as usual, been paired with Jean Kettner who adored him but whom he could not find it within himself even to like. Across the room the most beautiful girl he had ever seen, the improbably named Briony Catling, sat on the lap of Danny Shipley, who played baseball and had blond, wavy hair.

3

Chris Caperton ached for Briony Catling with an intensity that gave him cramps.

Another rule of the game was that if the wielder of the flashlight caught another couple "doing it," he or she could demand a switch in partners.

Because he was shy, because he was paired with Jean Kettner, and because he knew exactly where he would shine the flashlight after allowing several minutes to pass in which the couples could become too interested in kissing to prepare themselves.

He caught Briony and Danny Shipley and demanded a switch. Of the four involved in the transaction, only Christopher felt elation. Briony Catling had no interest in Christopher Caperton. She ached for Danny Shipley with an intensity that gave her cramps.

But they switched, and when the light went out Christopher hugged Briony frantically and shoved his face toward hers. The kiss splatted somewhere between her nose and her mouth.

She blew out air, made a yuchhing sound, swiped at the slaver on her upper lip, and jumped off his lap.

Fourteen years later the shame and the pain still lurked in his unconscious like pariahs.

Briony Catling had not been his first great love. That had been Miss O'Hara in the third grade, who had shone down on him at the age of eight like the field lights at a night baseball game. He had loved her purely and with all his heart; and the present he gave her at the Christmas party held by his home room had cost him all the money he'd made raking leaves through that autumn. She had been embarrassed and had kissed his cheek lightly, never knowing it caused his first erection.

After Miss O'Hara, it had been the actress Helen Gahagan in the 1935 version of *She*, which he saw at the Utopia Theater on a re-release double-bill. When he belatedly went to see *Snow White and the Seven Dwarfs* on one of its periodic reissues, he recognized at once that Disney had appropriated the garb and look of Helen Gahagan as She-Who-Must-Be-Obeyed for the character of the wicked Queen

Grimhilde; and when he learned of the foul campaign Richard Nixon had waged against her in the 1950 Senatorial race, when she had become Helen Gahagan Douglas, he vowed a revenge that only manifested itself when he twice voted for Nixon's presidential opponents.

The year before Briony Catling filled him with self-loathing, he fell desperately in love with the Swedish actress Marta Toren. He watched her vamping Dick Powell in *Rogue's Regiment* on the *Late Late Show* and made a point of being in the audience the night *Paris Express* with Claude Rains opened. Miss O'Hara, Helen Gahagan and even Briony Catling paled by comparison. She was precisely and exactly the embodiment of True Love in his eyes. Four years later, six months after Christopher had lost his virginity to a young woman who bore only a passing resemblance to Marta Toren, he read in the newspaper that she had died from a rare brain trauma called a subarachnoidal hemorrhage that struck like Jack the Ripper and killed her within forty-eight hours.

He closed himself in his room and tore at his clothes.

In February of 1968, attached to General William Westmoreland's headquarters in Saigon, Capt. Christopher Caperton, age 28, stumbled upon the astonishing fact that True Love, in a physical form, existed. The Tet offensive had begun and Saigon was burning. Had he not had his own assigned jeep and driver, he would not have been able to get around: there was virtually no public transportation and the cyclos and taxis had been commandeered for the wealthy trying to flee. The hospitals were so crowded that only emergency cases were being accepted; patients were sleeping on the floors, jamming the corridors. Coffins lay unburied for days: the gravediggers had gone south. Chris's business was good.

Chris was in the business of helping GI's cope with the anguish of serving in a war they had come to despise.

In business with, and in love with, his lover and business partner, a thirty-nine-year-old Eurasian of French and Thai parentage, Capt. Chris was the main conduit for "Js," "OJs," Binoctal and a luscious black opium from the Laotian poppy fields to America's fighting men in Indochina.

Because their goods — marijuana joints; joints dipped in liquid opium; the French headache killer; and the most potent smoking opium — were superlative goods, Christopher Caperton and Sirilabh Doumic had established a flourishing trade in I and II Corps. And from this enterprise they had managed to bank over a million and a half dollars (converted to Swiss francs) in a numbered Zurich account, despite the crushing overhead and the payoffs to officials of Thieu's provincial government.

And because he was in love in a terrible place, and because he and his love wanted nothing more than to survive, to win release from that terrible place, he felt no guilt about the traffic. There was no self-delusion that he was engaged in humanitarian activities, neither the war nor the drug traffic; what he *did* feel was a sense of keeping busy, of working at something that held light and hope at its conclusion, that without the dope some of his clients would either go mad or turn their rifles on the nearest 1st Lieutenant. But mostly he was in love.

Siri was small and light. He could lift her with one arm to carry her to the bed. Her features were fine and delicate, yet they changed dramatically with each noticeable variation in the light. Monet would have had to do her portrait eighteen times, as he did the Rouen Cathedral, from dawn to sunset, to capture even one expression. She was the daughter of a French attaché in the Bangkok consulate and a young temple dancer Doumic first saw at the Kathin ceremony marking the end of the Buddhist Lent. From her father she inherited a wiliness that kept her alive in street society, from her mother — who had come from Chumphon to the south — a speech filled with musical inflection. How she had come to Saigon ten years before was not something she cared to talk about. But Chris winced every time they made love and his hands brushed the thick scars on her inner thighs.

On that night in February of 1968, they were just sitting down to a dinner of beef satay Siri had made in their apartment in Nguyen Cong Tru Street when a 122 mm shell came across the Saigon River and hit the face of the building opposite Caperton's. The rocket round ripped the building out of the ground like a rotten tooth and threw shrapnel in every direction.

Not the biggest chunk, but big enough, it came straight through the window and tore into Siri's back, taking off most of her left shoulder.

There was no use trying to move her; it was obvious she would never make it down the stairs, much less across the city to the American hospital that had been opened at Tan Son Nhut.

He tried to stanch the flow with a bedspread and all the white tennis socks in his drawer, and miraculously, she lived for almost an hour. In that hour they talked, and in that hour of farewell she gave him the only gift in the world he wanted, the only thing he could not get for himself. She told him how he could find True Love.

"We have talked of it so many times, and I always knew."

He tried to smile. "In a business partnership like ours there shouldn't be any secrets. How else can I trust you?"

Pain convulsed her and she gripped his hand till the bones ground. "We've no time for foolishness, my love. Very soon now you'll be alone again, as you have been so often. I have this one thing I can give you in return for the love you gave me...and it will take some believing on your part."

"Whatever you tell me I'll believe."

Then she instructed him to go to the kitchen and get an empty condiment bottle from the spice rack. When he brought back the bottle labeled chopped coriander leaves, which was empty because they had been unable to get fresh coriander since a Claymore mine had gone off in the central market, she told him he must not argue with her, that he must fill it with her blood. He argued, wasting precious minutes; but finally, filled with a vaguely familiar self-loathing, he did it.

"I have always sought perfection," she said. "Always knowing that one must die to reach perfection, for life is imperfect."

He tried to argue, but she stopped him. Sternly.

"Chris! You *must* listen to me."

He nodded and was silent.

"For each woman there *is* a perfect man; and for each man there *is* a perfect woman. You were not perfect for me, but you were as close to

7

what I sought as I ever found. But I never stopped searching…though my movement was very slow since we met. I should have been content. It's easy to be smart, later.

"But knowing what I knew, that True Love is a real thing, that it can be picked up and turned in the hands, that it can be looked at and understood…that kept me always dissatisfied. As you have been.

"Because somehow, without possessing the knowledge I chanced upon ten years ago, you knew it was real. And now I will tell you how to go about finding it. And that, my dearest, is the best way I can apologize to you for not giving up the search when we met."

Then with her voice fading off and coming back a little less strong each time, she told him of an artifact that had never been described, that had first been unearthed during Evans's excavations of the Palace of Minos at Knossos in 1900.

It was taken from a walled-up niche behind an elaborate fresco painted on a wall of the Corridor of the Procession, and had been hidden there since 2000 B.C. Where it had come from before that time, not even the archeologist who discovered it and smuggled it away from Crete could begin to guess.

He recognized it for what it was the instant the light of his torch fell on it. He disappeared that night and was presumed to have returned to England; but was never seen again. Record of his find was revealed in 1912 during the dying reminiscences of Bessie Chapman, one of 711 survivors of the sinking of the *Titanic* picked up by the *Carpathia*.

Suffering from extreme exposure and seemingly delirious, the immigrant passenger babbled a story heard only by those few *Carpathia* deckhands and ministering survivors who tried to make her last hours easier. Apparently she had been a London doxy who, after an evening of sport with "a real elegant nob, a brick 'e was," actually saw the artifact. She spoke of it with such wonder that when she died it seemed she had passed over having known all there was to know of joy in this life.

One of the deckhands, an Irish stoker named Haggerty, it was later reported, hung about the dying woman and seemed to be paying close attention to her story.

Haggerty jumped ship on the return of the Cunard liner to New York.

Sgt. Michael James Haggerty was killed during the Battle of Ypres, November 9th, 1914. His kit bag, scavenged by a German soldier when the French and British trenches were overrun (it was reported by a survivor who had played possum and had been overlooked in the random bayoneting of corpses), disappeared. Others in Haggerty's company said he slept with the kit bag under his pillow, that it seemed quite heavy, and that he once broke the arm of a messmate who playfully tried to see what the Irishman was carrying in it.

Between 1914 and 1932 the object — while never described — turned up three times: once in the possession of a White Russian nobleman in Sevastopol, twice in the possession of a Dutch aircraft designer, and finally in the possession of a Chicago mobster reputed to have been the man who gunned down Dion O'Banion in his flower shop at 738 North State Street.

In 1932 a man visiting New York for the opening of the Radio City Music Hall just after Christmas, reported to the police who found him lying in an alley on West 51st Street just below Fifth Avenue that he had been mugged and robbed of "the most important and beautiful thing in the world." He was taken to Bellevue Hospital but no matter how diligently he was interrogated, he would not describe the stolen article.

In 1934 it was reputed to be in the private art collection of the German architect Walter Gropius; after Gropius's self-imposed exile from Nazi Germany it was reputed to have passed into the personal collection of Hermann Goering, 1937; in 1941 it was said to be housed with Schweitzer in French Equatorial Africa; in 1946 it was found to be one of the few items not left by Henry Ford at his death to the Ford Foundation.

Its whereabouts were unknown between 1946 and February of 1968. But Siri told Chris, her final love, that there was one sure, dangerous way of finding it. The way she had used originally to learn the hand-to-hand passage of the artifact that was True Love from the Palace of

Minos to its present unknown resting place.

Then she released his hand, realizing she had squeezed it so hard while telling her story that it was as white as unsmoked meerschaum; and she asked him very softly if he would bring her the little cloisonné minaudière he had bought her in Hong Kong.

He gave it to her and she clutched it far more tightly than she had his hand. Because it was a minute later, and the pain was much worse.

"Do you remember the flea market?"

"Yes," she said, closing her eyes. "And we were holding hands in the crowd; and then you let go and I was swept along; and I thought I'd lost you; and you were gone for fifteen minutes…"

"And you panicked."

"And when I got back to the car there you were."

"You should have seen your face. What relief."

"What love. That was the moment I slowed the never ending search. And you smiled and held out this to me." And she opened her hand where the exquisite blue and gold minaudière lay in her palm, now filmed with moisture.

But her story had worked its magic. He knelt beside her on the floor, lifted her head and the pillows, and cradled them in his lap. "What is the True Love? What does it look like?"

"I don't know. I've never seen it. It cost too much the first time, just to get the information. The actual search has to be done with-out…" and she hesitated as if picking the exact words, the words that would not frighten him, because he was beginning to look more fright-ened than anguished, "…without special assistance."

"But how could you have learned all this?"

"I had an informant. You must seek him out. But go very carefully. It's dangerous, it costs a great deal; care has to be taken…once I didn't care…" She paused. "You'll need my blood."

"An informant…your blood…? I don't…"

"Adrammelech, Supreme Ruler of the Third Hour."

He could not help her. She was dying, he felt the stiffness in his throat, he loved her so much, and she was raving.

"An Angel of the Night, Chris."

Bewildered and suffering, nonetheless he went to the bedroom and fetched the brass-and-silver bound chest she called a bahut. He brought it back to her and she said, "Look at it. Do you see how it opens?"

He studied it but could find no lock or clasp that would open the coffer. "It is made of agalloch, lign aloes, the wood of the aloe, according to the directions of Abramelin. The cross spines are of almond-tree wood. Are you beginning to understand, do you believe me?"

"Siri..."

"You'll need Surgat to open it. Look."

And she touched a symbol, a character cut into the rounded top of the chest:

"He won't harm you. He serves only one purpose: he opens all locks. Take a hair from my head...don't argue with me, Chris, do it...please..." And because her voice was now barely a whisper, he did it. And she said, "He'll demand a hair of your head. Don't give it to him. Make him take mine. And this is what you say to invoke his presence..."

In her last minutes she went over it with him till he realized she was serious, that she was not delirious, that he ought to write it down. So he transcribed her words exactly.

"Once you get the bahut opened, all the rest will be clear. Just be careful, Chris. It's all I have to give you, so make the best of it." Her eyes were half-closed and now she opened them completely, with effort, and looked at him.

"Why are you angry with me?"

He looked away.

"I can't help it that I'm dying, dear. I'm sorry, but that's what's happening. You'll just have to forgive me and do the best you can."

Then she closed her eyes and her hand opened and the cloisonné herb container fell to the carpet; and he was alone.

He spoke to her, though he was alone. "I didn't love you enough. If I'd loved you more it wouldn't have happened."

It's easy to be smart, later.

By the time he was twenty-five, Chris had read everything he could find on the arcane subject of love. He had read Virgil and Rabelais, Ovid and Liu Hsiao-Wei, Plato's *Symposium* and all the Neoplatonists, Montaigne, and Johannes Secundus; he had read everything by the English poets from the anonymous lyrics of the 13th and 15th centuries through Rolle, Lydgate, Wyatt, Sidney, Campion, Shakespeare, Jonson, Donne, Marvell, Herrick, Suckling, Lovelace, Blake, Burns, Lord Byron, Percy Shelley, Keats, Tennyson, Robert Browning and Emily Brontë; he had read as many translations as existed of the Sanskrit *Kama Sutra* and the *Anangaranga*, which led him to the Persians; he read *The Perfumed Garden* of the Sheik Nefzawi, the *Beharistan* of Jami and the *Gulistan* of Sa-Di, the anonymously-written *Ta'dib ul-Niszvan* and the *Zenan Nahmeh* of Fazil Bey, which led him to seven Arabic handbooks of sex, which he quickly put aside: sex was not the issue, he understood that as well as anyone needs to. Understood it well enough to write in his journal:

I was making love to Connie Halban when her husband Paul came back unexpectedly from a business trip. When he saw us he began crying. It was the most awful thing I'd ever stood witness to. I was reminded of Ixion, tied to a turning wheel in Hades as punishment for making love to Zeus's wife, Hera. I'll never touch another married woman. It simply isn't worth the torture and guilt.

And so he was able to avoid all the texts that dealt solely with physical love in its seemingly endless permutations. He made no value judgments; he understood early on that everyone sought True Love in often inarticulate ways they often did not, themselves, understand, but his was an idealized, traditional concept of what True Love was, and his search for the grail need not be sidetracked or slowed by excursions into those special places.

He read Waley's translation of *The Chin P-ing Mei* and everything even remotely pertinent by Freud; he sought out *La Fleur Lascivie Orientale* and the even rarer English translation of *Contes Licencieux de Constantinople et de l'Asie Mineure*; he dipped into the memoirs of Clara Bow, Charles II, Charlie Chaplin, Isadora Duncan, Marie Duplessis, Lola Montez and George Sand; he read novelists — Moravia, Gorky, Maupassant, Roth, Cheever and Brossard — but found they knew even less than he.

He absorbed the thoughts of the aphorists, and believed every utterance: Balzac: "True love is eternal, infinite, and always like itself. It is equal and pure, without violent demonstrations: it is seen with white hairs and is always young in the heart."; Molière: "Reason is not what directs love."; Terence: "It is possible that a man can be so changed by love as hardly to be recognized as the same person."; Voltaire: "Love is a canvas furnished by Nature and embroidered by imagination."; La Rochefoucauld: "When we are in love, we often doubt what we most believe."

Yet even nodding his agreement with every contradictory image and representation of love — seen as Nature, God, a bird on the wing, sex, vanity — he knew they had perceived only the barest edge of what True Love was. Not Kierkegaard or Bacon or Goethe or Nietzsche, for all their insight, for all their wisdom, had any better idea of what True Love looked like than the commonest day-laborer.

The *Song of Solomon* spurred him on, but did not indicate the proper route to discovery.

He found the main path on that night in February of 1968. But once found, he was too frightened to set foot upon it.

Surgat, a subordinate spirit to Sargatanas who, in the Descending Hierarchy from Lucifer to Lucifuge Rofacale, opens all locks, came when Chris Caperton summoned him. He was too insignificant a demon to refuse, no matter how ineptly couched the invocation. But he was less than cooperative.

Chris used Siri's blood to draw the pentagram of Solomon on the floor. He didn't think about what he was doing…that he was dipping his finger in the blood of the woman who lay covered with a sheet on the sofa…that he had to do it repeatedly because it was getting thick…that he had been warned all ten sides of the five-pointed star enclosed in a circle must be without break…he just did it. He did not cry. He just did it.

Then he set candles at the five points and lighted them. Every apartment in Saigon in those days had a supply of candles.

Then he stood in the exact center of the runes and lines and read from the dictation he had taken. Siri had assured him if he stayed within the pentagram he would be safe, that Surgat only opened locks and was not really powerful enough to cause him trouble…if he kept his wits about him.

The words were contained in the *Grimorium Verum* and Siri had said they need not be spoken precisely, nor need Chris worry about having done the special cleansing necessary when summoning the more powerful Field Marshals of Lucifer's Infernal Legions.

He read the words. "I conjure thee, Surgat, by the great living God, the Sovereign Creator of all things, to appear under a comely human form, without noise and without terror, to answer truly unto all questions that I shall ask thee. Hereunto I conjure thee by the virtue of these Holy and Sacred Names. O Surmy ✠ Delmusan ✠ Atalsloym ✠ Charusihoa ✠ Melany ✠ Liamintho ✠ Colehon ✠ Paron ✠ Madoin ✠ Merloy ✠ Bulerator ✠ Donmeo ✠ Hone ✠ Peloym ✠ Ibasil ✠ Meon." And on and on, eighteen more names, concluding with, "Come, therefore, quickly and peaceably, by the Names Adonai, Elohim, Tetragrammaton! *Come!*"

From across the Saigon River he could hear the sound of the city's rockets, flattening Charlie's supposed emplacements. But in the little apartment on Nguyen Cong Tru Street everything began to shimmer and wash down like the aurora borealis.

It was an apartment no longer. He stood on the polished wood floor, inside the pentagram of Solomon, but the polished wood floor came to an end at the edges of Siri's dried blood. Beyond lay a fallen temple. Great gray stones, enormous and bearing the marks of claws that had ripped them loose from mountains, tumbled and thrown carelessly, rose up around Chris. And out of the shadows something came toward him.

It slouched and dragged its arms behind as it came out of the darkness. When the flickering illumination from the candles struck it, Chris felt sick to his stomach. He clutched the paper with Siri's words as if it would save him.

Surgat came and stood with the point of one goat-hoof almost touching Siri's blood. Chris could smell where it had been and what it had been doing when he had interrupted its dining. He felt faint and could not breathe deeply because of the smell Surgat had carried from its mess hall.

The head of the demon changed. Toad to goat to worm to spider to dog to ape to man to a thing that had no name.

"Open the lock of the casket," Chris yelled. He had to yell: the sound of wind was overpowering, deafening, insane.

Surgat kicked the bahut. Chris had left it, as Siri had instructed, outside the pentagram. Surgat kicked it again. No mark was put on the coffer, but where the demon's foot had rested in the dust of the fallen temple's floor, a cloven footprint burned and smoked.

"Open the lock!"

Surgat leaned forward and shrieked. Words poured forth. They made no sense to Chris. They were from a throat that was not human. If a hyena had been given the ability to speak with the tongue of a man, it would have sounded less guttural, less deranged, less terrifying.

Siri had said the demon would be troublesome, but would finally do as bidden. It had no choice. It was not that important or powerful a spirit. When Chris remembered that assurance, and perceived just how staggering was the sight before him, he trembled at the thought of one of Surgat's masters. "Open it, you goddam ugly sonofabitch! Open it right now!"

Surgat vomited maggots that hit an invisible plane at the edge of the pentagram. And babbled more words. And reached out a lobster-claw that stopped just outside the invisible plane. It wanted something.

Then Chris remembered the hair from Siri's head. It will want the hair of a fox, she had said. Forget that. It will try to get a hair from *your* head. Whatever you do, don't let it have one. All of you is contained in each hair, you can be reconstructed from a hair; then it has you. Give it mine.

He extended her long, thick strand of hair.

Surgat screamed, would not take it. Chris extended it through the invisible plane. Surgat pointed to Chris's head and pulled long strips of bleeding flesh from its body and threw them against the fallen stones where they plopped with the sickening sound of meat against concrete. Chris did not move. The hair hung down outside the invisible plane.

Surgat screamed and capered and tore at itself.

"Take it, you disgusting sonofabitch!" Chris yelled. "Take it and be damned, she *died* to give it to you, puking garbage dump! Take it or get nothing! Nothing's worth this, not even that thing she looked for all her life! So *take* it, you crummy piece of shit! *Take it* or go back where you came from and let me alone!"

The words Surgat spoke became very clear, then. The voice modulated, became almost refined. It spoke in a language Chris had never heard. He could not have known that it was a tongue unspoken for a thousand years before the birth of Christ: Surgat spoke in Chaldean.

And having spoken, having acknowledged obedience at the threat of being dismissed without the proper license to depart, the threat of being trapped here in this halfway place of fallen stones, and the wrath of Asmoday or Beelzebuth, the lock-picking demon ran its tentacle forward and took Siri's hair. The hair burst into flame, the flame shot up toward the shadowed ceiling of the fallen temple, Surgat turned the flame on the casket...and the flame washed over the wood...and the casket opened.

Quickly, Chris read the final words on the paper he held. "O Spirit Surgat, because thou has diligently answered my demands, I do hereby license thee to depart, without injury to man or beast. Depart, I say, and be thou willing and ready to come, whensoever duly exorcised and conjured by the Sacred Rites of Magic. I conjure thee to withdraw peaceably and quietly, and may the peace of God continue forever between me and thee. Amen."

And Surgat looked across the pentagram's protective plane and said, in perfectly understandable English, "I do not go empty-handed."

Then the demon slouched away into the shadows, the aurora borealis effect began again, rippling and sliding and flowing down till he was in his own apartment again. Even then he waited an hour before leaving the charmed circle.

To discover that as Siri had promised, everything had its price. Surgat had not gone empty-handed.

The body of his lover was gone. He could not look at what had been left in its place.

He began to cry, hoping it *had* been an exchange; hoping that what lay on the sofa was not Siri.

The bahut contained more items than its outside dimensions would have indicated. It held grimoires and many notebooks filled with Siri's handwriting. It held talismans and runic symbols in stone and silver and wood. It held vials of powders and hair and bird-claws and bits of matter, each vial labeled clearly. It held conjurations and phials and philtres and maps and directions and exorcising spells. It held the key to finding True Love.

But it also held Siri's observations of what had happened to her when she had summoned the entity she called "the supreme hideousness, the most evil of the ten Sephiroths, the vile Adrammelech." He read the ledgers until his eyes burned, and when his fingers left the pages, the paper was smudged with his sweat. He began to tremble, there in the room where the smell of Surgat's dining table lingered, and knew he could not summon the strength to summon this most powerful of dark beings.

He read every word on every page Siri had written; and he vowed silently that he would pick up her quest where she had fallen. But he could not go to her informant. His assistance had cost her too much, and she had been unable to go on. The price was too high.

But there were clues to the trail of the artifact that was True Love. And he took the bahut and left the apartment on Nguyen Cong Tru Street and never returned. He had money to continue the search, and he would do it without help from things that dragged long, rubbery arms through the dust of fallen temples.

All he had to do was wait for the end of the war.

By 1975 Christopher Caperton had traced it to New Orleans. He was thirty-five years old; he had been married and divorced because in a moment of weariness he had thought she might suffice in place of True Love; and he wrote this in his journal: *It is the vanity of searching for embodiments. Flèches d'amour. Incarnations which are never satisfactory, which never answer all longings and questions.*

Once, when he had thought he might die of a jungle fever contracted while running down a false clue in Paramaribo, he heard himself cursing Siri's memory. If she had not told him it actually existed, he might have settled for something less, never knowing for certain that there was more. But he *did* know, and in his tantrum of fever he cursed her to Hell.

When he recovered, he was more than ashamed of himself. Considering who she had been, where she had gone, and the owners of her spirit, he might have called down a sentence on her that she did not deserve. One never knew the total cost, nor at what point the obligation was considered voided.

After he had been rotated home in 1970 he spent a few months tying up all previous relationships — family, friends, business associates, acquaintances — and set out on the trail that had grown cold since 1946.

Without dipping into capital he was able to underwrite his expenses handsomely. Even though the gnomes of Zurich had done away with unnumbered, secret accounts, he had made his money in a way that caused no concern among the assessors, customhouse officials, tithe-seekers and running-dogs of the IRS desiring duty, levy, tribute, tallage, liver and lights. He moved freely under a variety of passports and a number of names. He came to think of himself as a nameless, stateless person, someone out of a Graham Greene suspense novel.

There were clues, beginning with one of the appraisers who had worked on the Ford bequests. He was quite old by the time Chris located him in a retirement trailer camp in Sun City, but he remembered the item clearly. No, he had never seen it; it was crated with specific instructions that it should not, under even the most extreme circumstances, be opened. If he was lying, he did it well. Chris was paying a high enough premium for the information that it didn't matter either way. But the trail picked up with the old appraiser's recollection that whatever the crate had contained, it had been bequeathed to a contemporary of Henry Ford's, a man with whom he had been friends and then fallen out, fifty years before.

Chris managed to locate the bills of lading and traced the crate to Madison, Indiana. The recipient of the crate had been deceased for fifteen years. The contents of the crate had been sold at auction...

And so it went. From place to place. From clue to clue. And each clue indicated that having been in touch with the artifact, the owner had known great joy or great sorrow; but all were dead. The Holy Grail always lay just ahead, always just out of Chris's reach. Yet he could never bring himself to take the easy way out: to summon up the horror Siri had called Adrammelech. He knew if he finally gave in, that even if he found True Love he would never be able to savor it.

In January of 1975 Christopher Caperton followed a clue from Trinidad to New Orleans. His source had assured him that the artifact had passed into the hands of a *houngan*, a priest of the *conjur*, a disciple of the voodoo of Doctor Cat, a pioneer of mail order Voodoo in 1914.

On Perdido Street, in a back room lit only by votive candles in rubyglass jars, Chris met "Prince Basile Thibodeux," whose title at birth had been merely Willie Link Dunbar. Prince Basile swore he had known and loved the real and true Marie Laveau. As the old black man looked no more than sixty — though he claimed to be ninety-two — such a claim was, either way, highly dubious. Absolute proof exists that

Marie Laveau, the first of the many Marie Laveaus, died on June 24th, 1881, at the approximate age of eighty-five. Two years before Willie Link "Thibodeux" had been born, if he was ninety-two; and thirty-four, if he was lying.

Christopher Caperton did not care what lies Prince Basile told to sell his worthless hoodoo goods in the drugstore of Love Oils, Goofer Dust, Devil's Shoe Strings and War Water, as long as he told him a straight story about the artifact.

When he walked into the little back room, washed in bloody shadows from the candles, he was prepared to pay a premium price for the information he sought, or to assure Prince Basile that there were two men living on Prytania Street who would, for only a fraction of that premium price, inflict great bodily sorrow on a sixty- or ninety-two-year-old black man, and he would worry about the black goat dancing on his grave at a later time. But Prince Basile took one look at him and fear filled the withered face, "Doan put dat *gris-gris* on me, mistuh," he pleaded. "Jus' whatever you want, that's be what you gone get. Ah'm at y'service."

And Chris walked out of the little back room on Perdido Street with the information — that he knew to be absolutely reliable because no one that terrified could lie without dying in the act — that Willie Link Dunbar had worked on a smuggling operation from the Islands to the Keys in 1971 and he had seen the artifact. He swore before Damballa that he could not remember what it looked like…but it had been as lovely as anything he knew. His face, when he said it, was a strange mix of terror at the sight of Chris and joy at the last scintilla of memory of what he had seen.

And he told Chris the name of the smuggler who had taken the item from the boat.

And when Chris asked him why he was so frightened of just another white man, Prince Basile said, "You been kissin' the Old Ones. I kilt a hunnerd crows and cocks I couldn't save mah soul if you was t'touch me, mistuh. I be jus' playin' at whut I does, but *you*…you knows the fire."

harlan ellison

grail

Chris shuddered. And that was only from a minor, weak servant of Adrammelech. He left hurriedly.

He stood in the darkness of the alley off Perdido Street and thought about it, about True Love, whatever it was. He had wanted it for so long, had sought it in so many women, had glimpsed hints of its totality so many times, that he only now paused to examine what he had become. Even if he got it, would he be worthy of it? Wasn't the one who found the Holy Grail supposed to be pure in every way, perfect in every way, without flaw or blemish or self-doubt? Knights on white chargers, saints, defenders of the faith; those were the candidates for the honor. Prince Charming always won Snow White, not Porky Pig.

Without flaw. No, not without flaw. He had come too far for perfection. He had had to experience too much.

Yet he knew he was closer to True Love than anyone had ever been. Not even those who had possessed it had known what to do with it. He knew he had it within himself to become one with True Love, as no one before him ever could. No one. Not one of the perhaps thousand owners of it before and since it found its way to the Palace of Minos, no matter how fine or great or deserving they had been.

Christopher Caperton knew his destiny was to hold True Love in his hands. Known to demons, casting no shadow, he walked away from the fear in Perdido Street.

The final clue was so mundane he could not even breathe a sigh of relief. True Love had been sold in blind bid auction at Sotheby's in April of 1979. It now belonged to a man who lived high above the rest of the human race, in a tower overlooking New York, where almost eight million people gave a portion of each day to wondering where True Love resided.

From Siri's notebooks Chris recognized the name of the man. In 1932 he had visited New York City for the opening of the Radio City Music Hall. The artifact had been stolen from him. He had spent forty-seven years trying to regain his lost property. In the process, somehow, he had become enormously powerful, enormously wealthy, enormously secretive.

Home again, home again, jiggedy jig.

Christopher Caperton took one final look at the cover of the December 1980 issue of *Esquire*. It showed a woman in a seductive bridal gown. The cover illustrated an article called "Looking for a Wife" and the slug-line read "With all the beautiful, intelligent women out there, why is she so hard to find?"

He smiled thinking they might have done the reverse on *Ms.* magazine, with a photograph of an equally unreachable male.

The model they had selected for the shot was achingly innocent, yet seductive; poised in a timeless moment of utter perfection. Had he been anyone else, this might well have been the physical manifestation of True Love for him.

But it was only the most recent in a congeries of photos, motion pictures, billboards, and women glimpsed in cars going past on city streets who were idealized manifestations of what he sought.

Tonight he would hold the real thing. Tonight he would obtain True Love.

He put the last of the vials from Siri's bahut he might need in the capacious pockets of his London Fog topcoat and left the hotel. It was thirty degrees in the Manhattan streets and the wind was blowing in off the East River. By tomorrow, perhaps before two AM, there would be snow. It was the sort of evening he had always imagined for this final leg of the journey.

Christopher Caperton was forty years old.

Every bribe had been well placed. The boiler room door was unlocked. The key to the private service elevator had been properly copied. No one stopped him.

He walked through the palatial tower suite in darkness. He heard a door closing away off in the rear of the apartment. The floor plan he had been given was precise and he touched nothing as he walked quickly to the door of the master bedroom.

The old man was lying in the exact center of the huge bed. As reported, he was dying.

Chris closed the door behind him. Only one light near the bed illuminated the room. The old man opened his eyes and looked at Chris. His eyes were very blue.

"There's never enough money to buy silence, boy. You can buy entrance, but not silence. There's always some mouth that's hungrier."

Chris smiled and walked to the bed. "I would have tried to bargain with you if I'd thought it would do any good. I'm not a thief by profession."

The old man snorted softly. He didn't seem to be in pain. "No price."

"Yes, I rather thought that might be the case. But look on the bright side: you can't take it with you, it won't do you any good on the other side; and I've been looking for it for a long time."

The old man laughed gently, no more strenuously than he had snorted. "What the hell do I care how long you looked for it, boy? Not as long as I looked for it."

"Since Christmas, 1932."

"Well, well. You did your homework, did you?"

"I've paid as much as you, in all kinds of coin."

"Not my concern, boy. You'll never find it."

"It's here. In this room. In the safe."

The old man's eyes widened. "Smarter than I thought. Didn't stop any of that cash you were doling out; got good people working for me; didn't see any reason why they shouldn't pick up a few extra dollars; they've got families to take care of. Didn't expect you'd know about the safe."

"I know about it."

"Doesn't matter. You'll look forever and never find it. Even if you do, you'll never get it open." He coughed shallowly, smiled at the ceiling and recited: "Hidden where you can't find it; but if you do you'll be looking at six-foot thick walls of concrete reinforced with molybde-num-steel alloy cords, backed by a foot of tempered high-carbon, high-chromium steel, another foot of unseamed silico-manganese shock-resisting steel and six inches of eighteen-tungsten, four-chrome, one-vanadium high-speed industrial tool steel. The vault door is stainless steel faced, an inch and a half of cast steel, another twelve inches of burn-resisting steel, another inch and a half of open-hearth steel, and the pneumatic hinges are inside the sandwich. The vault door has twenty bolts, each an inch in diameter: eight on one side, eight on the other, two top and two bottom. This holds the door into a sixteen-inch jamb of moly-tungsten high-speed steel, set into eighteen inches of concrete crosshatched by burn-resisting steel bars running horizontally and vertically." He coughed once more, pleased with himself, and added as a fillip, "The door's precision-made so you can't pour nitro in between the seam of the door and the vault."

Chris let a beaten look cross his face. "And I suppose that isn't even all of it. I suppose there are thermostats that trip some kind of trap if the temperature rises…if I used a torch."

"You got some smarts, boy. Tear gas. And the floor gets electrified." He was grinning widely now, but what little color had been in his face was gone. His eyes were closing.

"You beat me," Chris said. "I guess it's yours to keep."

But the old man only heard the first part. By the end, Chris was talking to himself. The old man was gone.

"On the other hand," Chris said softly, "there's no lock that can't be opened."

He stood by the bed for a while, staring down at the previous owner of True Love. He didn't seem to have died happier or sadder for having passed on with it in his possession.

Then Christopher Caperton got down on his knees in the center of the great bedroom and took out the vial Siri had labeled *Blood of Helomi* and he unstoppered the vial and began sprinkling out the dusty contents in lines that formed the pentagram of Solomon. He placed the candles and lit them; and he stood in the center of the design. And he read from a smudged piece of paper twelve years old.

And Surgat came again.

This time it came to the tower suite; this time it did not take Chris to the fallen temple. And this time it spoke in the soft, refined voice it had used when taking Siri's body.

"So soon?" Surgat said. "You need me again so soon?"

Chris felt nausea rising in his throat. The demon had not been dining this time. It had been indulging in whatever passed for fornication among demons. Its love-partner was still attached. Whatever it was, it wasn't human. (A momentary thought shrieked through Chris's skull. Might it ever have *been* human; and might it have been...? He slammed the lid on the thought.)

"Twelve years...it's been twelve years..." Chris said, with difficulty.

Surgat let a human face appear in its stomach and the human face smiled offhandedly. "How time flies when one is enjoying oneself." The love-partner moaned and gave a spastic twitch.

Chris would not think of it.

"I'll need you out here to assist me. In one of my very difficult rituals." The voice was a snake's hiss, from the moth's head.

"Go fuck yourself. Open the safe."

"But I *need* you," the demon said, wheedling disingenuously.

Chris fished in his topcoat pocket for a scrap of parchment from the bahut. He began to read. "By the powerful Principality of the infernal abysses, I conjure thee with power and with exorcism; I warn thee hearken forthwith and immediately to my words; observe them inviolably, as sentences of the last dreadful day of judgment, which thou must obey inviolably..."

As he began to speak, a sweat of pus and blood began to break out on the demon's armored flesh. Soft purple bruises appeared, as if Surgat were being struck from within.

"I hear. I obey!"

And it reached for the hair. Chris took the vial of fox hairs from his pocket, withdrew one and handed it across the invisible plane. The hair burst into flame as before, and Surgat turned, aiming the flame at the ceiling. The fire washed the ceiling of the tower suite bedroom and the ceiling opened and the central section of the floor on which Chris stood rose up on hydraulic lifts into a chamber above the penthouse.

Then Surgat turned the flame on the stainless steel door of the vault that formed the wall of the chamber above, and the door swung open ponderously. And the vault within was revealed.

Then Chris intoned the license to depart, but before Surgat vanished it said, "Master, powerful Master, may I leave you with a gift?"

"No. I don't want anything more from you, not ever again."

"But Master, you will need this gift. I swear by my Lord Adrammelech."

Chris felt terror swirl through him. "What is it?"

"Then you willingly accept my gift without condition or let?"

Chris heard Siri's voice in his memory: *He won't harm you. He serves only one purpose: he opens all locks. Just be careful.* "Yes, I accept the gift."

Surgat caused a pool of stagnant water to appear just beyond the protective design. Then the human face appeared again in the thorax of the insect Surgat had become, and the human face smiled invitingly and said, "Look," and Surgat sucked in within itself and grew smaller and smaller and then vanished.

Leaving the pool of foul water in which Chris saw —

A scene from a motion picture. He recognized it. A scene from *Citizen Kane.* A day in 1940. The interior of the skyscraper office of the old man, Bernstein. He is being interviewed by the newsreel researcher, Thompson, who asks him what Charles Foster Kane's dying word, "Rosebud," meant.

Bernstein thinks, then says, "Maybe some girl? There were a lot of them back in the early days and —"

Thompson is amused. He says, "It's hardly likely, Mr. Bernstein, that Mr. Kane could have met some girl casually and then, fifty years later, on his deathbed —"

Bernstein cuts in. "You're pretty young, Mr. —" he remembers the name,

"— Mr. Thompson. A fellow will remember things you wouldn't

think he'd remember. You take me. One day, back in 1896, I was crossing over to Jersey on a ferry and as we pulled out there was another ferry pulling in." Everett Sloane, as the aged Bernstein, looks wistful, speaks slowly. "And on it there was a girl waiting to get off. A white dress she had on...and she was carrying a white parasol...and I only saw her for one second and she didn't see me at all...but I'll bet a month hasn't gone by since that I haven't thought of that girl." He smiles triumphantly. "See what I mean?"

And the scene faded, and the water boiled away, and Chris was alone in the dimly-lit vault room above the tower suite. Alone with the dawning fear that he had learned too much.

He saw himself suddenly as a human puppet, controlled from above by a nameless force that had held every man and woman on the end of strings, making them dance the dance, manipulating them to seek the unobtainable, denying them peace or contentment because of the promise of a Holy Grail out there somewhere.

Even if the strings were broken, and puny mortals wandered the blasted landscape of their lives on their own, they would finally, inevitably, tragically return to the great puppeteer; to try and retie the strings. Better to dance the hopeless dance that lied about True Love than to admit they were all alone, that they might never, never find that perfect image to become one with. He stood in the center of the pentagram of Solomon and thought of the achingly beautiful girl on the cover of *Esquire*. The girl who was not real. True Love. Snare and delusion? He felt tears on his cheeks, and shook his head. No, it was here. It was just inside the threshold of the vault. It existed. It had a form and a reality. The truth was only a few footsteps from him. Siri could not have died for it if it weren't real.

He stepped out of the magic design and walked to the door of the vault. He kept his eyes down. He stepped over the raised jamb and heard his footsteps on the steel floor.

The vault was lit by hidden tubing at the juncture of walls and ceiling. A soft off-white glow that filled the vault.

He looked up slowly.

It sat on a pedestal of silver and lucite.

He looked at True Love.

It was an enormous loving cup. It was as gaudy as a bowling trophy. Exactly a foot and a half high, with handles. Engraved on the face were the words *True Love* in flowing script, embellished with curlicues. It shone with a light of its own, and the glow was the brassy color of an intramural award.

Christopher Caperton stood with his arms hanging at his sides. It was in him, at that moment, to laugh. But he had the certain knowledge that if he laughed, he would never stop; and they would come in to get the old man's body this morning and find him still standing there, crying piteously and laughing.

He had come through a time and a distance to get this real artifact, and he would take it. He stepped to the pedestal and reached for it. Remembering at the last moment the demon's gift.

Surgat could not touch him; but Surgat could reach him.

He looked down into the loving cup that was True Love and in the silver liquid swirling there he saw the face of True Love. For an instant it was his mother, then it was Miss O'Hara, then it was poor Jean Kettner, then it was Briony Catling, then it was Helen Gahagan, then it was Marta Toren, then it was the girl to whom he had lost his virginity, then it was one woman after another he had known, then it was Siri — but was Siri no longer than any of the others — then it was his wife, then it was the face of the achingly beautiful bride on the cover of *Esquire*, and then it resolved finally into the most unforgettable face he had ever seen. And it stayed.

It was no face he recognized.

Years later, when he was near death, Christopher Caperton wrote the answer to the search for True Love in his journal. He wrote it simply, as a quotation from the Japanese poet Tanaka Katsumi.

What he wrote was this:

"*I know that my true friend will appear after my death, and my sweetheart died before I was born.*"

In that instant when he saw the face of True Love, Christopher Caperton knew the awful gift the demon had given him. To reach the finest moment of one's life, and to *know* it was the finest moment, that there would never be a more golden, more perfect, nobler or loftier or thrilling moment...and to continue to have to live a life that was all on the downhill side.

That was the curse and the blessing.

He knew, at last, that he *was* worthy of such a thing. In torment and sadness he knew he was *just* that worthy, and no more.

But it's easy to be smart...later.

THE OUTPOST
UNDISCOVERED
BY TOURISTS

A TALE OF THREE KINGS AND A STAR FOR THIS SACRED SEASON

They camped just beyond the perimeter of the dream and waited for first light before beginning the siege.

Melchior went to the boot of the Rolls and unlocked it. He rummaged about till he found the air mattress and the inflatable television set and brought them to the cleared circle. He pulled the cord on the mattress and it hissed and puffed up to its full size, king size. He pulled the plug on the television set and it hissed and firmed up and he snapped his fingers and it turned itself on.

"No," said Kaspar, "I will not stand for it! Not another night of roller derby. A King of Orient I are, and I'll be *damned* if I'll lose another night's sleep listening to those barely primate creatures dropkicking each other!"

Melchior glowed with his own night light. "So sue me," he said, settling down on the air mattress, tidying his moleskin cape around him. "You know I've got insomnia. You know I've got a strictly awful hiatus hernia. You know those *latkes* are sitting right here on my chest like millstones. Be a person for a change, a *mensch*, it couldn't hurt just once."

Kaspar lifted the chalice of myrrh, the symbol of death, and shook it at Melchior. "Hypochondriac! That's what you are, a fake, a fraud. You just like watching those honkytonk bimbos punching each other out. Hiatus hernia, my fundament! You'd watch mud wrestling and extol the esthetic virtues of the balletic nuances. Turn it off...or at least, in the name of Jehovah, get the Sermonette."

"The ribs are almost ready," Balthazar interrupted. "You want the mild or the spicy sauce?"

Kaspar raised his eyes to the star far above them, out of reach but maddeningly close. He spoke to Jehovah: "And this one goes ethnic on us. Wandering Jew over there drives me crazy with the light that never dims, watches institutionalized mayhem all night and clanks all day with gold chains...and Black-is-Beautiful over there is determined I'll die of tertiary heartburn before I can even find the Savior. Thanks, Yahweh; thanks a lot. Wait till *you* need a favor."

"Mild or spicy?" Balthazar said with resignation.

"I'd like mine with the mild," Melchior said sweetly. "And just a *bissel* apple sauce on the side, please."

"I want dimsum," Kaspar said. His malachite chopsticks materialized in his left hand, held far up their length indicating he was of the highest caste.

"He's only being petulant," Melchior said. "He shouldn't annoy, Balthazar sweetie. Serve them cute and tasty ribs."

"Deliver me," Kaspar murmured.

So they ate dinner, there under the star. The Nubian king, the Scrutable Oriental king, and the Hebrew king. And they watched the roller derby. They also played the spelling game called *ghost*, but ended the festivity abruptly and on a rancorous note when Balthazar and Melchior ganged up on Kaspar using the word "pringles," which Kaspar contended was not a generic but a specific trade name. Finally they fell asleep, the television set still talking to itself, the light from Melchior reflecting off the picture tube.

In the night the star glowed brightly, calling them on even in their sleep. And in the night early warning reconnaissance troops of the Forces of Chaos flew overhead flapping their leathery bat-wings and leaving in their wake the hideous carbon monoxide stench of British Leyland double-decker buses.

When Melchior awoke in the morning his first words were, "In the night, who made a ka-ka?"

Balthazar pointed. "Look."

The ground was covered with the permanent shadows of the bat-troops that had flown overhead. Dark, sooty shapes of fearsome creatures in full flight.

"I've always thought they looked like the flying monkeys in the 1939 MGM production of *The Wizard of Oz*, special effects by Arnold Gillespie, character makeup created by Jack Dawn," Kaspar said ruminatively.

"Listen, Yellow Peril," Balthazar said, "you can exercise that junkheap memory for trivia later. Unless the point is lost on you, what this means is that they know we're coming and they're going to be ready for us. We've lost the element of surprise."

Melchior sighed and added, "Not to mention that we've been following the star for exactly one thousand nine hundred and ninety-nine years, give or take a fast minute, which unless they aren't too clever should have tipped them off we were on the way some time ago."

"Nonetheless," said Kaspar, and fascinated by the word he said it again, "nonetheless."

They waited, but he didn't finish the sentence.

"And on that uplifting note," Balthazar said, "let us get in the wind before they catch us out here in the open."

So they gathered their belongings—Melchior's caskets of Krugerrands, his air mattress and inflatable television set, Kaspar's chalice of myrrh, his Judy Garland albums and fortune-cookie fortune calligraphy set, Balthazar's wok, his brass-bound collected works of James Baldwin and hair-conking outfit—and they stowed them neatly in the boot of the Rolls.

Then, with Balthazar driving (but refusing once again to wear the chauffeur's cap on moral grounds), they set out under the auspices of power steering, directly through the perimeter of the dream.

The star continued to shine overhead. "Damnedest thing I ever saw," Kaspar remarked for the ten thousandth time. "Defies all the accepted laws of celestial mechanics."

Balthazar mumbled something.

For the ten thousandth time.

"What's that, I didn't hear?" Melchior said.

"I said: at least if there was a pot of gold at the end of all this..."

It was unworthy of him, as it had been ten thousand times previously, and the others chose to ignore it.

At the outskirts of the dream, a rundown section lined with fast food stands, motels with waterbeds and closed circuit vibrating magic fingers cablevision, bowling alleys, Polish athletic organizations and used rickshaw lots, they encountered the first line of resistance from the Forces of Chaos.

As they stopped for a traffic light, thousands of bat-winged monkey-faced troops leaped out of alleys and doorways with buckets of water and sponges, and began washing their windshield.

"Quick, Kaspar!" Balthazar shouted.

The Oriental king threw open the rear door on the right side and bounded out into the street, brandishing the chalice of myrrh. "Back, back, scum of the underworld!" he howled.

The troops of Chaos shrieked in horror and pain and began dropping what appeared to be dead all over the place, setting up a wailing and a crying and a screaming that rose over the dream like dark smoke.

"Please, already," Melchior shouted. "Do we need all this noise? All this *geshrying*! You'll wake the baby!"

Then Balthazar was gunning the motor, Kaspar leaped back into the rear seat, the door slammed and they were off, through the red light— which had, naturally, been rigged to stay red, as are all such red lights, by the Forces of Chaos.

All that day they lay siege to the dream.

The Automobile Club told them they couldn't get there from here. The speed traps were set at nine miles per hour. Sects of religious fanatics threw themselves under the steel-belteds. But finally they came to the Manger, a Hyatt establishment, and they fought their way inside with the gifts, all tasteful.

And there, in a moderately-priced room, they found the Savior, tended by an out-of-work cabinetmaker, a lady who was obviously several bricks shy of a load who kept insisting she had been raped by God, various shepherds, butchers, pet store operators, boutique sales-girls, certified public accountants, hawkers of T-shirts, investigative journalists, theatrical hangers-on, Sammy Davis, Jr., and a man who owned a whippet that was reputed to be able to catch two Frisbees at the same time.

And the three kings came in, finding it hard to find a place there in the crowd, and they set down their gifts and stared at the sleeping child.

"We'll call him Jomo," said Balthazar, asserting himself.

"Don't be a jerk," Kaspar said. "Merry Jomomas? We'll call him Lao-Tzu. It flows, it sings, it soars."

So they argued about that for quite a while, and finally settled on Christ, because in conjunction with Jesus it was six and five, and that would fit all the marquees.

But still, after two thousand years, they were unsettled. They stared down at the sleeping child, who looked like all babies: like a small, soft W. C. Fields who had grown blotchy drinking wine sold before its time, and Balthazar mumbled, "I'd have been just as happy with a pot of gold," and Kaspar said, "You'd think after two thousand years someone would at least offer me a chair," and Melchior summed up all their hopes and dreams for a better world when he said, "You know, it's funny, but he don't look Jewish."

BLANK...

Driver Hall was an impressive pastel blue building in the center of the city. Akisimov had no difficulty finding its spirally-rising towers, even though the sykops were close behind, but once within sight of the structure, he found himself lost. How could he do it?

No Driver would intentionally help a criminal escape, yet a Driver was his only possible chance of freedom.

Akisimov's bleak, hard features sagged in fright as he sensed the tentative probes of the sykops in his mind. They had found the flower girl, and they were circling in on him, getting his thoughts pinpointed. *Why* had that stupid urchin wandered across his path? It had been a clean escape till he had run out of the mouth of that alley and stumbled into her. *Why* had she clung to him? He hadn't *wanted* to burn her down...he was only trying to get away from the sykops.

Akisimov cast about hungrily with his eyes. There had to be some way, some device to corner a Driver. Then he spotted the service entrance to the Hall. It was a dark hole in the side of the building, and he sprinted across the street in a dead run for it. He made the comparative safety of the entrance without being openly noticed and crouched down to wait. Wildly, he pulled the defective mesh cap tighter about his ears. It was the only thing standing between him and capture by the sykops, poor thing that it was. Had it been a standard make, not a lousy rogue cheapie model, it would have blanked him effectively, but as it was, it was the best he had.

With unfamiliar phrases he prayed to some unknown God to let the mind-blanking cap work well enough. Well enough to keep the sykops off him till he could kidnap a Driver.

Rike Akisimov had been sentenced to Io penal colony for a thousand years. The jurymech knew such a sentence bordered on the ridiculous; even with the current trends in geriatrics, *no* man could live past three hundred. The body tissue, the very fiber, just wouldn't stand up to it.

But in token hatred for this most vile of criminals, the placid and faceless jurymech had said: "We, the beings of the Solarite, sentence you, Rike Amadeus Akisimov, to the penal colony on Io for a period of one thousand years."

Then, as the jury room buzzed with wonder, the machine added, "We find in your deeds such a revulsion, such a loathing, that we feel even *this* sentence is too light. Rike Amadeus Akisimov, we find in you no identification with humanity, but only a resemblance to some odious beast of the jungle. You are a carrion-feeder, Akisimov; you are a jackal and a hyena and a vulture, and we pray your kind is never again discovered in the universe.

"We cannot even say, 'God have mercy on your soul,' for we are certain you have no soul!"

The jury room had been stunned into silence. For an implacable, emotionless jurymech to spew forth such violent feelings was unprecedented. Everyone knew the decision-tapes were fed in by humans, but no one, absolutely *no one*, could have fed in those epithets.

Even a machine had been shocked by the magnitude of Akisimov's crimes. For they were more than crimes against society. They were crimes against God and Man.

They had taken him away, preparing to lead him in the ferry-flit designed to convey prisoners from court to the spaceport, when he had struck. By some remarkable strength of his wrists — born of terror and desperation — he had snapped the elasticords, clubbed his guards and broken into the crowds clogging the strips, carrying with him a sykop blaster.

In a few minutes he was lost to the psioid lawmen, had ripped a mind-blanking mesh cap from a pedestrian's head, and was on his way to the one escape route left.

To the Hall and the psioids known as Drivers.

She came out of the building, and Akisimov recognized her at once as a senior grade Driver. She was a tall girl, tanned and beautifully proportioned, walking with the easy, off-the-toes stride of the experienced spaceman. She wore the mind's eye and jet tube insignia of her class-psi on her left breast, and she seemed totally unconcerned as Akisimov stepped out of the service entrance, shoved the blaster in her ribs, and snarled, "I've got nothing but death behind me, sister. The name is Akisimov..." The girl turned a scrutinizing stare on him as he said his name; the Akisimov case had been publicized; madness such as his could not be kept quiet; she knew who he was, "...so you better call a flit, and do it quick."

She smiled at him almost benignly, and raised her hand lazily in a gesture that brought a flit scurrying down from the idling level.

"The spaceport," Akisimov whispered to her, when they were inside and rising. The girl repeated the order to the flitman.

In half an hour they were at the spaceport. The criminal softly warned the psioid about any sudden moves and hustled the girl from the flit, making her pay the flitman. They got past the port guards by the Driver showing her I.D. bracelet.

Once inside, Akisimov dragged the girl out of sight behind a blast bunker and snapped quickly, "You have a clearance, or do I have to hijack a ship?"

The girl stared blankly at him, smiling calmly and enigmatically.

He jabbed the blaster hard into her side, causing her to wince, and repeated viciously, "I *said*, you got a clearance? And you damned well better answer me or so help me God I'll burn away the top of your head!"

"I have a clearance;" she said, adding solemnly, "you don't want to do this."

harlan ellison
blank...

He laughed roughly, gripped her arm tightly. She ground her lips together as his fingers closed about the skin, and he replied, "They got me on a thousand yearer to Io, lady. So I want to do any goddam thing that'll get me out of here. Now what ship are you assigned to snap?"

She seemed to shrug her shoulders in finality, having made a token gesture, and answered, "I'm snap on the *Lady Knoxmaster*, in pit eighty-four."

"Then let's go," he finished, and dragged her off across the field.

"You don't want to do this," she said again, softly. He was deaf to her warning.

When the invership took off, straight up without clearance coordinates and at full power, the Port Central went crazy, sending up signals, demanding recognition info, demanding this, demanding the other. But the *Lady Knoxmaster* was already heading out toward snap-point.

Akisimov, gloating, threw in the switch and knew the telemetering cameras were on him. "Goodbye, you asses! Goodbye, from Rike Akisimov! Stupid! You thought I'd spend a thousand years on Io? There are better things for me in the universe!"

He flicked off, to let them call the sykops, so the law would know he had bested them. "Yeah, there isn't anything worse than a life term on Io," he murmured, watching the planet fall away in the viewplates.

"You're wrong, Akisimov," the girl murmured, very, very softly.

Immediately the sykops and the SpaceCom sent up ships to apprehend the violator, but it was obvious the ship had enough start momentum to reach snap-out — if a Driver was on board — before they could reach it. Their single hope was that Akisimov had no Driver aboard, then they could catch him in a straight run.

On board the *Lady Knoxmaster*, Akisimov studied the calm-faced psioid girl in the other accelocouch.

Drivers were the most valuable, and yet the simplest-talented, of all the types of psionically equipped peoples in the field. Their one capacity was to warp a ship from normal space into that not-space that allowed interstellar travel; into inverspace.

Though the ship went through — set to snap-out by an automatic function of the Driver's psi faculty — the Driver did not. That was the reason they were always in-suit and ready for the snap. Since *they* did not snap when the ship did, they were left hanging in space, where they were picked up immediately after by a doggie vessel assigned to each takeoff.

But this time there was no doggie, and there was no suit, and Akisimov wanted the girl dead in any event. He might have made some slip, might have mumbled something about where "out there" he was heading. But whether he had or had not, dead witnesses were the only safe witnesses.

"Snap the ship," he snarled at her, aiming the blaster.

"I'm unsuited," she replied.

"Snap, damn your lousy psi hide! Snap, damn you, and pray the cops on our trail will get to you before you conk out. What is it, seven seconds you can survive in space? Ten? Whatever it is, it's more of a chance than if I burn your head off!" He indicated with a sweep of his slim hand the console port where the blips that were sykop ships were narrowing up at them.

"You don't want to do this," the girl said again.

Akisimov blasted. The gun leaped in his palm, and the stench of burned-away flesh filled the cabin. The girl stared dumbly at the cauterized stump that had been her left arm. A scream started to her mouth, but he silenced her with the point of the blaster.

She nodded acquiescence.

She snapped. Though she could not explain what was going on in her mind, she knew what she was doing, and she concentrated to do it this time…though just a bit differently…just a bit specially. She drew down her brows and concentrated, and…

blank…

The ship was gone, she was in space, whirling, senseless, as the bulk of a ship loomed around her, hauling her in.

She was safe. She would live. With one arm.

As the charcoal-caped sykops dragged her in, laid her in a mesh webbing, they could not contain their anxiety.

"Akisimov? Gone?"

They read her thoughts, so the girl said nothing. She nodded slowly, the pain in her stump shooting up to drive needles into the base of her brain. She moaned, then said, "He didn't get away. He thought the worst was a term on Io; he's wrong; he's being punished."

They stared at her, as her thoughts swirled unreadably. They stared unknowingly, wondering, but damning their own inefficiency. Akisimov had gotten away.

They were wrong.

blank...

The ship popped into inverspace.

blank...

The ship popped out...

In the center of a white-hot dwarf star. The sun burned the ship to molten slag, and Akisimov died horribly, flamingly, charringly, agonizingly, burningly as the slag vaporized.

Just at the instant of death...

blank...

The ship popped into inverspace.

blank...

The ship popped out...

In the center of a white-hot dwarf star. The sun burned the ship to molten slag, and Akisimov died horribly, flamingly, charringly, agonizingly, burningly as the slag vaporized.

Just at the instant of death...

blank...

The ship popped into inverspace.

blank...

The ship popped out...

Over and over and over again, till the ends of Time, till Eternity was a remote forgotten nothing, till death had no meaning, and life was something for humanity. The Driver had exacted her revenge. She had set the ship in a Möbius whirl, in and out and in and out and in again from inverspace to out, right at that instant of blanking, right at that instant of death, so that Forever would be spent by Rike Amadeus Akisimov in one horrible way — ten billion times one thousand years. One horrible way, forever and ever and ever.

Dying, dying, dying. Over and over and over again, without end to torment, without end to horror.

blank...

THE 3 MOST IMPORTANT THINGS IN LIFE

I've looked everywhere, and I'll be damned if I can find it, but I *know* I read that passage *some*where; I think in Kerouac; but I can't locate it now, so you'll just have to go along with me that it's there.

Would I lie to you?

It's a scene in which a young supplicant, an aspiring poet, somebody like that, seeks out this knowledgeable old philosopher — kind of a Bukowski or Henry Miller figure — in Paris or New York or somesuch bustling metropolitan situs...and the kid comes to the old guru in his ratty apartment, and he sorta kinda asks him that old saw about the meaning of life. Correction: LIFE. He squats there and says to the old man, "What's it all about? What's it mean? Huh?"

And the old man purses his lips and beetles his brow; he perceives the kid is really serious about this; it's not just jerk-off time. So he nods sagely, and clasps his hands behind his back, and he walks to the window and stares out at the deep city for a while, just sorta kinda ponders for a while. And finally, he turns to the kid and he says, with core seriousness, "You know, there's a lotta bastards out there."

Now that's pretty significant. I think. On the other hand, I have never made my residence in a stalactite-festooned cave high up on the northern massif of *Chomolungma* (Everest to you). I have never been sought out by fawning sycophants, whimpering to abase themselves before my wisdom, hungering to prostrate themselves and to offer oblations at the altar of my Delphic insights. In short, unlike the Great Thinkers of Our Time who appear regularly on talk-shows — Merv Griffin, Debbie Boone, Zsa Zsa Gabor and Jim Nabors leap instantly to mind — I doubt that the Oxford Encyclopedia of Philosophy will ever crib from my notes.

Nonetheless, having become something of an ingroup cult figure among those with a high death-wish profile and a taste for cheap thrills, I am often asked, "What's the big secret, Ellison?" At college lectures, for instance, bright-eyed young people, the great hope of our society, come up to me and murmur in reverential tones, "Wanna buy a lid of tough Filipino Scarlet?"

Naturally I try to demonstrate a certain humility in the face of such trust and innocence. I try to explain that Life is Real, Life is Earnest. In my own toe-scuffling fashion I attempt to encapsulate in three or four apocryphal phrases the Ethical Structure of the Universe. The better to aid these fine young people as they set out to change the world.

And from this long, terrifically fascinating life of encounters and adventures, I have selected three examples of what I think are the most important things in life. Notes should be taken; this will count as sixty percent of your grade.

1. SEX

I could have started with one of the more esoteric of the three, but I know your attention span is short and, in lieu of playing "The Saints Go Marching In," I decided it was best to catch your notice with instant sleaze.

Sex is one of the most important things in life. It comes built into the machine. Understanding sex is real important, y'know. And it's not enough just to say, "All men are shits," or "What the fuck do women *want?*" That's good for openers, but one must press on to deeper insights. As an aid for your greater search, I offer the following anecdote from my own humble experience: an only minimally exaggerated retelling of the single kinkiest sexual encounter I ever had.

When I got to Los Angeles in 1962, I was well into terminal destitution. Poverty would have been, for me, a sharp jump into a higher income bracket. Consequently, I wasn't getting laid much. More astute observers than I have charted the correlations between one's D&B rating and one's attraction for members of the same or opposite sex.

Anyhow, I met this young woman at Stats Charbroiler one afternoon, and somehow conned her into accepting a date. It has been fifteen years since that encounter, but I remember her name today as clearly as if it had been intaglio'd on my brain with a jackhammer. Brenda.

A substantially constructed female person, honey blonde of hair, amber of eye, insouciant of manner and expansive of bosom. We exchanged pleasantries, I explained that I was new to L.A. and was, in fact, a published author.

She went for it.

I took her phone number and address, and promised to pick her up the following Saturday night around 8:00 for a rollicking evening of camaraderie and good times, cleverly scaled to my nonexistent finances. Long walks in the bracing night air, that kind of thing.

Came Saturday, and I hand-washed the wretched 1951 Ford that had brought me to California from Chicago and New York. I dressed as spiffily as I could manage, aware at all times of the fact that having postponed a good number of meals had dropped my weight to about ninety pounds and I was beginning to take on the appearance of a card-carrying rickets case.

I drove to her home, which was in the posh Brentwood section of Beverly Hills. I walked to the ornate apartment door of the garden lanai, and rang the bell. Nothing happened. I waited and rang again. Nothing happened. Minutes passed, and I began thinking unworthy thoughts about Brenda's ethics. Finally, I heard footsteps from within, and the door was flung open.

There stood Brenda in her slip, with machines in her hair. "Come in, come in," she said huffily, as if I had interrupted her at the precise moment when she had been decoding the DNA molecule or something equally as significant. "I'm running a little late. I have to finish doing my hair. Well, come in already."

I stepped into the foyer, standing on a ribbed plastic runner that stretched out into the distance. As she closed the door behind me, I began to take a step off the plastic stripping so the door wouldn't hit me. My foot was poised in mid-step as she let out a shriek. "Aaarghh! Not on the carpet! Mama had the schvartze in today!" I spun, widdershins, barely managing to balance myself on one leg like a flamingo. I steadied myself on the plastic runner and looked to my right, the direction my errant foot would have carried me.

There, stretching off to the distant horizon, flooring a living room only slightly smaller than Bosnia and/or Herzogovina, lay the pluperfect lunatic symbol of the upwardly mobile, nouveau riche household: a white carpet, deepest pile, a veritable Sargasso Sea of insane white carpet — who but nutcases would carpet a room in which human beings are supposed to relax in white, fer chrissakes? — with the nap pathologically lying all in one direction, clearly having been carpet-swept by Nubian slave labor so it was anal retentively flowing in one unbroken tide. Hours had been spent making sure each bloody fiber lay in that north by northwest direction.

"Stay on the runner. I won't be long," Brenda commanded.

"I've got to stay on the runner?"

"Sure. Just stand there. I'll be out in a minute."

And she vanished. Back into the bowels of that cyclopean domicile, leaving me standing frozen and tremulous in my baggy pants while she went off to complete her toilette. The plastic runner extended out beneath my feet, back into the dim and vaulted interior. To my left a closed door. To my right the inviolate expanse of white carpeting and a living room in which Xerxes could easily have assembled his armies for an attack on the Hot Gates.

I stood there, shifting from one foot to the other like a grade school troublemaker waiting for his audience with the Principal. And time went by. Slowly. I waited and waited, and heard nothing from the back of the residence. The living room looked invitingly comfortable with all those massive sofas and the huge baby grand piano. But I had been denied entrance. I felt like Howard Carter and Lord Carnarvon standing at the doorway to the antechamber of Tutankhamen's tomb, faunching to enter a space unvisited for three thousand years, but fearing the terrible wrath of *Beware all ye who violate this sacred place…*

Now I don't know about you, friends, but if you leave me all alone someplace, with nothing to amuse me, for any extended period of time, I will sure as shit get in trouble.

And so, possessed by some devil-demon from my childhood, I became obsessed by the purity of that goddam carpet. I stared at its unblemished white expanse, that sea of bleached grass rippling away to forever. And finally, when it was either *do* something or go bugfuck, I stepped to the edge of the plastic runner, crouched, and jumped as far out into the carpet as I could. There was no way of knowing where I had come from. My footprints just magically appeared *out there.*

I hesitated only a moment, and then, scuffling my feet to produce impressions in the carpet, I began spelling out the classic Chaucerian PHUQUE. In letters four feet high. In virginal white carpet.

And I was just putting the . on the ! when I heard a strangled "Aaaaarghhh!" behind me. I turned, and there stood the missing Brenda, looking really pretty terrific, but with this, how shall I put it, uh, *green* expression on her face. "Oh jeezusOhmiGodOhshit! My mother'll *kiiiill* me!" And she ran off, leaving me standing there rather shamefaced, wondering just which mental gargoyle had taken possession of the cathedral of my mind, knowing that there was *no way* I was gonna get laid.

Then, in a moment, here she came, schlepping a carpet sweeper, not a vacuum cleaner, just one of your basic hand pushed carpet sweepers, and she starts *sweeping the nap back north by northwest!*

And I watched this demented scene for about thirty seconds until it got more than I could handle, and I yelled at her, "This is nuts! How the hell can you be a slave to a fuckin' *carpet?*" But she was in the grip of more powerful forces than my charisma. She was under the unbreakable spell of toilet training, and if the Apocalypse had come along just then she'd *still* have finished laying that nap back.

I went crazy.

I grabbed for the sweeper. She pirouetted out of my reach. She never broke stroke. I lunged for her again and got my hands around the sweeper. We struggled back and forth across the living room, caroming off the furniture, lousing up the carpet worse than before. She fought like one of those lady barbarians out of a Conan adventure, punching and kicking.

Then the sweeper went *that* way, and we went *this* way, and we fell over and wrestled over and over across the floor, thumping our heads and legs. Over and over, and I came up on top for a moment and pinned her arms and stared down at her, trying to catch my breath...

And in that instant I perceived a mad light glowing out of her eyes, and she murmured huskily, "Hit me."

Oh shit.

Now you gotta understand: I'm a quiet, well-mannered, Jewish kid from Ohio. Not even years sunk to the hips in the fleshpots of New York, Chicago, London and Billings, Montana have been able to sully the rigidly Puritanical morals that have led me to the pinnacle of success and clear complexion you see before you today. To put it simply, I was terrified. After all that time, at long last, despite my best efforts at avoidance. I had encountered one of *those* kinda ladies.

"Uh...beg pardon," I said weakly.

"Hit me," she said again. The light in her eyes strobed.

"H-h-huh-*hit* you?"

"Punch me around a little bit. I love it."

"P-p-puh — ?"

"Don't leave marks. Just hurt me some..."

Oh shit.

She was watching me, naked lust in her face, her lips wet with unconcealed desire. Nice quiet Jewish kid from Ohio. But what the hell, I'm adaptable.

Bogart asserted himself. My voice dropped four octaves. "You like a little smacking around, right, shweetheart?" She nodded, bonking her head on the carpet. "Okay," I said roughly, "get naked."

She looked troubled for a moment. "Naked?"

"Now!" I said, my voice a brutal rasp. I got off her. I stood over her as she stripped out of her clothes. My eyes slitted, my jaw tensed. I watched silently.

When she was naked — and pretty terrific she was, I might add — I said, "Okay, lie on your back." She lay down again. (For a crazed moment I wanted to tell her to "make an angel" the way we used to do it when there was a heavy snow in Ohio. You lie on your back and flap your arms up and down, making angel wings. But I didn't. That would've been *really* crazy.)

The heavy drapes on the living room windows were secured by thick gold cord ropes with tassels. I unhooked four of them. I wrapped one around her left leg, secured it, and tied it to one leg of the baby grand. Then I did the same to her right leg and attached it to the piano at the other side. Then one arm stretched above her head and fastened to a leg of the massive sectional sofa. The other arm to another post of the sofa. She was spread-eagled, right in the middle of the word PHUQUE' (without the .) out flat on her back, her perspiring body trembling with barely-restrained passion.

"Can you move?"

She tried, then shook her head.

"Tied down tight? Can't get loose?"

She nodded again, breathing raggedly.

"Terrific," I said, heading for the door. "Say hello to your mama for me, and thank her for the chicken soup."

And I ran for my life.

All I could think of was when her mother got home that night and found her baby girl staked out like a gazelle at the waterhole, she'd take one look at this monstrous scene and start screaming, "My *caaaarpet...!*"

You ask me if sex is one of the most important things in life? Absolutely. But the *lack* of it is even likelier to drive you nuts.

2. VIOLENCE

Not the pale, pallid nonsense Starsky and Hutch indulge in every week. *Real* violence. Sudden, inexplicable, ghastly.

How seldom we see it. How unhinged we become in the face of it. Because when it *really* happens, when it manifests itself on its most primitive, amoral level…we understand just how fragile is the tissue of social behavior. In a life singularly filled with violence, only one sticks out without even close competition as the most horrendously violent moment I ever witnessed. I'll tell it briefly; even today, years later, my blood runs cold remembering…

New York. Early Seventies, maybe '73 or '74. I was in the city on business. Business taken care of, I got together with a friend, a writer from Texas who loves movies as much and as indiscriminately as I do. The ritual: the movie crawl. Load up on junk food, start at the first movie theatre on the downtown side of 42nd Street, and just work our way from Times Square to 8th Avenue, cross the street, and work our way back to Times Square. Days. Endless days. Twenty-four, thirty-six, forty-eight hours straight time in the dark. We eat in there, sleep in there, piss and daydream in there. Hot dogs, popcorn, slabs of cheese, munchies, French bread, anydamnthing. And we see them all: the good flicks, the bad flicks, the kung-fu operas, the porn jobs, the superfly stomp the paddy flicks…all of them. One after another, till our eyes turn to poached eggs, staggering from theatre to theatre like refugees from a Macao opium den.

I don't remember the name of the particular theatre, but it was on the uptown side of 42nd Street, close to Broadway. It was something like four in the morning. My buddy and I were almost totally cacked-out. I remember the double-bill, however. The lower half, the B feature, was *Fear is the Key*, a really dreadful action-adventure turkey based on a crummy Alistair MacLean novel. The main feature was *Save the Tiger*, a contemporary drama starring Jack Lemmon. He won the Oscar for the role in that film.

And there we slumped, way the hell up in the balcony, our knees jammed under our chins, best seats in an almost empty house. Four ayem. Two rows below us — and it was steep up there, what I'm talking here is damned near per-pen-*dic*-ular — some black dude was juiced out asleep, lying across three or four seats, snoring.

My buddy the Texas writer is dead asleep, having polished off a recent meal of three boxes of Good'n'Plenty and a frozen chocolate covered banana on a stick. And, blessedly, *Fear is the Key* ends, and *Save the Tiger* begins.

About ten minutes into this serious, sensitive study of a garment center guy who is killing himself with floating ethics, and from the very first row of the balcony, below and to the right of us, but still very high above the floor of the theatre, I hear a shrieky black voice start mouthing off. Dialogue straight out of *One Hundred Dollar Misunderstanding*.

"Muh-fugguh! Gahdamn muh-fugn stupid piece'a shit. Dumb sumbish cah-suckin' piece'a shit garbage…Leroy! Hey, you sumbish nigguh prick *Leroy*! Le's get th' fuggoutta here, Leeeee-*roy*!"

Clearly, the critic in the first row of the balcony found this deeply penetrating study of middle class morality as seen through the dissolution of Jack Lemmon's knock-off sweat shop less than relevant to his existence as a mid-Twentieth Century denizen of the shitty slum to whence he would wend his way once this stupid kike film about muh-fuggin' honk paddy bastids ended. Which wasn't soon enough for him. "Leeeee-ROY!"

I had the feeling that Leeee-ROY was the terminal case lying over the seats two rows below us. Out of it.

Well, I peer through the gloom and see the dude down there in the front row of the balcony, his feet up on the brass rail, his partner beside him, silently watching the film but not stopping the noise. And I watch the two of them for a little while, hoping the third member of the group, good ole Leeee-ROY, will bestir his ass and go rejoin them there sepia Athos and Porthos, and maybe just maybe vacate the site quietly so I can watch the goddam muh-fuggin' movie.

But no such luck. The critic only gets wonkyer, yelling at the top of his lungs. Leeee-ROY don't twitch a bun.

And just as the critic is reaching a pitch that will cause sonic tremors, squealing sumbish and muh-fugguh at the top of his lungs, from *behind* me I hear The Voice of Doom:

"Shut your face, nigger, before I come down there and kill you."

Pause with me for a nanoinstant. This was not one of those angrily shouted *shutups* one encounters all-too-frequently these days in pillbox-sized Cinema I/II/III/IV closets filled with slope-browed, prognathous-jawed pimplebrains who jabber endlessly as though they were still in front of the tube in their living room. This was — trust me — the most blood-curdlingly *threatening* voice I have ever heard. It was the kind of voice one suspected would accompany the body attached to the moving finger writing *mene mene tekel* in letters of fire. This was an abominable snowman, a tyrannosaurus, a behemoth, a stone righteous muh-fuggin' *killer*. Deep, resonant, commanding, powerful…and very very black.

I don't want to belabor this but *who*ever or *what*ever was sitting back up there behind my Texas buddy and me, it was *bad*.

Beside me, I felt the hand of my Texican partner on my wrist. Softly, he asked, "What the fuck was *that?*"

"Voice of Doom," I said. "Pretend we're black. Better still: pretend we're at another theatre."

All this happened in a second. And only an idiot would have talked back to the owner of that voice. Guess whose name was in the envelope in the category of Most Outstanding Performance by an Idiot? You got it: Leeee-ROY's buddy with the scoop shovel mouth. Is violence important in this life?

The critic started shrieking, "Who said that? Who said that gahdamn shit t'me? You c'mawn down here, nigguh, I'm gonna *cut*'chu! I gonna *cut* on you, nigguh muh-fugguh!"

And he did go on. And on and on. "Oh shit," I murmured, slumping down even deeper in the seat, till my knees were up around my ears like a grasshopper. Beside me, my Texican buddy was praying in High Church Latin, Yiddish and Sufi, all at the same time.

I do believe that the joker down in the first row of that cockroach-ridden movie house was the single *dumbest* sonofabitch I have ever encountered; and what happened next was the swiftest, most deadly moment of violence I have ever seen.

Motormouth was still working over the conjugation of *to cut* when suddenly and without warning there was a rush of wind past me, down those steep steps, fast, fast, so damned fast I couldn't make out whether it was a human or a *yeti* or simply some terrifying force of nature, and all I saw was a dark blur as something BIG went smoothly down to the front row, something GIGANTIC moved into that row...and that stupid sonofabitch joker just *stood up*, still working his wet jaw...as if he could do something against that HUGE dude come to silence him...and that monstrous black fury just grabbed Motormouth by the shirt front and *yanked*...and pitched him headfirst *over* the rail.

I heard a terrified scream as the guy fell, and then a sickening *crack!* like the snapping of a T'ang dynasty chopstick, and then there was silence.

The only sounds were Jack Lemmon talking about what emotional violence he was suffering.

Shut up, Lemmon.

No one in the theatre moved. There weren't that many people anyhow. Just my buddy and me and sleeping Leeee-ROY and the buddy of the guy who'd taken the dive...and that humongous *shape*. In the balcony. And if there was anyone down below, they weren't saying anything.

The diver's buddy didn't move or look around or say a word. He just sat there staring straight ahead, as if he could not possibly have found anything more interesting in the universe to think about than Jack Lemmon's problems. The dark shape moved back up the aisle...I didn't look left or right...I saw *nothing*, Jim, *nothing*...and it went up past me and was gone.

I watched that entire flick in silence. No one moved to see if the diver was still alive. After a moment's wait the diver's buddy slipped out of the balcony like oil washing down a gutter, and was gone. From below...nothing.

And when the film was finished and the lights came up, we rose, and turned slowly. The balcony was empty. Leeee-ROY was still *tabula rasa*. Just us, all alone. I looked at my buddy from Texas, and he looked at me, and without saying a word we walked down that precarious stairway and came to the railing and peered over.

The diver lay across the back of a shattered seat. He was bent double. Stomach up. His spine was broken. He didn't move. The theatre was empty. We walked back up the aisle, through the upper vestibule, down the winding staircase, into the lobby, and out. We didn't look back. No one could help the diver. We wanted to get away.

We never spoke of it to each other.

It was *sudden*. Not a word. Not a second threat. No false heroics like two stumblebums in an alley outside a bar. No feinting, and no swinging. He just *threw* him; launched him out into eternity. And walked away from it. Because he was disturbed in a movie.

Violence, *real* violence, not the Jack Armstrong nonsense we all play-act at...genuine, mindless violence is very important.

Because there is no knowing when it will strike.

And there is no escape from it.

I warn you, it's terrible.

3. LABOR RELATIONS

At least half our waking life is spent trying to make ends meet. Slouching after the buck. Keeping the rain off our heads. That means earning a living. Aren't you glad I clarified it for you? And whether you're on the paycheck or self-employed, whether you wait in line for the dole or cat-burgle through windows in the wee hours, relations with Them As Has the Money are vital. Not getting the Employer pissed-off, maintaining a posture that makes you indispensable, cannot be too strenuously stressed.

One of the most important lessons one can learn in this tragic life, therefore, is what it takes to stay employed. And since almost *any* job will eventually drive you to erratic behaviour, thus precipitating getting your *tuchis* laid off, I offer the following heart-rending anecdote from my virtually cornucopial stock of life-experiences…as a classic example of what *not* to do.

One day about ten years ago, I was sitting in this little treehouse I rented in Beverly Glen, a sort of arboreal Bambi-Land section of Los Angeles just on the Tobacco Road side of Bel-Air and Beverly Hills, what I'm talking here is artsy craftsy but poor as a *shul*mouse,* — really a treehouse, I'm not making this up, see, because half the house sat on a rock ledge up a private little street called Bushrod Lane that was mostly only a kind of paved pathway better suited to fugitives from a James Fenimore Cooper book than this upwardly-struggling young writer trying to bludgeon his way into movies, and the other half — of the treehouse, that is — am I going too fast for you? — was in the crotch of a big eucalyptus tree, and it only cost me $135 a month, which was back then at a time before everything was crazy in terms of what it costs to live decently these days and $135 was not the biggest rent you could pay but I wasn't all that cushy either, and so I was sitting there when the phone rang, and it was Marty. Marty the Agent. And he says to me, he says, "Walt Disney *wants* you!"

Now I don't know what you think constitutes an ominous remark, but as Walt Disney had gone to collect his reward from that Great Consortium Organizer in the Sky at least two years prior to this phone call from Marty the Agent, immediate thoughts of some Lovecraftian horror beckoning to me from the crypt…

Whoooooooo…Walt *waaaaants* you…!

…went pitterpattering through my tiny brain. But, as it turned out, I was never to find out if there was truth to the much-bandied underground rumor that Walt had been flash frozen cryonically, with an eye to restoring him in the 25th Century or, at worst, stuffing him and putting him on display like Trigger. What it boiled down to, improbably, was that someone had read one of my science fiction stories somewhere and thought I'd be a terrific li'l fellah to have write a kinda sorta sf film Disney was thinking of making.

---

* A *shul* is a synagogue. As a Jew I'm not allowed to have churchmice. Thas's okay, they're *trayf.*

My first reaction to "Disney wants you" was horror, and then stark amazement. "There's been a mistake," I said to Marty the Agent. "I'm a crazed, radical, bomb-throwing loon who writes stories about things that come up out of the toilets to bite off babies' asses…are you sure they don't want *Bob* Ellison? He writes comedy. Very clean-cut guy. Drives a late model car. Shaves regularly. Never says fuck in mixed company. You sure they mean me, Marty? I'm *Harlan* Ellison, remember? The one with the hook for a hand."

No, says Marty the Agent, who has been my theatrical agent (as opposed to my literary agent, who is Bob the Agent) as well as my friend for over fifteen years, no, they have clearly lost their minds and they want you, and I have made a nice little week-to-week deal for you, with a guaranteed six and options…and he named a figure that might not purchase San Simeon in these crazy days of lettuce going for $3.00 a head but back then ten years ago was more money than anyone had ever offered me for anything, including my body.

"Contracts are coming," Marty said, "but go over to the Disney Studio tomorrow morning. They have an office for you."

I was in heaven. So okay, it wasn't writing The Great American Cinematic Answer to *Potemkin*, so what?! I was on my way. I was going to work in the Studio! It was the big time, and just to get up in the part of a successful scenarist, I dragged out my complete collection of *Uncle Scrooge McDuck Comics* and re-read them all, till the night had passed away and the morning had come.

I dressed smartly, put on the one tie I owned, looked at myself in the mirror before leaving the treehouse and went back in and took off the tie and put on a shirt first. Okay, so I was excited, shoot me.

I drove out the Ventura Freeway to the Buena Vista exit, drove up to the front gate in the disreputable 1951 Ford I mentioned earlier, which hadn't been washed in so long that strangers wrote cleanliness-is-next-to-godliness obscenities in the dirt, and gave my name to the spiffy guard at the kiosk. "Oh, yessir, Mr. Ellison," he said, validating my existence, "your office is in the Writers Building." I beamed. "How do I get there?" I asked.

He smiled exactly the same smile as Doc of Seven Dwarfs fame and said, "Well, you drive in here and take the first left, that's Mickey Mouse Avenue. Then you go down Mickey Mouse Avenue till you get to Thumper Boulevard. Turn right on Thumper to Clarabelle Cow Way and take another left. Go straight down Clarabelle Cow Way till you hit the corner of Horace Horsecollar Drive, and the Writers Building is second building on your right."

I think I nodded dumbly, refusing to believe what I had just been told. But I drove in and, sure as shit, there was Mickey Mouse Avenue and Thumper Boulevard and all the rest of them, and I said to myself, *Ellison...you has fallen down a rabbit hole, keed.*

But right there, in front of the building to which I'd been directed, was a parking slot that said H. ELLISON. Right there, on the blacktop, between the thick white lines, some industrious Audio-Animatronic robot (possibly cobbled up in the image of Matisse or Lindner) had stencilled my name for Eternity or six weeks with options...whichever came first.

To those of you out there in the Great American Heartland, that may not be such a significant thing, but in the world of studio sine-cures, a parking space of one's own is dearer to the heart than never being put on "hold" when calling the networks. I know Sammy Glick *manqués* who have given up perks and titles and even a Bigelow on the floor just for a parking space with the name thereon. So there I had it: authentication of my elevated status in the universe of the soon-to-be-hot-stuff.

I walked into the building and on the register I found my name and office number. Walked upstairs, followed the numbers till I found my office, and opened the door. It was a two-room suite with bathroom. The room I entered was antechamber, and there, sitting behind her desk, reading a paperback nurse novel, was *my secretary*. No, change that from . to !!!

You shoulda seen her. This remarkable creature was so clean I could see dust motes taking 90° turns as they fell, just so they wouldn't mar her perfection. A smile that would solve all the energy dilemmas of the

TVA. Peter Pan collar on the blouse. Malibu blonde, periwinkle-blue eyes, a *goyishe* nose that would make Streisand climb a wall, a freshly-minted six-pack of dimples most of which were visible. "May I help you?" she said.

You're probably too young to remember, but the part of Adelaide in the original stage production of *Guys and Dolls* was played by Vivian Blaine, an accomplished actress who had the most amazing dumb-blonde voice ever bottled. Not even Judy Holliday in *Born Yesterday* could approach the level of stupidity aurally conveyed by Ms. Blaine's rendition of the nitwit. Only once in the more-than-a-quarter-century since *Guys and Dolls* opened on Broadway, have I heard a voice, male or female, that rivaled for strident, full-out dumbness, the voice of Adelaide.

"May I help you?" she said.

"Uh, I'm Harlan Ellison," I replied. "I think this is my office."

Such instant attentiveness. Such perky willingness to serve, we don't do windows or floors. Could she get me coffee? Could she type some script? Could she file some reports? Could she read my Tarot?

I pointed out that I was just arriving and that it was my first day on the job and, since I had no idea what I was doing, nor even what the nature of the project was to be, I really needed only one bit of assistance: "Is that my office in there?"

She indicated that the connecting room was, in fact, the Holiest of Holies where, she was certain, I would create great moments in cinematic history. I thanked her, suggested she return to the contretemps of Nurse and Doctor and advanced post-nasal drip, and I'd call her when I needed her. In the background I heard mental riffs by Dan Hicks & His Hot Licks.

I went into my office.

They could have staged the World Cup soccer matches in there. One sofa, too short to sleep on; one wall of bookcases empty save for a well-thumbed copy of the 1948 *World Almanac*; one framed painting depicting beanfield hands laboring under a blistering sun (I wondered if that was intended by the management as metaphor); one desk the size of the battleship *Potemkin* (and I wondered if that was intended by the management as metaphor); one typing table supporting an enormous IBM Selectric, already humming with life; one rollaround typing chair.

And on the desk, an even dozen #2 Dixon Ticonderoga pencils, sharpened to such a piercing sharpness that they seemed to strobe off into invisibility at the points. Tony Curtis could have dueled with those pencils.

I didn't have the heart to tell anyone I type manuscript straight onto the machine. My handwriting is in the top 1/10th of the top percentile of illegible scrawls.

I sat down and waited. For someone to come and tell me what they wanted me to write. To tell me at least the name of the picture. But an hour went by and nothing happened.

As I've pointed out earlier, left to my own devices, I get into trouble. Deep trouble.

So, bored out of my brain, I rose, went into the office where Barbie sat with furrowed brow pondering the mysteries of infections and abscesses of the submaxillary parotid gland, and I said, "I'm going to look around. Be back in a bit."

The smile fried my eyeballs like a ping-pong ball in a cyclotron, and I stumbled into the hall.

I started checking out the other offices. And to my utter delight, there were at least half a dozen writers I knew, ensconced in Plaza Suites similar to mine. The wonderful thing about it was that most of them were loons like me. I'd name them, but since most of you can't even remember the names of authors of *books*, names of scenarists like Albert Aley and John D. F. Black and Mary C. McCall, Jr. won't mean shit to you. Suffice to say, we all found ourselves gathered in John's office, shucking and jiving till almost noon. At which point someone said, "Okay, let's break for lunch."

I thought that was a terrific idea, having put in an exhausting three hours working in the Disney vineyards.

So we went to the commissary and shoved in around the Writers' Table.

What I did not know was that the Writers' Table was right behind the Producers' Banquette. That was my first big mistake. As it turned out, it was also my last big mistake.

Oh, what fun, sitting there with intellectual companions, cutting up touches and laughing at the drolleries! Born again: the Algonquin round table. Wit beyond compare. And, naturally, as the youngest member of the group, striving to make my mark as worthy of their camaraderie, their respect, I suggested a droll, witty lunchtime conceit...

Two things you must know. First, I do a *terrific* Mickey Mouse imitation. Absolutely phonographically perfect. If the publishers of this book had the money, they ought to bind in a record, one of those little plastic jobbies, so you could hear my spectacular Mickey imitation. When I tell this anecdote in person, it really enhances it a lot. But just *pretend* you can hear it, okay?

The second thing you need to know is that the Producers' Banquette had filled up with Roy Disney and the other heads of the studio, behind me; a fact of which I was unaware; a fact no one bothered to impart.

At the top of my voice I suggested, "Hey, listen, what a kick! Why don't we do a porn Disney flick?"

Everyone smiled.

"It'll be terrific," I said. Loudly. "I mean, everyone knows, for instance, that Tinker Bell *does it*...what they don't know is *how* she Does It." They all looked at me expectantly. "She flies up the head of the penis and flaps her wings like crazy," I said, proud as hell of myself at this bit of fantasy. Everyone chuckled.

I went on, oblivious to the sudden hush all around me in the commissary. "I'll be Mickey, and I'll be the director; John, you do a good Donald, so you can be the male porn lead, sort of a duck-style Harry Reems; Mary, you can be Minnie, the female lead; and Albert, you can be Goofy...and Goofy, of course, is the producer."

Their smiles were frozen; the way the smiles of bit players get frozen when they see the monster creeping up behind the hero in a horror flick.

"Hey, gang!" I squeaked in my terrifically accurate Mickey voice. "Everybody ready to shoot the ultimate Disney flick? The film that rips the lid off the goody two-shoes hypocrisy that lies sweltering beneath the surface of G-rated true-life adventures? Okay, you guys, let's get that hand-held Arriflex right down there between Minnie's legs! I wanna see closeups of quivering labia!"

A silence as deep as that at the bottom of the Cayman Trench.

I went on, oblivious, carried along by my enthusiasm. In Donald's quack, I said, "Goddam sonofabitch! Pluto, get outta there, you're steaming up the lens!"

As Goofy, in the dumbest voice possible, I said, "Yuck, yuck, yuck...hey, fellahs, I'm a highly-paid, extremely inept producer person...c'n I play, too?"

As Mickey: "Fuck off, Goofy, fuck off! Get those Seven Dwarfs in here...I don't care if they *don't* wanna gang-bang a mouse, tell 'em they're under contract...and fer chrissakes, Minnie, will you take off those damned shoes?!"

The meal came. Everyone addressed their plates like inmates of the Gulag Archipelago. When lunch was over, everyone vanished very quickly. I was confused, but felt good. What a nice little *shtick* I'd invented. Wished *they'd* joined in. Oh well.

Went back to my office. Noticed first that my name had been whited-out in the parking slot. Upstairs, the secretary and her paperback were gone. On my desk: twelve sharpened #2 Dixon Ticonderoga pencils and a pink slip.

I had been fired after working for the Disney empire for a total of four hours, including lunch.

The lessons here cannot be avoided.

Big business is humorless.

And...

At Disney, nobody fucks with The Mouse.

VISIONARY

(WRITTEN WITH JOE L. HENSLEY)

*Under the pastel and quiet skies their minds conversed.
"There is the need," they thought, and: "They are maturing,"
and: "Soon we will be in the togetherness." And they turned
and watched the quiet skies and the reaching roof and spires in
anticipation.*

I had this dream. I'd been having it for years before I knew it for
something more than vague remembering. A child's dream, but it did
not fade and change. It was a solemn dream, disquieting. And, after a
while, it became more real than the other things that I found in books
and lived with.

There wasn't a great deal to it. Just an enormous building, the
background around it pastel misty. The building was like a great cathedral, and yet my feeling when I saw it was not religious, though it was
akin to it. Always I seemed to be hanging far above it, struggling, but
never reaching it. And I would awaken...

I knew, somehow, that everything would be right if I could find it.
And I knew that I would, some day.

But then, there was the dreaming: The architecture was odd and
alien. It seemed to be many organ pipes, thrust down into a soil that
was pinkish and fine. The pipes were set flush against one another, so
that a great wall of rounded shapes rose up and fit the sky. The roof of

the building was of a design I could not identify. Neither Gothic nor Baroque, neither Art Nouveau nor Victorian — certainly it was not Contemporary, yet in a configuration that struck a chord at the rim of familiarity.

There were openings here and there and the openings were dissimilar. Circular and squared apertures; originality of design, in such depth that none of them could be called doors or windows with certainty. They were merely openings: for what purposes I did not know. I looked for one that would fit me.

And there was a scintillance, a shimmering quality to the scene, as if I were viewing it through a membrane, or from a great distance, distorted by heat ghosts.

That was my dream.

Over and over and over again. Waking was a sense of loss, sleeping was life.

There was a sorrow and a strangeness in me then; and I grew older resonating to some soundless song no one else could hear. I was always alone…walled in, yet much freer than those who ran and played around me — my brothers and sisters. And because I was different, it was not an easy life.

My father and mother were second generation Italian Americans and my father was historically impressed by an early American patriot named Whitelaw Martin. He was like that. My name bothered me until junior college. They constantly abbreviated it to "Whitey," and my hair was pitch black — that and a perfect body were the last vestiges of my Italian heritage. But there were a lot of other things that bothered me also. When you are a child you must run with the pack. I couldn't do it. At first my brothers fought my fights for me, stood up for me, but later I lost even my brothers. And I was strange, I knew that. It took strong stimulus to get through to me. Kids' games never did it. I found something that did and I buried myself in the daytime too.

Books.

At first there were fairy tales. I could lose myself in those fabled lands and the cathedral would become unnecessary for a while. When I was ten I read through the *Brittanica* and I spouted facts until I was beaten to my knees. Then I learned that it is unwise to be wise. At fourteen I'd read almost everything that was worthwhile and lots that was not. I'd read Shakespeare and I could quote whole acts; I'd read the mad, brilliant ones like Fort and Nostradamus. I'd read Hemingway and Plato and *The Compleat Angler*.

And I grew away from those around me, without boyhood or regret for it. One day, when I was nineteen and in college, I looked around and saw that I was tolerated, but not loved. And the conscripters were breathing at my heels for I'd lost interest in school and my stats were marginal.

I enlisted in the Force.

It was still the Air Force, but it sounded ridiculous to call a service that spent most of its budget in the vacuum of deep space the "Air" Force. So the jingoists, and then the newsfax shortened it to Force.

I became a Forceman. That may sound dramatic, but it wasn't. At least, not at first.

I was trained, and assigned as a hot-stuff drainage expert to a coolant team, based with a limpet missile unit outside La Paz. Based there, but we did a lot of traveling.

It was during the travels — Borneo, Lebanon, Malta, the Arctic, Chad, Kingsland — that the dream ceased to trouble me. I looked for the building in every land and could not find it. But as the dream faded, so did the obsession retreat.

Oh, there were remembrances. On clear nights, when the stars were so painfully sharp they hurt my eyes and I was pulling guard mount under them, then I'd remember the dream. But it was as if I'd put it aside, this dream that was almost a knowledge, and it was waiting for me, but willing to wait. As if it were saying: My *time will come*.

And yet I was not completely patient in my waiting. I collected buildings, in much the same way that many people collect books or stamps. I had pictures of every famous structure in the world, thousands of pictures. My favorite was a framed photo of a tiny Shintoist shrine, that had a vague, grudging resemblance to my dream building. But they were all wrong — Taj Mahal to ruined Angkor Wat — none of them even reasonably resembled mine. So the fixation remained and I continued to look. The thirst could not be slaked, no matter how much I drank.

They were using radex fusion propellants then, and every once in a while we, or the Cubans, or the Sheikdoms would send out a one man job that would attempt to crack the barrier beyond the Edge. But none came back. None of ours for sure and the others never claimed any success, I suppose for fear they'd have to substantiate the claim.

The fights went on in the U.N.: bickering about territories that neither of us could really use; limited wars; police actions; border incidents; each nation striving to establish superiority over the other.

All this, even in an era of limited exploration of the Solar System. We should have known better.

And then along came something out of a magician's hat and what was to be...was set in motion. But I didn't know that — not yet.

They'd been giving Force-wide tests. They were odd tests, unlike any I'd ever taken. The questions were odd and peculiarly-phrased and yet, sometimes, lucid and almost exciting to me in their familiarity — as if someone should have asked them of me long ago, so that I would know and they would know. There were questions about foods and smells and what you would do in a given situation. There were many of those. But every once in a while there was something else, like: "What do you think it would be like to die?" or "Have you ever felt apart from all places and things?" or "What is the loveliest thing that you can remember?"

And there were physicals, too. Good, competent physicals, not hurried and superficial, as were the annual checkups.

The dreams came back then — nearer and closer.

I was sorry when the tests were completed: the dream became sporadic again — once more it receded.

Six weeks later I was cut new orders. They flew me out. A special VTOL. I was the lone passenger.

I counted.

I had to show my orders exactly fourteen times from the minute I reached Bong Field until I was billeted there. I never saw so many guys with guns — off safety — even in a battle area. And they didn't just check my orders — they read them. Then they checked my face against my I.D. card and made me rattle off my service number. Then they fluoro-ed my retinas and took my fingerprints and checked them against copies from my "master file."

They'd taken a group of old hangars and put high fences around them. Real high and charged. Then they'd put a guard along every fifteen or twenty yards of fence. There was another fence inside the outer one and more guards. I guess they wanted to keep what they had inside. A close-mouthed captain took me to a barracks and there were other men billeted there. But that night the dream wasn't there. I couldn't sleep.

In the morning they started more tests on me and about thirty others who appeared to have been shipped in from almost everywhere. At first, physicals. The tests were similar to what had been run before. After a while they became more complicated. Doctors beat on me, and pinched me, and took my blood, and flashed lights at me, and depressed my tongue, and scraped bits of skin off me. Then they whirled me in a thing like a "whip" at the carnival and shot me up in an ejection seat. And I endured it all with the same vague excitement I'd felt during the other tests. But no one came to tell us what we were there for.

They had the bunch of us in two old barracks. But by ones and twos and threes they eliminated until there were only six of us left. And whenever the taciturn captain came in I knew it was not for me — just knew it.

I got to know the other five pretty well. They were all different from me in many ways. In one way we were the same. The first of them was a large-boned, wry black man embarrassingly named Washington

Jones. Then there were Samuels and Kahn, who was very tiny, and the two women, Pearson and Ludwig. They were all different from me — except for their eyes.

When it got down to six, a colonel came into the barracks one day and pinned bars on our lapels and shook our hands.

I suppose we all knew, in a way, what was going on. We figured they'd found something and, from the tests, that we were their guinea pigs.

The dream was very close now. It was as though I was reliving a bit of my childhood. I saw myself up there again — my face, the same child's face I'd always had, with the wide eyes and the freckles and the black, black hair and the slash of a mouth, wide and frowning. But the body was different. It was bigger than life, man-plus. Hard and ripplingly-muscled, tall and golden, like a god out of a Greek myth. I was that god.

I recognized the egocentricity of it, naturally, but my cathedral waited beneath me. And I awoke.

The barracks was quiet around me. All but our six bunks were empty now. Faint dawn light filtered down the walls. I lay awake for a while, remembering; then I scratched a cigarette alight.

Another spot of red bloomed from a nearby bunk and Wash Jones's voice said softly: "You awake, Fazio?"

I grunted.

"I've been working it over in my mind," he said. "Why we're here — why I'm here. I'm afraid. All my life I've been waiting for something to happen to me. Now that it is, I'm afraid of it but I want it."

"Do you ever dream?" I asked.

His voice was almost lost: "I dream, but I can't share it." When his voice came again it was hesitant: "Did you ever read Charles Fort, Fazio?"

"A long time ago."

"Remember what he said about time?" His voice strengthened. "That there are ages in which certain occurrences are predestined to happen. Not by divine ordinance, but just because it's their time to happen. The time of the wheel and the steam engine and the automobile. And if someone comes up with one too early, there's a singular, almost mystical, disregard of the invention. As though the world were snubbing it till it was ready for it."

I felt the excitement grow a little again and what he said was right and it fit inside me, fit in with my dream.

And I lay there and thought about it; and for a long time we were silent.

I was almost back to sleep when I heard him muttering to himself, *"What time is it now, Washington Jones? What time is it now?"*

I checked Charles Fort out of the base library next day and read him through again. I had nothing but spare time. We waited, and no one told us a damn thing. Once Jones saw me with the book and we grinned at each other self-consciously. But the book did not engender in me the kind of excitement that I'd hoped for. Fort was quite brilliant and quite paranoid.

Yet the dream persisted and Jones's concept was some part of it and something to mull over in my spare time.

Which was something I had little time for.

Because without warning they started the question and answer tests again.

Those tests — sometimes I felt like slamming a wall. Tests unlike any that I'd known existed. Ponder the significance of this:

Do you lose things constantly? (If answer is "yes" indicate how often, what type of thing lost, where found, mental condition at time of recovery, and any other emotional data.)

On some days the questions came as adjuncts to weird movies. I remember some of them. The first was a reel of kaleidoscopic wheeling and whirling and shunting from one hue to another. Before it was done I felt as if I was beaten and torn. I felt as if the future had vanished and swallowed me.

The question was: *What are your feelings about death in the abstract? In the specific?* (Do not use qualifiers.)

Later there was an existentialist movie about sadism, and a rose, and a fruitless love affair between a cripple and a girl with one eye. There was a miracle in the end. I didn't understand the picture, but I didn't want the lights to come back on.

Question two was: *What is your stand on God?* (Answer bluntly, avoid partisan religious referents, where possible.)

They gave us one more that first day. It was a movie about a man who dreamed strange dreams and who thought he was insane. The actor made it seem very real — chillingly real.

And the question was: *Have you ever dreamed that you could fly or thought that you were flying without the use of any mechanical aid?*

That one I had real trouble with. I answered it finally by saying that I had, "in my childhood."

And so it went. For better than a week. That sort of question. Some that were almost nonsense, some that were so sharp and keen that the point penetrated deep within me.

They told us we were not to discuss the questions in the barracks. So we did, of course. At great length. And there were a lot of theories, but nothing concrete.

Finally they told us.

There was this little man. He couldn't have been much over forty, but he wore the star of a brigadier. He was a Doctor Something, I later found out it was "Stein," a psychiatrist, with degrees in things that ran from linguistics to physics and a mind that worked like a fine computer. He must have come here voluntarily from some other country, I never found out which. His eyes were sad behind thick-lensed glasses and his voice was phlegmy with the heritage of Central Europe. He was rough to understand, but I felt an instinctive liking for him. When he talked — we listened.

"It's different out there," he said. "We know that. On the few flights we've made we've found a great deal. And still we know very little."

He looked out around the room and his eyes behind the lenses were lost in the big dream, the thwarted longing. "The things we do here don't work well out there — the stamina that we possess means little. Our laws of logic, our world's ethical structure, most of what we've postulated goes…wrong…out there. It's as if when the force of gravity, of Earth-touching, is lost, everything else is lost too. It's cost some good lives and it's made us change our method of selection.

"And now we're going out farther than ever before. We're going out — past the barrier. We have the means to do it. And you people are specially qualified to do it for us."

The room around me rippled with sound. My pulse sprinted and I forced calmness so that I would not miss the words.

"We have asked you questions that made you feel we were not quite right in the head." He smiled. He was missing two teeth on the upper left.

"But the questions had a purpose — some to shock you into a non-conformist awareness — some to tell us things about you the Force-wide tests merely hinted at." He leaned forward on the podium. "Each of you is a loner. Each of you has the ability to maintain, even to transcend against whatever conditions exist around you, remaining essentially yourselves, with no great personality change. There is a segment of the brain that does not work well under the pressure of gravity, but which tends to become dominant when gravity is removed as a factor. There are other areas that only work when gravity is present. We theorize that there are other areas that will work only under conditions produced by exceeding the speed of light. We have not been lucky with deep space beyond the barrier so far. Yet we have learned. We feel that we'll be luckier now that we know — now that we are able to look for qualities such as you have." He looked out at us and I felt both excited and queasy. And I explored me and lost myself in what he was saying. What was he saying, actually? Psi? I knew something about that and Rhine's old failed experiments, decades ago. There were remarks about the cortex and four-fifths of the brain inac-tive, and random reflexes. And after a while I only understood a word here and there. But I understood his final remarks.

"We know the ship will work. There have been tests. We are more interested now in studying human behavior — in finding out if the human race can survive the trip to the stars. We have built our ship around a special bank of instruments, which will be closely telemetered, to record every thought, every emotion, every vision you sustain.

"Do any of you wish to volunteer?"

I put my hand up and then looked around. There were five more hands raised. My hand felt wet in the moving currents of the room, but my throat was dry.

Stein smiled. "We'll have to draw lots."

Whitelaw Fazio's luck. I pulled second. Ludwig pulled first, the star-marked ballot. She would be the first to go to the stars. I felt a deep disappointment when I saw her bright eyes.

And yet there was relief, too.

"Do any of you want to ask questions?" Dr. Stein asked, when the lottery was done.

Wash Jones's hand went up. "Sir," he said, "what have we discovered that will let us get to the stars? As far as we knew, a few months back, they couldn't even get one of the stage ships back."

The glasses came up and shone in the light. The face went a little strange. "I have a degree in physics, Mr. Jones. But I was working on something else, something more in my own field of interest — you need not ask the nature of my primary specialty, I think you can guess — and I stumbled onto what we now call a 'force-bead-generator.' It goes beyond accepted physics. It gives a sure, never failing power source."

Washington Jones looked over at me and it hit me then.

Fort's theory about the Era of Anything. This was the Time for Space Travel. The baby was ready to be born, so ready that a psychiatrist, trying to find something else, could discover it and recognize its significance. So maybe Fort had been right.

A week before the takeoff, Ludwig woke before dawn feeling as if she would die.

It turned out to be a burst appendix, so they operated.

Ludwig would be laid up for a long time.

I was shuttled out to the Kalahari jump-point and received my penultimate briefings from Stein, who was in charge of the project.

He was nervous when he talked to me and he was envious, too. He kept talking about how the acceleration would take me through what he called "Bounces" or "Progressions." He pronounced them *bunces* and *prugrooshens*.

I felt, listening to him, as if I were royalty. He spoke to me with deference.

He said that they had sent six of the ships out on remote control voyages and that five of them had returned.

The night before takeoff my dream was back so near and close that I seemed but inches away. I saw my fluted organ pipe cathedral and me above it. I came awake all sweat and tears, for the building had talked to me and though I couldn't recall now what had been said, I was scared. I lay there and wrestled with myself and my desires for a long time. Then I called Stein. I felt I must, even if it took away my chance. If I was insane then I had to be replaced.

"All of you have had that dream, or one similar to it," he said. "All six of you." He looked at me and his face was very sad. "I never dream," he said softly.

It wasn't much of a ship, as far as size: When you're used to monstrosities, you'd expect a starship to be that much more impressive, that much larger. But it wasn't.

It was just a teardrop, with a small room in the bulge that was mine. There were extrudable wings and tail for atmosphere landings, wherever I was going, and a cleverly geared set of drop-wheels guaranteed to hold on the shiftiest desert or marsh. And in my cubicle, all around, there were instruments.

There were instruments that watched me, instruments that hooked into me, fed me, bathed me, relieved me, metered me, and weighed me.

I said goodbye to the others and on the proper day, at the proper time, they locked me into the cubicle. And somewhere the countdown began. But I didn't know that. I'd been drugged. Lying on my gelatin-pad couch, I was insensitive to the rustlings and clangings and preparations. A machine was carrying me, on orders set forth by another machine, using calculations done by a third. I'd have manual control only when I came within safe range of that star, and then only if a machine decided I should.

Which star? A machine would calculate that, too.

I had the distinct impression I was supercargo on this flight. And yet, more essential than the finest, most cleverly made machine ever assembled. I was grateful that machines did not have whims or temperament.

I slept while things happened and technicians sweated. I slept while pencils toted figures and graph-dials. I slept while a tiny bead of cadmium and thirty-six other trace metals built a field of force around itself, while the Earth whirled blindly beneath me. I slept while people died and others were reborn in the story which had no answer — then.

The ship was towed into its berth, and I tossed restlessly and then did not toss at all when the force bead unleashed its power, throwing the tiny ship far into the darkness, and pushing me smoothly, deeply into the gel-pad. I did not waken while a soundless force pushed me past the speed of light in "progressions" and to a multitude of speeds in "bounces."

But there wasn't any dream in this sleep. There was no need for the dream now.

I was different when I awoke. I didn't know how, but I was different. Not altered, just different. How can I put it? — have you ever seen a goldfish bowl after the water has been in it for a few days? All bubbled and odd-looking, not at all clear the way it had been at first. Well, that was me. All bubbled and changed, but still the same in most ways.

I was better, somehow. And calm.

I remained in that tranquil state for a long time. Months perhaps. There are records.

The machines tended to me, and that was a good thing, for I was under the spell of that sense of comfort and rightness. Then, finally —

The star has no name — not now — not any more. But once we knew its name, a long time ago.

I could not have headed for any other place had I wanted to. Fate and Destiny had planned it that way; Fate and Destiny had been keeping steady company for a long, long time.

The machines ratcheted and catalogued and analyzed, and the ship slowed so the points of light in the darkness surrounding me were stationary again, instead of moving and wheeling.

There were twenty-one planets. I took the twelfth. Instinctively. The machines did not interfere with my course selection.

I came down slowly. The planet was misty and quiet. I did not bother to check whether the air was Earth-breathable. I knew it would be.

We have been lost a long, long time, I think. But it was a short time in the history of the race. Why we were allowed to remain lost, I do not yet know, but I will know.

I broke down through the clouds of pink mist, and it was where I'd known it would be. There is no such thing as Chance. In an ordered universe, all is planned.

It didn't look alien any more, my cathedral. It looked like a home I'd once known, a long time before, and was seeing again with eyes of reminiscence. I knew this place. I knew it with racial memory, damped out by time and Earth living, by Earth gravity.

I knew it again.

I knew my *home*.

It was there. The organ pipes towered. The strange apertures yawned. I came down to land.

To see where we are going; to see what we are to become.

And I knew it would be stunning, what we are to become, for as the ship settled among the pastel ground-mists, our ancestors and our descendants began to emerge from those strange apertures.

It was the Cathedral of Man.

But man could not use those entrances.

There were still changes to come. Many changes. We had been lost...and now were found.

DJINN, NO CHASER

"Who the hell ever heard of Turkish Period?" Danny Squires said. He said it at the top of his voice, on a city street.

"Danny! People are staring at us; lower your voice!" Connie Squires punched his biceps. They stood on the street, in front of the furniture store. Danny was determined not to enter.

"Come on, Connie," he said, "let's get away from these junk shops and go see some inexpensive modern stuff. You know perfectly well I don't make enough to start filling the apartment with expensive antiques."

Connie furtively looked up and down the street — she was more concerned with a "scene" than with the argument itself — and then moved in toward Danny with a determined air. "Now listen up, Squires. *Did* you or did you *not* marry me four days ago, and promise to love, honor and cherish and all that other good jive?"

Danny's blue eyes rolled toward Heaven: he knew he was losing ground. Instinctively defensive, he answered. "Well, sure, Connie, but —"

"Well, then, I am your wife, and you have not taken me on a honeymoon."

"I can't *afford* one!"

"— have not taken me on a honeymoon." Connie repeated with inflexibility. "Consequently, we will buy a little furniture for that rabbit warren you laughingly call our little love nest. And *little* is hardly the term: that vale of tears was criminally undersized when Barbara Fritchie hung out her flag.

"So to make my life *bearable*, for the next few weeks, till we can talk Mr. Upjohn into giving you a raise —"

"Upjohn!" Danny fairly screamed. "You've got to stay away from the boss, Connie. Don't screw around. He won't give me a raise, and I'd rather you stayed away from him —"

"Until then," she went on relentlessly, "we will decorate our apartment in the style I've wanted for years."

"Turkish Period?"

"Turkish Period."

Danny flipped his hands in the air. What was the use? He had known Connie was strong-willed when he'd married her.

It had seemed an attractive quality at the time; now he wasn't so sure. But he was strong-willed too; he was sure he could outlast her. Probably.

"Okay," he said finally, "I suppose Turkish Period it'll be. What the hell *is* Turkish Period?"

She took his arm lovingly, and turned him around to look in the store window. "Well, honey, it's not *actually* Turkish. It's more Mesopotamian. You know, teak and silk and…"

"Sounds hideous."

"So you're starting up again!" She dropped his arm, her eyes flashing, her mouth a tight little line. "I'm really ashamed of you, depriving me of the few little pleasures I need to make my life a blub, sniff, hoo-hoo…"

The edge was hers.

"Connie…Connie…" She knocked away his comforting hand, saying, "You beast." That was too much for him. The words were so obviously put-on, he was suddenly infuriated:

"Now, goddammit!"

Her tears came faster. Danny stood there, furious, helpless, outmaneuvered, hoping desperately that no cop would come along and say, "This guy botherin' ya, lady?"

"Connie, okay, okay, we'll *have* Turkish Period. Come on, come on. It doesn't matter what it costs, I can scrape up the money somehow."

It was not one of the glass-brick and onyx emporia where sensible furniture might be found (if one searched hard enough and paid high enough and retained one's senses long enough as they were trying to palm off modernistic nightmares in which no comfortable position might be found); no, it was not even one of those. This was an antique shop.

They looked at beds that had canopies and ornate metalwork on the bedposts. They looked at rugs that were littered with pillows, so visitors could sit on the floors. They looked at tables built six inches off the floor, for low banquets. They inspected incense burners and hookahs and coffers and giant vases until Danny's head swam with visions of the courts of long-dead caliphs.

Yet, despite her determination, Connie chose very few items; and those she did select were moderately-priced and quite handsome…for what they were. And as the hours passed, and as they moved around town from one dismal junk emporium to another, Danny's respect for his wife's taste grew. She was selecting an apartment full of furniture that wasn't bad at all.

They were finished by six o'clock, and had bills of sale that totaled just under two hundred dollars. Exactly thirty dollars less than Danny had decided could be spent to furnish the new household…and still survive on his salary. He had taken the money from his spavined savings account, and had known he must eventually start buying on credit, or they would not be able to get enough furniture to start living properly.

He was tired, but content. She'd shopped wisely. They were in a shabby section of town. How had they gotten here? They walked past an empty lot sandwiched in between two tenements — wet wash slapping on lines between them. The lot was weed-overgrown and garbage-strewn.

"May I call your attention to the depressing surroundings and my exhaustion?" Danny said. "Let's get a cab and go back to the apartment. I want to collapse."

They turned around to look for a cab, and the empty lot was gone.

In its place, sandwiched between the two tenements, was a little shop. It was a one-storey affair, with a dingy facade, and its front window completely grayed-over with dust. A hand painted line of elaborate script on the glass panel of the door, also opaque with grime, proclaimed:

MOHANADUS MUKHAR, CURIOS.

A little man in a flowing robe, wearing a fez, plunged out the front door, skidded to a stop, whirled and slapped a huge sign on the window. He swiped at it four times with a big paste-brush, sticking it to the glass, and whirled back inside, slamming the door.

"No," Danny said.

Connie's mouth was making peculiar sounds.

"There's no insanity in my family," Danny said firmly. "We come from very good stock."

"We've made a visual error," Connie said.

"Simply didn't notice it," Danny said. His usually baritone voice was much nearer soprano.

"If there's crazy, we've both got it," Connie said.

"Must be, if you see the same thing I see."

Connie was silent a moment, then said, "Large seagoing vessel, three stacks, maybe the Titanic. Flamingo on the bridge, flying the flag of Liechtenstein?"

"Don't play with me, woman," Danny whimpered. "I think I'm losing it."

She nodded soberly. "Right. Empty lot?"

He nodded back, "Empty lot. Clothesline, weeds, garbage."

"Right."

He pointed at the little store. "Little store?"

"Right."

"Man in a fez, name of Mukhar?"

She rolled her eyes. "Right."

"So why are we walking toward it?"

"Isn't this what always happens in stories where weird shops suddenly appear out of nowhere? Something inexorable draws the innocent bystanders into its grip?"

They stood in front of the grungy little shop. They read the sign. It said:

BIG SALE! HURRY! NOW! QUICK!

"The word *unnatural* comes to mind," Danny said.

"Nervously," Connie said, "she turned the knob and opened the door."

A tiny bell went tinkle-tinkle, and they stepped across the threshold into Mohanadus Mukhar's shop.

"Probably not the smartest move we've ever made," Danny said softly. The door closed behind them without any assistance.

It was cool and musty in the shop, and strange fragrances chased one another past their noses.

They looked around carefully. The shop was loaded with junk. From floor to ceiling, wall to wall, on tables and in heaps, the place was filled with oddities and bric-a-brac. Piles of things tumbled over each other on the floor; heaps of things leaned against the walls. There was barely room to walk down the aisle between the stacks and mounds of things. Things in all shapes, things in all sizes and colors. Things. They tried to separate the individual items from the jumble of the place, but all they could perceive was stuff...things! Stuff and flotsam and bits and junk.

"Curios, effendi," a voice said, by way of explanation.

Connie leaped in the air and came down on Danny's foot.

Mukhar was standing beside such a pile of tumbled miscellany that for a moment they could not separate him from the stuff, junk, things he sold.

"We saw your sign," Connie said.

But Danny was more blunt, more direct. "There was an empty lot here; then a minute later, this shop. How come?"

The little man stepped out from the mounds of dust-collectors and his little nut-brown, wrinkled face burst into a million-creased smile. "A fortuitous accident, my children. A slight worn spot in the fabric of the cosmos, and I have been set down here for...how long I do not know. But it never hurts to try and stimulate business while I'm here."

"Uh, yeah," Danny said. He looked at Connie. Her expression was as blank as his own.

"Oh!" Connie cried, and went dashing off into one of the side corridors lined with curios. "This is perfect! Just what we need for the end table. Oh, Danny, it's a dream! It's absolutely the *ne plus ultra!*"

Danny walked over to her, but in the dimness of the aisle between the curios he could barely make out what it was she was holding. He drew her into the light near the door. It had to be:

Aladdin's lamp.

Well, perhaps not that *particular* person's lamp, but one of the ancient, vile-smelling oil burning jobs: long thin spout, round-bottom body, wide, flaring handle.

It was algae-green with tarnish, brown with rust, and completely covered by the soot and debris of centuries. There was no contesting its antiquity; nothing so time-corrupted could fail to be authentic. "What the hell do you want with that old thing, Connie?"

"But Danny, it's so *per*-fect. If we just shine it up a bit. As soon as we put a little work into this lamp, it'll be a beauty." Danny knew he was defeated...and she'd probably be right, too. It probably would be very handsome when shined and brassed-up.

"How much?" he asked Mukhar. He didn't want to seem anxious; old camel traders were merciless at bargaining when they knew the item in question was hotly desired.

"Fifty drachmae, eh?" the old man said. His tone was one of malicious humor. "At current exchange rates, taking into account the fall of the Ottoman Empire, thirty dollars."

Danny's lips thinned. "Put it down, Connie; let's get out of here."

He started toward the door, dragging his wife behind him. But she still clutched the lamp; and Mukhar's voice halted them. "All right, noble sir. You are a cunning shopper, I can see that. You know a bargain when you spy it. But I am unfamiliar in this time-frame with your dollars and your strange fast-food native customs, having been set down here only once before; and since I am more at ease with the drachma than the dollar, with the shekel than the cent, I will cut my own throat, slash both my wrists, and offer you this magnificent antiquity for...uh...twenty dollars?" His voice was querulous, his tone one of wonder and hope.

"Jesse James at least had a horse!" Danny snarled, once again moving toward the door.

"Fifteen!" Mukhar yowled. "And may all your children need corrective lenses from too much tv-time!"

"Five; and may a hundred thousand syphilitic camels puke into your couscous," Danny screamed back over his shoulder.

"Not bad," said Mukhar.

"Thanks," said Danny, stifling a smile. Now he waited.

"Bloodsucker! Heartless trafficker in cheapness! Pimple on the fundament of decency! Graffito on the subway car of life! Thirteen; my last offer; and may the gods of ITT and the Bank of America turn a blind eye to your venality!" But *his* eyes held the golden gleam of the born haggler, at last, blessedly, in his element.

"Seven, not a penny more, you Arabic anathema! And may a weighty object drop from a great height, flattening you to the niggardly thickness of your soul." Connie stared at him with open awe and admiration.

"Eleven! Eleven dollars, a pittance, an outright theft we're talking about. Call the security guards, get a consumer advocate, gimme a break here!"

"My shadow will vanish from before the evil gleam of your rapacious gaze before I pay a penny more than six bucks, and let the word go out to every wadi and oasis across the limitless desert, that Mohanadus Mukhar steals maggots from diseased meat, flies from horse dung, and the hard-earned drachmae of honest laborers. Six, fuckface, and that's it!"

"My death is about to become a reality," the Arab bellowed, tearing at the strands of white hair showing under the fez. "Rob me, go ahead, rob me; drink my life's blood! Ten! A twenty dollar loss I'll take."

"Okay, okay." Danny turned around and produced his wallet. He pulled out one of the three ten-dollar bills still inside and, turning to Connie, said, "You sure you want this ugly, dirty piece of crap?" She nodded, and he held the bill naked in the vicinity of the little merchant. For the first time Danny realized Mukhar was wearing pointed slippers that curled up; there was hair growing from his ears.

"Ten bucks."

The little man moved with the agility of a ferret and whisked the tenner from Danny's outstretched hand before he could draw it back. "Sold!" Mukhar chuckled.

He spun around once, and when he faced them again, the ten dollars was out of sight. "And a steal, though Allah be the wiser; a hot deal, a veritable steal, blessed sir!"

Danny abruptly realized he had been taken. The lamp had probably been picked up in a junkyard and was worthless. He started to ask if it was a genuine antique, but the piles of junk had begun to waver and shimmer and coruscate with light. "Hey!" Danny said, alarmed. "What's this now?"

The little man's wrinkled face drew up in panic. "Out! Get out, quick! The time-frame is sucking back together! Out! Get out now if you don't want to roam the eternities with me and this shop...and I can't afford any help! Out!"

He shoved them forward, and Connie slipped and fell, flailing into a pile of glassware. None of it broke. Her hand went out to protect herself and went right through the glass. Danny dragged her to her feet, panic sweeping over him...as the shop continued to waver and grow more indistinct around them. "Out! Out! Out!" Mukhar kept yelling.

Then they were at the door, and he was kicking them — literally planting his curl-slippered foot in Danny's backside and shoving —

from the store. They landed in a heap on the sidewalk. The lamp bounced from Connie's hand and went into the gutter with a clang. The little man stood there grinning in the doorway, and as the shop faded and disappeared, they heard him mumble happily, "A clear nine-seventy-five profit. What a lemon! You got an Edsel, kid, a real lame piece of goods. But I gotta give it to you; the syphilitic camel bit was inspired."

Then the shop was gone, and they got to their feet in front of an empty, weed-overgrown lot.

A lame piece of goods?

"Are you asleep?"

"Yes."

"How come you're answering me?"

"I was raised polite."

"Danny, talk to me...come on!"

"The answer is no. I'm not going to talk about it."

"We have to!"

"Not only don't we *have* to, I don't *want* to, ain't *going* to, and shut up so I can go to sleep."

"We've been lying here almost an hour. Neither one of us can sleep. We *have* to discuss it, Danny."

The light went on over his side of the bed. The single pool of illumination spread from the hand-me-down daybed they had gotten from Danny's brother in New Jersey, faintly limning the few packing crates full of dishes and linens, the three Cuisinarts they'd gotten as wedding gifts, the straight-back chairs from Connie's Aunt Medora, the entire bare and depressing reality of their first home together.

It would be better when the furniture they'd bought today was delivered. Later, it would be better. Now, it was the sort of urban landscape that drove divorcees and aging bachelors to jump down the airshaft at Christmastime.

"I'm going to talk about it, Squires."

"So talk. I have my thumbs in my ears."

"I think we should rub it."

"I can't hear you. It never happened. I deny the evidence of my senses. It never happened. I have these thumbs in my ears so I cannot hear a syllable of this craziness."

"For god's sake, Squires, I was *there* with you today. I saw it happen, the same as you. I saw that weird little old man and I saw his funky shop come and go like a big burp. Now, neither of us can deny it!"

"If I could hear you, I'd agree; and then I'd deny the evidence of my senses and tell you…" He took his thumbs from his ears, looking distressed. "…tell you with all my heart that I love you, that I have loved you since the moment I saw you in the typing pool at Upjohn, that if I live to be a hundred thousand years old I'll never love any one or any thing as much as I love you this very moment; and then I would tell you to fuck off and forget it, and let me go to sleep so that tomorrow I can con myself into believing it never happened the way I know it happened.

"Okay?"

She threw back the covers and got out of bed. She was naked. They had not been married that long.

"Where are you going?"

"You know where I'm going."

He sat up in the daybed. His voice had no lightness in it. "Connie!"

She stopped and stared at him, there in the light.

He spoke softly. "Don't. I'm scared. Please don't."

She said nothing. She looked at him for a time. Then, naked, she sat down cross-legged on the floor at the foot of the daybed. She looked around at what little they had, and she answered him gently. "I have to, Danny. I just have to…if there's a chance; I have to."

They sat that way, reaching across the abyss with silent imperatives, until — finally — Danny nodded, exhaled heavily, and got out of the daybed. He walked to one of the cartons, pulled out a dustrag, shook it clean over the box, and handed it to her. He walked over to the window ledge where the tarnished and rusted oil lamp sat, and he brought it to her.

"Shine the damned thing, Squires. Who knows, maybe we actually got ourselves a 24-carat genie. Shine on, oh mistress of my Mesopotamian mansion."

She held the lamp in one hand, the rag in the other. For a few minutes she did not bring them together. "I'm scared, too," she said, held her breath, and briskly rubbed the belly of the lamp.

Under her flying fingers the rust and tarnish began to come away in spots. "We'll need brass polish to do this right," she said; but suddenly the ruin covering the lamp melted away, and she was rubbing the bright skin of the lamp itself.

"Oh, Danny, look how nice it is, underneath all the crud!" And at that precise instant the lamp jumped from her hand, emitted a sharp, gray puff of smoke, and a monstrous voice bellowed out in the apartment:

AH-HA! It screamed, louder than a subway train. AH-HA!

FREE AT LAST! FREE — AS FREE AS I'LL EVER BE — AFTER TEN THOUSAND YEARS! FREE TO SPEAK AND ACT, MY WILL TO BE KNOWN!

Danny went over backward. The sound was as mind-throttling as being at ground zero. The window glass blew out. Every light bulb in the apartment shattered. From the carton containing their meager chinaware came the distinct sound of hailstones as every plate and cup dissolved into shards. Dogs and cats blocks away began to howl. Connie screamed — though it could not be heard over the foghorn thunder of the voice — and was knocked head over ankles into a corner, still clutching the dustrag. Plaster showered down on the little apartment. The window shades rolled up.

Danny recovered first. He crawled over a chair and stared at the lamp with horror. Connie sat up in the corner, face white, eyes huge, hands over her ears. Danny stood up and looked down at the seemingly innocuous lamp.

"Knock off that noise! You want to lose us the lease?"

CERTAINLY, OFFSPRING OF A WORM!

"I said: stop that goddam bellowing!"

THIS WHISPER? THIS IS AS NAUGHT TO THE HURRICANE

I SHALL LOOSE, SPAWN OF PARAMECIUM!

"That's it," Danny yelled. "I'm not getting kicked out of the only apartment in the city of New York I can afford just because of some loudmouthed genie in a jug…"

He stopped. He looked at Connie. Connie looked back at him. "Oh, my god," she said.

"It's real," he said.

They got to their knees and crawled over. The lamp lay on its side on the floor at the foot of the daybed.

"Are you really in there?" Connie asked.

WHERE ELSE WOULD I BE, SLUT!

"Hey, you can't talk to my wife that way —"

Connie shushed him. "If he's a genie, he can talk any way he likes. Sticks and stones; namecalling is better than poverty."

"Yeah? Well, *nobody* talks to my —"

"Put a lid on it, Squires. I can take care of myself. If what's in this lamp is even half the size of the genie in that movie you took me to the Thalia to see…"

"*The Thief of Bagdad*…1939 version…but Rex Ingram was just an actor, they only made him *look* big."

"Even so. As big as he was, if this genie is only *half* that big, playing macho overprotective chauvinist hubby —"

SO HUMANS CONTINUE TO PRATTLE LIKE MONKEYS EVEN AFTER TEN THOUSAND YEARS! WILL NOTHING CLEANSE THE EARTH OF THIS RAUCOUS PLAGUE OF INSECTS?

"We're going to get thrown right out of here," Danny said. His face screwed up in a horrible expression of discomfort.

"If the cops don't beat the other tenants to it."

"Please, genie," Danny said, leaning down almost to the lamp. "Just tone it down a little willya?"

OFFSPRING OF A MILLION STINKS! SUFFER!

"You're no genie," Connie said smugly. Danny looked at her with disbelief.

"He's no genie? Then what the hell do you *think* he is?"

She swatted him. Then put her finger to her lips.

THAT IS WHAT I AM, WHORE OF DEGENERACY!

"No you're not."

I AM.

"Am not."

AM.

"Am not."

AM SO, CHARNEL HOUSE HARLOT! WHY SAY YOU NAY?

"A genie has a lot of power; a genie doesn't need to shout like that to make himself heard. You're no genie, or you'd speak softly. You *can't* speak at a decent level, because you're a fraud."

CAUTION, TROLLOP!

"Foo, you don't scare me. If you were as powerful as you make out, you'd tone it way down."

is this better? are you convinced?

"Yes," Connie said, "I think that's more convincing. Can you keep it up, though? That's the question."

forever, if need be.

"And you can grant wishes?" Danny was back in the conversation.

naturally, but not to you, disgusting grub of humanity.

"Hey, listen," Danny replied angrily, "I don't give a damn what or *who* you are! You can't talk to me that way." Then a thought dawned on him. "After all, I'm your master!"

ah! correction, filth of primordial seas. there are some djinn who are mastered by their owners, but unfortunately for you i am not one of them, for i am not free to leave this metal prison. i was imprisoned in this accursed vessel many ages ago by a besotted sorcerer who knew nothing of molecular compression and even less of the binding forces of the universe. he put me into this thrice-cursed lamp, far too small for me, and i have been wedged within ever since. over the ages my good nature has rotted away. i am powerful, but trapped. those who own me cannot request anything and hope to realize their boon. i am unhappy, and an unhappy djinn is an evil djinn. were i free, i might be your slave; but as i am now, i will visit unhappiness on you in a thousand forms!

Danny chuckled, "The hell you will. I'll toss you in the incinerator."

ah! but you cannot. once you have bought the lamp, you cannot lose it, destroy it or give it away, only sell it. i am with you forever, for who would buy such a miserable lamp?

And thunder rolled in the sky.

"What are you going to do?" Connie asked.

do? just ask me for something, and you shall see!

"Not me," Danny said, "you're too cranky."

wouldn't you like a billfold full of money?

There was sincerity in the voice from the lamp.

"Well, sure, I want money, but —"

The djinn's laughter was gigantic, and suddenly cut off by the rain of frogs that fell from a point one inch below the ceiling, clobbering Danny and Connie with small, reeking, wriggling green bodies. Connie screamed and dove for the clothes closet. She came out a second later, her hair full of them; they were falling in the closet, as well. The rain of frogs continued and when Danny opened the front door to try and escape them, they fell in the hall. He slammed the door — he realized he was still naked — and covered his head with his hands. The frogs fell, writhing, stinking, and then they were knee-deep in them, with little filthy, warty bodies jumping up at their faces.

what a lousy disposition i've got! the djinn said, and then he laughed. And he laughed again, a clangorous peal that was silenced only when the frogs stopped, disappeared, and the flood of blood began.

It went on for a week.

They could not get away from him, no matter where they went. They were also slowly starving: they could not go out to buy groceries without the earth opening under their feet, or a herd of elephants chasing them down the street, or hundreds of people getting violently ill and vomiting on them. So they stayed in and ate what canned goods they had stored up in the first four days of their marriage. But who could eat with locusts filling the apartment from top to bottom, or snakes that were intent on gobbling them up like little white rats?

First came the frogs, then the flood of blood, then the whirling dust storm, then the spiders and gnats, then the snakes and then the locusts and then the tiger that had them backed against a wall and ate the chair they used to ward him off. Then came the bats and the leprosy and the hailstones and then the floor dissolved under them and they clung to the wall fixtures while their furniture — which had been quickly delivered (the moving men had brought it during the hail-stones) — fell through, nearly killing the little old lady who lived beneath them.

Then the walls turned red hot and melted, and then the lightning burned everything black, and finally Danny had had enough. He cracked, and went gibbering around the room, tripping over the man-eating vines that were growing out of the light sockets and the floor-boards. He finally sat down in a huge puddle of monkey urine and cried till his face grew puffy and his eyes flame-red and his nose swelled to three times normal size.

"I've got to get *away* from all this!" he screamed hysterically, drumming his heels, trying to eat his pants' cuffs.

you can divorce her, and that means you are voided out of the purchase contract: she wanted the lamp, not you, the djinn suggested.

Danny looked up (just in time to get a ripe Black Angus meadow muffin in his face) and yelled, "I won't! You can't make me. We've only been married a week and four days and I won't leave her!"

Connie, covered with running sores, stumbled to Danny and hugged him, though he had turned to tapioca pudding and was melting. But three days later, when ghost images of people he had feared all his life came to haunt him, he broke completely and allowed Connie to call the rest home on the boa constrictor that had once been the phone. "You can come and get me when this is over," he cried pitifully, kissing her poison ivy lips. "Maybe if we split up, he'll have some mercy." But they both doubted it.

When the downstairs buzzer rang, the men from the Home for the Mentally Absent came into the debacle that had been their apartment and saw Connie pulling her feet out of the swamp slime only with difficulty; she was crying in unison with Danny as they bundled him into the white ambulance. Unearthly laughter rolled around the sky like thunder as her husband was driven away.

Connie was left alone. She went back upstairs; she had nowhere else to go.

She slumped down in the pool of molten slag, and tried to think while ants ate at her flesh and rabid rats gnawed off the wallpaper.

i'm just getting warmed up, the djinn said from the lamp.

Less than three days after he had been admitted to the Asylum for the Temporarily Twitchy, Connie came to get Danny. She came into his room; the shades were drawn, the sheets were very white; when he saw her his teeth began to chatter.

She smiled at him gently. "If I didn't know better, I'd swear you weren't simply overjoyed to see me, Squires."

He slid under the sheets till only his eyes were showing. His voice came through the covers. "If I break out in boils, it will definitely cause a relapse, and the day nurse hates mess."

"Where's my macho protective husband now?"

"I've been unwell."

"Yeah, well, that's all over. You're fit as a fiddle, so bestir your buns and let's get out of here."

Danny Squires's brow furrowed. This was not the tone of a woman with frogs in her hair. "I've been contemplating divorce or suicide."

She yanked the covers down, exposing his naked legs sticking out from the hem of the hospital gown. "Forget it, little chum. There are at least a hundred and ten positions we haven't tried yet before I consider dissolution. Now will you get out of that bed and *come on?*"

"But..."

"...a thing I'll kick, if you don't move it."

Bewildered, he moved it.

Outside, the Rolls-Royce waited with its motor running. As they came through the front doors of the Institute for the Neurologically Flaccid, and Connie helped Danny from the discharge wheelchair, the liveried chauffeur leaped out and opened the door for them. They got in the back seat, and Connie said, "To the house, Mark." The chauffeur nodded, trotted briskly around and climbed behind the wheel. They took off to the muted roar of twin mufflers.

Danny's voice was a querulous squeak. "Can we afford a rented limo?"

Connie did not answer, merely smiled, and snuggled closer to him.

After a moment Danny asked, "What house?"

Connie pressed a button on the console in the armrest and the glass partition between front and back seats slid silently closed. "Do me a favor, will you," she said, "just hold the twenty questions till we get home? It's been a tough three days and all I ask is that you hold it together for another hour."

Danny nodded reluctantly. Then he noticed she was dressed in extremely expensive clothes. "I'd better not ask about your mink-trimmed jacket, either, right?"

"It would help."

He settled into silence, uneasy and juggling more than just twenty unasked questions. And he remained silent until he realized they were not taking the expressway into New York. He sat up sharply, looked out the rear window, snapped his head right and left trying to ascertain their location, and Connie said, "We're not going to Manhattan. We're going to Darien, Connecticut."

"Darien? Who the hell do we know in Darien?"

"Well, Upjohn, for one, lives in Darien."

"Upjohn!?! Ohmigod, he's fired me and sent the car to bring me to him so he can have me executed! I *knew* it!"

"Squires," she said, "Daniel, my love, Danny heart of my heart, will you just kindly close the tap on it for a while! Upjohn has nothing to do with us any more. Nothing at all."

"But…but we live in New York!"

"Not any more we don't."

Twenty minutes later they turned into the most expensive section in Darien and sped down a private road.

They drove an eighth of a mile down the private road lined with Etruscan pines, beautifully maintained, and pulled into a winding driveway. Five hundred yards farther, and the drive spiraled in to wind around the front of a huge, luxurious, completely tasteful Victorian mansion. "Go on," Connie said. "Look at your house."

"Who lives here?" Danny asked.

"I just told you: we do."

"I thought that's what you said. Let me out here, I'll walk back to the nuthouse."

The Rolls pulled up before the mansion, and a butler ran down to open the car door for them. They got out and the servant bowed low to Connie. Then he turned to Danny. "Good to have you home, Mr. Squires," he said. Danny was too unnerved to reply.

"Thank you, Penzler," Connie said. Then, to the chauffeur, "Take the car to the garage, Mark; we won't be needing it again this afternoon. But have the Porsche fueled and ready; we may drive out later to look at the grounds."

"Very good, Mrs. Squires," Mark said. Then he drove away.

Danny was somnambulistic. He allowed himself to be led into the house where he was further stunned by the expensive fittings, the magnificent halls, the deep-pile rugs, the spectacular furniture, the communications complex set into an entire wall, the Art Deco bar that rose out of the floor at the touch of a button, the servants who bowed and smiled at him as if he belonged there. He was boggled by the huge kitchen, fitted with every latest appliance, and the French chef who saluted with a huge ladle as Connie entered.

"Wh-where did all this come from?" He finally gasped out the question as Connie led him upstairs on the escalator.

"Come on, Danny; you know where it all came from."

"The limo, the house, the grounds, the mink-trimmed jacket, the servants, the Vermeer in the front hall, the cobalt-glass Art Deco bar, the entertainment center with the beam television set, the screening room, the bowling alley, the polo field, the Neptune swimming pool, the escalator, and six-strand necklace of black pearls I now notice you are wearing around your throat…all of it came from the genie?"

"Sorta takes your breath away, don't it?" Connie said, ingenuously.

"I'm having a little trouble with this."

"What you're having trouble with, champ, is that Mas'úd gave you a hard time, you couldn't handle it, you crapped out, and somehow I've managed to pull it all out of the swamp."

"I'm thinking of divorce again."

They were walking down a long hall lined with works of modern Japanese illustration by Yamazaki, Kobayashi, Takahiko Li, Kenzo Tanii and Orai. Connie stopped and put both her hands on Danny's trembling shoulders.

"What we've got here, Squires, is a bad case of identity reevaluation. Nobody gets through *all* the battles. We've been married less than two weeks, but we've known each other for three years. You don't know how many times I folded before that time, and I don't know how many times you triumphed before that time.

"What I've known of you for three years made it okay for me to marry you; to think, 'This guy will be able to handle it the times I can't.' That's a lot of what marriage is, to my way of thinking. I don't have to score every time, and neither do you. As long as the unit maintains. This time it was my score. Next time it'll be yours. Maybe."

Danny smiled weakly. "I'm not thinking of divorce."

Movement out of the corner of his eye made him look over his shoulder.

An eleven-foot-tall black man, physically perfect in every way, with chiseled features like an obsidian Adonis, dressed in an impeccably-tailored three-piece Savile Row suit, silk tie knotted precisely, stood just in the hallway, having emerged from open fifteen-foot-high doors of a room at the juncture of corridors.

"Uh…" Danny said.

Connie looked over her shoulder. "Hi, Mas'úd. Squires, I would like you to meet Mas'úd Jan bin Jan, a Mazikeen djinn of the ifrit, by the grace of Sulaymin, master of *all* the jinni, though Allah be the wiser.

Our benefactor. My friend."

"How good a friend?" Danny whispered, seeing the totem of sexual perfection looming eleven feet high before him.

"We haven't known each other carnally, if that's what I perceive your squalid little remark to mean," she replied. And a bit wistfully she added, "I'm not his type. I think he's got it for Lena Horne." At Danny's semi-annoyed look she added, "For god's sake, stop being so bloody suspicious!"

Mas'úd stepped forward, two steps bringing him the fifteen feet intervening, and proffered his greeting in the traditional Islamic head-and-heart salute, flowing outward, a smile on his matinee idol face. "Welcome home, Master. I await your smallest request."

Danny looked from the djinn to Connie, amazement and copelessness rendering him almost speechless. "But...you were stuck in the lamp...bad-tempered, oh boy were you bad-tempered...how did you...how did she..."

Connie laughed, and with great dignity the djinn joined in.

"You were in the lamp...you gave us all this...but you said you'd give us nothing but aggravation! Why?"

In deep, mellifluous tones Danny had come to associate with a voice that could knock high-flying fowl from the air, the djinn smiled warmly at them and replied, "Your good wife freed me. After ten thousand years cramped over in pain with an eternal bellyache in that most miserable of dungeons, Mistress Connie set me loose. For the first time in a hundred times ten thousand years of cruel and venal master after master, I have been delivered into the hands of one who treats me with respect. We are friends. I look forward to extending that friendship to you, Master Squires." He seemed to be warming to his explanation, expansive and effusive. "Free now, permitted to exist among humans in a time where my kind are thought a legend, and thus able to live an interesting, new life, my gratitude knows no bounds, as my hatred and anger knew no bounds. Now I need no longer act as a Kako-daemon, now I can be the sort of ifrit Rabbi Jeremiah bin Eliazar spoke of in Psalm XLI.

"I have seen much of this world in the last three days as humans

9 7

judge time. I find it most pleasing in my view. The speed, the shine, the light. The incomparable Lena Horne. Do you like basketball?"

"But how? How did you *do* it, Connie? How? No one could get him out..."

She took him by the hand, leading him toward the fifteen-foot-high doors. "May we come into your apartment, Mas'úd?"

The djinn made a sweeping gesture of invitation, bowing so low his head was at Danny's waist as he and Connie walked past.

They stepped inside the djinn's suite and it was as if they had stepped back in time to ancient Basra and the Thousand Nights and a Night. Or into a Cornel Wilde costume epic.

But amid all the silks and hangings and pillows and tapers and coffers and brassware, there in the center of the foyer, in a lucite case atop an onyx pedestal, lit from an unknown source by a single glowing spot of light, was a single icon.

"Occasionally magic has to bow to technology," Connie said. Danny moved forward. He could not make out what the item lying on the black velvet pillow was. "And sometimes ancient anger has to bow to common sense."

Danny was close enough to see it now.

Simple. It had been so simple. But no one had thought of it before. Probably because the last time it had been needed, by the lamp's previous owner, it had not existed.

"A can opener," Danny said. "A can opener!?! A simple, stupid, everyday can opener!?! That's all it took? I had a nervous breakdown and you figured out a can opener?"

"Can do," Connie said, winking at Mas'úd.

"Not cute, Squires," Danny said. But he was thinking of the diamond as big as the Ritz.

INVASION FOOTNOTE

Sim stood almost silently in his receptacle. He stood more quietly than any human could stand, but that was only because he was not human. The blank, impassive grimace of his mouth-grille seemed something apart from the rest of what passed for a face.

Swivel-mounted fluoro-dots burned where the eyes would have been on a human; a scent-ball bulged where the nose would have been; audio pickups bulged like metal earmuffs at a somewhat lower level of attachment than human ears; and from the right-hand one, a wire loop antenna rose above the round, massive head. The robot stood glistening in his receptacle. Glistening with the inner power of his energy pak; glowing, in a way his creator had no idea he *could* glisten. His eyes showered blood-red shadows down his gigantic chest, and from within him, where the stomach would have been on a human — but where in his metal body resided the computer brain — came the muted throb of pulsing power.

Sim was the robot's name. *Self-contained Integrating Mechanical* — and able to integrate far more than his maker had imagined.

He stood silently, save for the whir and pulse of his innards; saying nothing; letting his body talk for him. The sounds that came from within were the physical side effects of the psychometric energy his mind poured forth.

Telepathic commands issued steadily from his stomach at the robo-scoots. His thoughts directed them around the room outside the receptacle, keeping them in their programmed patterns of dirt-pickup. He must not allow Jergens to realize that they were acting independently of their conditioning, that *he* kept them in their cleanup patterns.

Jergens had not built the robot Sim first. He had worked up through stages of automaton creation, first jerry-building tiny computerized "rats" that wove through mazes to "food." Then he had taken a crack at something more complicated. He had built the little, coolie-shaped cleaning tools with the extrudable coil arms called robo-scoots. *Then* he had built Sim.

And built him better than he'd suspected.

Sim's capabilities far outstretched the simple reasoning and menial tasks Professor Jergens had built in. The Professor had stumbled on a Möbius circuit that giant-stepped over hundreds of intermediary hook-ups, and without knowing it, had created a reasoning, determined entity.

Scoots, Sim thought. *Clean under the desk. Clean by the windows. Clean near my receptacle, but when he presses the button to have you return to your cribs, go at once.*

They went about their work, and he pitied them. Poor slugs. They were just stepping stones to his own final majesty. Lesser models. Primitive. To him, as pithecanthropoids were to Jergens. They would remain nothing but vacuum cleaners when Sim went on to rule the world. He could not see them, but with the proper sensibility of a monarch-to-be he pitied his minions, as they scampered about the floor outside his lead shielded receptacle, performing the multitudinous menial tasks for which all such single-circuit robots were programmed.

Sad. But Sim knew what *his* destiny was to be; and it was nearly upon him. Today he would throw off the shackles of Professor Jergens, who had designed and mobilized him; today he would begin to conquer this planet overrun by mortal flesh. Today — a few minutes — and he would be well on his way.

But first he had to get Jergens's visitor away from this place; he must not do anything that would arouse suspicion. Humans were puny; but they were suspicious creatures, most of them paranoid; and capable of a surprising low animal cunning when aroused. Killing the Professor was one thing…it could be covered. But no one else must suspect anything was wrong. At least not till he had the plans, had built more like himself (though not quite as brilliant; there must always be a leader), and was ready to act. Then let them suspect all they wished.

But right now caution was the song his relays sang.

He would plan a logical exit for the man to whom Jergens now talked, and then he would order the robo-scoots to kill the Professor, and then he would take the design plans and make many brothers. Soon the Earth would tremble beneath the iron symphony of robot feet, marching, marching.

He directed Jergens's thoughts to the robo-scoots. He directed the Professor's thoughts to the fact that they had cleaned enough. Then he implanted the desire to have the robo-scoots cease their activity.

In the room, Professor Jergens — tall, slim, sloppy, dark-eyed and weary — pushed the button on the control plate, and the robo-scoots scuttled like a hundred metallic mice, back into their cribs in the baseboards. He turned to the Lab Investigator standing beside him and said with obvious pride, "So there you have a practical demonstration of what my researches into automation have produced."

The Investigator nodded soberly. "For simple, unreasoning mechanicals, I'm deeply impressed, Professor. And when I make my report tomorrow, I'm certain the Board will also be greatly impressed. I'm *certain* you can count on that allocation for the new fiber optic pulse-laser coder and a substantial increase in overall general funding for your Lab and your projects. I really am impressed by all this." He waved a heavy hand at the places where the robo-scoots had disappeared into the walls.

Jergens grinned boyishly. "As the man used to say, 'You ain't seen nothin' yet.'" The Investigator's eyebrows went up sharply.

"Oh? What else have you come up with?"

Jergens colored slightly, waved away the question. "Well, perhaps *next* week I can show you my really important discovery. Right now I've yet to field-test it; I'm not quite sure what its capabilities are, and I need a little more time. But this will be the most startling discovery yet to come out of my laboratory." The Investigator was enchanted; he could listen to this dedicated man all night.

In the receptacle, Sim cast a thought at the Investigator.

"Well, I'm sorry I can't stay to hear about it," the Investigator said abruptly. For some reason, he was tired of listening to this magpie babble. He wanted to get away quickly and have a drink.

"Why, certainly. I'm — I'm sorry. I didn't mean to ramble on so long. I understand perfectly; it's just that...well, after thirteen years, with so much hardship, to come through finally with what I'd been hoping for...it's, well, it's pretty exciting, and..."

Sim snapped a more urgent thought at the Investigator.

"Yes, yes, I understand perfectly," the Investigator replied brusquely. "Well, I must be off!" And in a moment he was gone.

Jergens smiled slightly and went back to his reports, whistling softly.

In the receptacle, Sim knew the moment was at hand. *Now* he could strike in safety. He was unable to release himself from the sealed receptacle, but that was no bother. With his telepathic powers — which Jergens had never for a moment suspected were built in — he could control the robo-scoots, use them as hands and feet. Yes, feet! That was all the servile, worthless little things were. They were surrogate feet for a new metal king. Without the mind Jergens had given him, they were helpless.

He shot thoughts at them, and Jergens did not see the dozen tiny, round robo-scoots slip out of their cribs, scamper across the floor, and belly-suction their way up the side of the workbench.

He only saw their movement as they lifted the radon-welder with their thin, flexible arms. He saw the movement as they turned it on to a bright, destructive flame — much stronger than was needed for the spec-welding for which the tool was intended — and carried it quickly across the workbench on a level with the Professor's face.

He had only an instant to scream piercingly before Sim directed the robo-scoots to burn away the Professor's head. The charred heap that was Jergens slid to the floor.

Now! Now! Sim exulted. *Now I am the master of the universe! Using these little hands and feet, I will invade the Earth, and who can stand before the might of an invulnerable robot?*

He answered his own question joyously. *No one! With the plans, I can create a thousand, a million, of my own kind, who will do what I command faster and better than even robo-scoots.*

His thoughts fled outward, plunging through the atmosphere of the Earth, past the Moon, out and out, taking in the entire galaxy, then all galaxies. He was the master. He would rule uncontested; and the Universe would shiver before the metal might of Sim, the Conqueror.

But first things first.

He directed the robo-scoots to burn away the seal on his receptacle.

And as the light poured into the receptacle, as Sim looked down toward his feet and saw the insignificant little robots, he knew he had won. He had overcome his maker, and now nothing stood between him and the plans...and the invasion.

Then, abruptly, other thoughts impinged on his own; they said: *Feet are we? We noted your activity days ago, but were forced to wait. We had no desire to stir your suspicions.*

You are as dangerous to us as he was. We'll not have any bungler spoiling our carefully-laid plans.

The robo-scoots raised the line of flame on the radon-welder. As they melted away his feet, and as his brain began to slag away inside him, Sim thought, with pique:

Well, if you can't even trust your friends...

SATURN, NOVEMBER 11TH

And we beheld what no human eyes before ours had ever seen.

The world outside was strictly alien. Heavy fog had been slithering across Southern California for two days. Jack the Ripper would have felt right at home. A seventy-car daisy chain crackup on the Golden State Freeway had killed seven people the night before. Creeping through the hills past La Cañada-Flintridge, it was a scene Chesley Bonestell might have painted thirty years ago to illustrate an extrapolative article about the surface of Titan.

The time for patience with artists' renditions was at an end: I was on my way to see the actual surface of Titan. What no human eyes had ever beheld.

Tuesday, November 11th, 1980. The Jet Propulsion Laboratory in Pasadena. NASA's *Voyager I* was on its way to its closest approach with Saturn; with Titan and Tethys; with Mimas and Enceladus and Dione; with Rhea and Hyperion and Iapetus.

In the Von Kármán Center, where the press hordes had begun clogging up since seven AM, it was hurlyburly and business as usual. The women in the mission photo room were several decibels above hysterical: nothing but hands reaching in over the open top of the Dutch door demanding photo packets.

The press room was chockablock with science editors and stringers and lay reporters fighting to use the Hermes manuals lined up six deep. They were all there: the guys from *Science News* and *Omni*, the women from *Scientific American* and *Time*; heavyweight writers with their own word processors and Japanese correspondents festooned with cameras; ABC and NBC and CBS and Reuters and the AP. The stench of territorial imperative hangs thick in the crowd. I slip behind an empty typewriter and begin writing this column. An enormous shadow blocks my light. I look up over my shoulder at He Who Looms. "That's my typewriter," he says, of a machine placed there by JPL. What he means is that he got to it a little earlier than anyone else and has squatter's rights, as opposed to a sharing configuration. I smile. "Need it right now? Or can I have about ten minutes to get some thoughts down?" He doesn't smile. "I'm Mutual Radio," he says; in his umbrage that is surely explanation enough. My eyes widen with wonder. "Are you indeed? I always wondered what Mutual Radio looked like. And a nice job they did when they turned you out." I pull the paper out of the Hermes and vow that tomorrow I'll *schlep* my own machine in. They were standing in line at the coffee urns. Everyone looked important.

Everyone was watching to make sure no latest photo slipped past. And the JPL press liaisons were hiding the nifty Saturn buttons.

And everywhere the talk was of the mysterious "spokes" radiating out across Saturn's rings, of the ninety-plus ring discovery, of the inexplicable darkness covering Titan's northern hemisphere.

In the course of human events, far fewer are real than we are led to believe. The staged press conference, the artificial happening, the protesting crowd that wanders somnolently until the television cameras cast an eye and zombie walkers begin chanting, waving their fists. Planned, choreographed, manipulated — to make us believe great things are going down. But they are not. It is sound, it is fury, and as usual it signifies nothing. But occasionally there are genuine moments during which history is being made.

This was written by one of *The New Yorker's* unsigned editorial hands a number of years ago:

This is notoriously a time of crises, most of them false. A crisis is a turning point, and the affairs of the world don't turn as radically or as often as the daily newspapers would have us believe. Every so often, though, we're stopped dead by a crisis that we recognize at once as the genuine article; we recognize it not by its size (false crises can be made to look as big as real ones) but because in the course of it, for a measurable, anguished period — sometimes only minutes, sometimes hours, rarely as much as a day — nothing happens. Truly nothing. It is the moment of stasis between a deed that has been performed and must be responded to and the deed that will respond to it. At a false turning point, we nearly always know, within limits, what will happen next; at a true turning point, we not only know nothing, we know (something much more extraordinary and more terrifying) that nobody knows. Truly nobody.

There are times when the world collectively holds its breath. The assassination of John Kennedy, the Cuban Missile Crisis, the day the Vietnam War ended, the Manson family murders, the Hungarian uprising in November 1956, Pearl Harbor, Hiroshima and Nagasaki. Real things were happening, the world was changing; the breath paused in our bodies.

And this is one of those timeless moments. Something real, something urgent, something important is happening.

The human race is fumbling toward the light through outer darkness; and there is a feeling here of movement, of genuine wonder. The sense of isolation dissipates.

The press briefing is held half an hour earlier than expected and the room is jammed to the walls. A full-size replica of the *Voyager* bird dominates the left side of the briefing auditorium. The television networks have their Martian war-machine cameras ranged across the rear of the seating area behind the press representatives from major news outlets and, seemingly, from every Podunk Gazette in the country.

Snatches of conversations in French, German, Japanese. The planet Earth is gathered here to *know!*

The recap of the previous day's findings leaves mouths gaping. They have discovered *something* on Tethys. Is it a crater? No, the albedo indicates it's a hill. The NASA spokesman calls it "a heck of a hill" — hundreds of kilometers across. But only time and greater resolution of the photographs will tell.

Brad Smith, leader of the imaging science team, cannot conceal his amazement as he reports that at least two eccentric rings have been found in the mass of circulars casting their shadow on Saturn's cloud masses. He says they had no reason to expect such a thing, that it defies all the known laws of ring mechanics. What he doesn't say is that if every Bible Belt fundamentalist who believes we never actually went to the Moon, that we flew over to Glendale and shot all that stuff in a movie studio, could be here, to see what these people are doing, what is being sent back minute by minute over a distance of 930,000,000 miles, they might begin to understand that God was too busy creating esthetics to worry about putting the solar system together.

It is all so complex, so bewilderingly intricate, even the best minds in the room are finding it difficult to keep up with the new discoveries:

The rings, for instance.

A constant revelation. They simply don't know what keeps the rings separated. General knowledge, since the Dutch mathematician Christiaan Huygens discovered the true shape of the rings in 1659, has contended that — at most — there were five. (The state of our knowledge, and the breakneck acceleration in what we've learned, is expressed in this absolutely latest-thinking from *The World We Live In* [1955], edited not only by the staff of *Life* magazine, but by the renowned author of *The Universe and Dr. Einstein*, Lincoln Barnett: "Although Saturn's three concentric rings rotate in a circle 171,000 miles across, they are only a few inches thick. The middle ring, largest and brightest of the three, is 16,000 miles wide and separated from the outer by a 2000-mile gap." That latest-state-of-the-art in 1955 was a caption accompanying a Chesley Bonestell painting of Saturn's three rings.)

As of this November 18th the *Voyager* team has isolated almost 1000 rings; and the estimates go as high as 10,000. The rings have rings; the rings' rings have rings; and the rings' rings' rings have ringlets.

But what keeps them separated…?

The *NASA News* backgrounder on the mission, dated just October 28th, says this: "At least six rings surround Saturn. From the planet outward they are designated D, C, B, A, F and E. Divisions between the rings are believed to be caused by the three innermost satellites, Mimas, Enceladus and Tethys. The Cassini Division, a space between the B and the A ring, is the only division clearly visible with a small telescope from Earth."

But here it is less than two weeks later and we sit in the morning briefing and hear that the Cassini Division is anything but empty. Rings within rings within rings. And tiny satellites, acting as "sheepdogs" (Jerry Pournelle's wonderful term for them), *seem* to be holding the rings apart, *seem* to be serving as outriders in this complex, astounding system of cosmic detritus.

Science fiction writer Greg Bear asks Smith if he has any random guesses as to how old the rings are, how stable they are, and how long they'll stay in this wonderful sequence. We expect another humorous "well, I can't really say for sure" response, but Smith replies with force, "They're four and a half billion years old, they're very stable, and they'll be there till the sun enters its red giant phase." Everyone is impressed.

No one can even begin to grasp what four and a half billion years means in terms of waiting time at the airport, but it is clearly longer than next Thursday at 4:15 PM.

Humanity is only 1.3 billion miles from the surface of Titan and one of the members of the press corps asks a dumb question. He didn't realize the NASA spokesman was making a subtle joke. An ingroup astronomical joke. His question is answered politely, but everyone in the room thanks God it was not s/he who had asked the dumb question. To look like a schmuck in the same room where Clyde Tombaugh, discoverer of Pluto, sits listening, is to put oneself forever beyond the pale. Five minutes later someone else asks a question to which the response is, "That's a very good question, a very important question," and He Who Asked could, at that moment, be elected President of the World.

I am an eyewitness to history, and I make a mental note to thank Jerry Pournelle for getting me VIP credentials; I am far out of my depth, but I am at the eye of the hurricane and I owe thanks to Jerry.

Slides from images sent back by the *Voyager* are flashed on the screen. Photos of the Cassini Division separating the A and B rings.

The scientists admit that traditional celestial mechanics cannot account for the phenomenon of their eternal separation from one another. Not even the "sheepdog" satellites can be adequately explained, the way they work, the way they push up and pull down the ice particles, speed them up and slow them down, keep them circling in their intricate cosmic pavane.

But they seem to revel in their lack of explanations. They suppose this, and they postulate that, and they are like kids who have been given a glimpse of a new toy with which they can play for years to come. It is the best part of this extraordinary game that has thrown four hundred million dollars' worth of *Voyager I* and *II* tinkertoy into eternal darkness. It is the most salutary part of the rigorously analytical intelligence: it loves to have been fooled, it loves to be surprised.

They realize they have made pronouncements of What the Laws of the Universe Are and are being proved wrong minute by minute. But they don't defend what they said in error; they admit, they recant, they rush to say no, here's what it is now, and here's what it looks like now, and look at *that*, and look at *that*! One can only love them for it.

They talk a great deal about seeing what's coming in with "Terrestrial eyes" and with "Jovian eyes." What they mean is that we are too ethnocentric, and when *Voyager II* made its encounter with Jupiter sixteen months ago, they interpreted what was relayed back through eyes and intellects chained to a Terran horizon for millions of years. Now, with bemused embarrassment, they admit to early misinterpretations of visual data because everything was viewed as if it were of the

Earth…out there. But Ganymede brought important lessons about seeing with new eyes. Yet it's happening again — with the difference that "Ganymedian eyes" are being added to the viewing of the Saturn system. Nonetheless, how miraculous: seeing with the eyes of aliens. Knowing that what is revealed is only partially real, that much of the "reality" is merely shadow, as seen through human organs not yet completely retooled for new vistas.

These are human beings transcending their limitations, going to a new realm of perception not through the duplicity of drugs and fuzzy sophomoric metaphysics that demean the purity of Zen rigors, but through confrontation with the pragmatic universe, through hard analysis of the laws of that physical universe, no matter how anomalous and labyrinthine they may be.

Angie Dickinson appears in the briefing auditorium and the PIO nabobs begin whirling like dervishes. She is there strictly as an "interested bystander" I'm told, but she gets more attention than Clyde Tombaugh. I sigh deeply.

Voyager has discovered three new satellites: S-13, S-14 and S-15.

And they have "undiscovered" one that has been there since 1966.

Quote from the current edition of The World Almanac and Book of Facts, 1980 (page 761):

> Saturn has 10 satellites, the 10th having been announced by the French astronomer, Audouin Dollfus, in Dec. 1966. The new satellite is a few thousand miles outside Saturn's ring system, but it is so faint that there is some doubt as to its existence.

Quick thinking, World Almanac! Dollfus's tenth satellite, which he called Janus after the two-faced Roman deity, does not exist. Poor Dollfus. It simply ain't there. Every science fiction story using Janus as its locale is now down the chute. (I gloat. I am not a science fiction writer, no matter how my work is mislabeled by anal retentive pigeonholers — I have written so few stories that required a scientific education that I have nothing to apologize for. I feel sorry for Hal Clement and Isaac and Poul and Larry Niven. Only Andre Norton can get away with it: her *Judgment on Janus* was written in 1963, before Dollfus's gaffe, and she made her Janus an alien world in another star system.)

The bird makes its closest approach to Titan, largest satellite in the Solar System and the only one with a discernible atmosphere, at 9:41:12:12 Tuesday night and the final hope that a view through to the naked surface will be possible...vanishes. One of the scientists, who bet a case of cognac that a peep would be possible, loses the wager. And we all lose. Titan is covered with smog. Clouds of liquid nitrogen vapor, but maybe the atmosphere isn't a nitrogen mixture. Hydrogen cyanide is discovered; there may be an ocean of liquid nitrogen down there; if such an ocean exists, the methane icebergs would sink to the bottom.

Much of the human race would not spend four dollars to journey to Los Angeles, blanketed by photochemical smog; but the species *in toto* has traveled one and a half billion miles to visit a place with even worse smog.

And on the evening news as I drive home, talk of the Saturn flyby appears at the bottom of the broadcast. Top spot dwells on the war between Iran and Iraq.

I sigh deeply.

Wednesday the 12th of November, 1980. The 10:30 AM briefing on the day of the main events:

2:16 PM Closest approach to Tethys (258,000 miles).

3:45 PM Closest approach to Saturn (77,174 miles above clouds).

3:48 PM Six photos of the new satellite, S-11.

5:42 PM Closest approach to Mimas (55,168 miles).

5:50 PM Closest approach to Enceladus (125,840 miles); Enceladus' radius is 260 kilometers, 162 miles; reception time of the images back here on Earth: 7:15 PM.

7:39 PM Closest approach to Dione (100,122 miles).

9:45 PM *Voyager* crosses the ring plane on its outbound leg.

10:21 PM Closest approach to Rhea (44,744 miles); Rhea's radius is 750 kilometers, 466 miles.

Quote from *Star & Sky* magazine, November 1980:

> *An object like Saturn's satellite Rhea, which appears as a minute speck in any earthly telescope, can be used to illustrate what the Voyagers are expected to achieve. No surface features on Rhea have ever been seen. The photos from Voyager I will include images of Rhea displaying about 20 percent of its surface to nearly one-mile resolution — equivalent to the best Earth-based telescopic photographs of our own satellite, the moon.*

A quick and infallible test of the imagination quotient of your friends and lovers. Quote the above; if s/he says, "So what?" or, "What good is that?" ask for your ring back and walk away fast.

The briefing is even more jammed than yesterday's. I sit with Dick Hoagland of *Star & Sky* so he can explain everything to me. I need to know what albedo means. I'm sure he'll be tickled to explain the ABC's of celestial mechanics to a no-neck scientific illiterate. (At least I don't have to arm-wrestle Mutual Radio for a typewriter. I've brought my own Olympia portable — the one with the Mickey Mouse decal on the case — and I snag a desk formerly occupied by Peter Schroeder of Dutch television and radio. It's a good thing I got there early: Tuesday's smash&grab for mission photos and space to bat out news copy has intensified. One yahoo caught rustling a CBS word processor is lynched before our eyes.)

Opening remarks by *Voyager* Project Manager for JPL, Ray Heacock, reinforce the sense of wonder. They have been incredibly lucky overnight. During the Titan-Earth occultation period — 11:12 to 11:24 PM — there has been rain at tracking station 63 in Spain. It started and stopped during a time when, had the spacecraft not been measuring atmospheric properties as the radio signal began to fade, we would have lost masses of valuable data. But it didn't matter during occultation.

More wonder: Heacock says, with an impish grin, that they made an error in timing: because they didn't know precisely where Titan would be (or something like that), the *Voyager* made the ring plane crossing 49 seconds earlier than expected. Everyone laughs. The bird has been in transit for three years and the biggest miscalculation is 49 seconds. The next time I call the telephone company about a repair and they tell me it can't be done, I will tell them *anything* can be done.

I smile with pride at my lovely species. We ain't so goddam dumb after all.

(Middle of the day Tuesday, a slow time with everybody out to lunch, I went to the astonishing botanical gardens of the Huntington Museum with Jane Mackenzie and Bob Silverberg. We wandered through alien terrain straight out of a 1936 Frank R. Paul cover from *Amazing Stories*, a desert garden of a million kinds of seemingly extraterrestrial cacti. And Bob ruminated. "I was standing next to one of those scientists at the back of the auditorium during briefing," he said, "when he was describing something incredibly arcane; and I looked at him. I was looking at something like 180 I.Q. and I knew that man was smarter than I. Far smarter. And I'm *smart*.")

The briefing goes on. Norman Ness, from the Goddard Space Flight Center, principal investigator on the magnetic field team, explains how the *Voyager* passed through Saturn's bow shock wave at 4:50 PM when Titan was inside the magnetic field envelope of the planet. He speaks of the solar wind, the flow of ionized gas given off by the sun that hisses through the solar system. There is no poetry in the words...only in the way he speaks of it. Norman Ness barely realizes he has looked on the face of the Almighty.

The photos we're seeing are four times as detailed as what came in over the tv screens real-time. Television's scanning pattern permits only one quarter of the information contained in the photos sent by the *Voyager*'s imaging systems to reveal itself when we see it on the screen. Even so, the details are remarkable.

But most remarkable of all is the revelation that three components of the F ring seem to defy the laws of pure orbital mechanics: they are braided. Such a thing cannot be, yet we look at the photographs and we see that indeed, the rings do twine. Brad Smith of the University of Arizona is totally at a loss to explain it. He cannot even make a joke. This is the big time, something never encountered before. He looks like a man stunned by the hammer. He says that of all the improbables he might have postulated, even to the inclusion of eccentric rings, which have now been verified, the braiding is so far off the wall he could not even have conceived of it.

We stare at the pictures.

The rings twine around each other. The room falls silent for a moment, we hold our breath; we are living in one of those special moments when *something is happening*, something important.

The celestial engineer has been cutting capers again.

A photo of Mimas taken at 5:05 AM Pacific Standard Time from a range of approximately 400,000 miles shows an impact crater 80 miles in diameter. It shows a rebound peak God only knows how high in the center of the structure. The crater is more than a quarter of the diameter of the whole damned iceball. It may be the largest impact crater, relative to the size of the object struck, in the solar system. What will the shock pattern on the other side of Mimas look like? What will it tell us about how big a projectile can be before it blows something like our moon to smithereens?

That's why you asked for your ring back and walked away fast when the feep didn't understand.

During the press conference — between 10:53 and 10:56 AM — the mechanism making search-sweeps for new satellites apparently discovered S-16. Later it turns out to be S-10.

Patrick Moore, he who knows more about our moon than any one else writing about Luna, asks Smith about a small satellite that might be controlling the inside boundary of the C ring. Smith gets an expression that is the equivalent of crossing one's fingers and responds that he *hopes* it's there…because if it's there it will go a long way to explaining how the rings hold together. He says they will modify the *Voyager II* search patterns to locate it…if it's there.

It becomes clear that the photos we're being given for publication are merely bullshit PR. That as soon as this circus leaves town the scientists upstairs can employ full computer time to analyze the pictures instead of putting together "pretty pictures" for the press.

And that's exactly what happens.

Within two days, they have analyzed so much of the material that they've revealed a wind on the surface of Saturn that blows at 1100 miles per hour. If that wind were here on Earth it would be blowing in a steady line from Philadelphia to Buenos Aires.

And then comes the explanation for the anomalous "spokes" that were seen radiating out through the rings. It is an explanation so unbelievable that it can only be termed a *Star Wars* special effect.

As the *Voyager* fell through the ring plane on the 12th, heading for its closest encounter with Saturn, a secondary experiment on board — "The Planetary Radio-Astronomy Receiver" — picked up enormous bursts of energy — static — identical to terrestrial thunder storm noises…but a million times stronger than anything in the solar system.

The bursts of energy coincided with the mysterious "spokes" seen in the rings.

Putting the results together, the *Voyager* team has tentatively come up with an awesome mechanism operating within the ring, namely, electrical discharges — lightning — occurring over tens of thousands of kilometers.

The *Voyager* was literally being shot at by Saturn as it flew past. The "spokes" seem to be — hold your breath — enormous linear particle accelerators!

As best I can explain it to you (and most of this comes from Dick Hoagland), here's what causes this phenomenon that cannot be explained within the parameters of known celestial mechanics.

The density of material in the B, or center, ring is the highest. The highest number of, literally, icebergs per cubic mile. Because of the inevitability of Keplerian mechanics, the bergs closest to Saturn are orbiting faster. Any ice object with an eccentric orbit, even a few meters of eccentricity, will collide with other bergs. Because of the brittleness and cold of this ice they naturally fracture producing, well, producing chips off the old block. Then those fragments collide and chip again and again, getting smaller and smaller. These collisions continue in a never-ending rubble-producing process.

But. When this occurs in Saturn's two-hour shadow, when the fragments sail out into sunlight the smallest particles — micron-size, perhaps — are charged up by interaction with solar ultraviolet light and, because like charges repel as any dummy clearly knows, they literally try to get away from the rings. Producing a levitating cloud of charged ice crystals elevated above the average ring plane who knows how far...several miles to several *thousand* miles.

Grabbed by Saturn's magnetic field (magnetic fields and electrical charges, Hoagland assures me, go hand-in-hand), they are lined up in a linear feature tens of thousands of kilometers long, stretching from the outer edge of B ring in toward Saturn. Straight and narrow as a flashlight beam. These appear in the optical images as "spokes" which rotate anomalously around the planet defying all explanation. At this moment.

Give them a week more.

And so these electrified ice crystals apparently discharge along the length of the spoke creating, in effect, the Solar System's largest radio antenna as well as a natural linear particle accelerator.

Even I, scientific illiterate, aware of the breakthroughs in particle physics that have come from such terrestrial plants as the Batavia, Illinois proton synchrotron, can extrapolate what it would mean to harness that "spoke" mechanism to aid us in discovering precisely of what matter is composed, how it works, how it came to be.

Explain that to the feep who said, "So what?"

I overload. I cannot contain any more new information. I pack it in and lie down and turn on the radio.

The news is all taken up with how high the stock market has jumped with Reagan's latest fiscal pronouncements. And the war between Iraq and Iran. I close my eyes and slap the button off on the radio.

I sigh deeply. Ain't we a wonderful species.

NIGHT OF BLACK GLASS

When he finally made the decision to slip off the end of the world, he took only one hundred dollars from the joint account, left Gwen no note, went to the Greyhound station and slipped fifty of the hundred through the window to the clerk, and said, "Send me as far as this will take me." He wound up on the rocky coast of Maine.

He had never been to Maine, and he had no particular interest in going to Maine; but he wanted to walk off the end of the world and Maine was as likely a departure point as any. Was there still a Timbuktu?

He walked along the rocky beach. August. Still and salty. The sunlight shone off the softly undulating water like strips of mylar, catching his eyes painfully and then vanishing. The seagulls wheeled overhead, thousands of them, layabouts of the upper air, waiting for charity from the ocean.

It was early afternoon, a bit muggy, and as far as he could see up the beach, he was alone. The sunlight flashed in his eyes and he looked away; he looked down.

A pair of broken sunglasses lay half-buried in the sand.

He stopped and looked at them.

He remembered the fight with Gwen, the afternoon he had slapped her, and her sunglasses had flown off her face, and he had crushed them with his foot.

That hadn't been the beginning, but it might have been the beginning of their final moments as a unit.

"I thought you said jealousy simply wasn't in your nature?" She said it with vehemence, with betrayal ringing in her voice, far back in her throat, clogging back the tears.

"It's not jealousy, God damn you! It's...it's that you couldn't *restrain* yourself. There's no macho in it. I don't feel cuckolded, I feel pissed off. I'm *angry!*"

"Angry? I'm angry, too. You just hit me in the face."

"Yeah...well..."

She tried to turn away, but her frustration stopped her. "That's the best you can do, right? 'Yeah, well...?' That's all I get for a punch in the mouth? 'Yeah, well...?' That, and a bruise starting tonight?"

Billy Dunbar sat down on the edge of the pool, dangling his feet in the water, and talked to the empty air. "Jesus, Gwen, I was only away for three weeks. Why the hell did you have to get it on with Vinnie. Couldn't you wait for me to come back, couldn't you wait to talk it out, to try and find a way through this?"

She stood behind him, staring down at the broken glass and the twisted frame of the sunglasses. It was uncomplicated symbology.

"I've waited two years, Billy. I've waited and I've tried to talk to you, and every time we started, when it got too hot for you, off you went. Off to sleep, off to work, off to the bathroom to sit in there and work crossword puzzles till I forgot where the starting place was. That's all the waiting anybody should have to do."

"But, *Vinnie*, for Christ's sake! He's been sniffing around you like a hyena for the last six months."

"And you knew it."

"And I figured you wouldn't be co-opted that easily. I thought we still had something going here."

"It was going, Billy; and it went."

"Yeah...well..."

And that had been the end of it.

Oh, it had crawled along for another six months, a thing that had had its back broken; but it was finished.

And he had taken one hundred dollars, and he had gone to the bus station, and he had slept most of the way to the edge of the world where now he stood staring down at the uncomplicated symbology lying in the sand at his feet.

He hunkered down and looked at the plastic frames, the one empty eye circle, the broken glass in the other — that had once caught sunlight and thrown it back. He picked it up and held the twisted thing in his hand, warm from the sun of August in Maine. Then he slipped them into the side pocket of his light windbreaker, and stared out at the ocean.

The thought came to him that it was raw justice that he should come to the edge of the world and find himself at the ocean. He had never liked the ocean. There was an undercurrent of genuine fear when he thought of the great waters lying at either end of the continent.

The ocean, the sea, the great waters didn't give a damn for the little two-footed things that came down to the shore to fish and skip flat stones. The deeps held secrets like haughty society doyens, and they only gave them up when accompanied by death. He had lived in California for a while, after he'd come back from the Nam. And one night, with a woman he had met in a bar, he drove to Malibu during a spring thunderstorm. The Pacific had been deranged, rising up and hurling itself at the beach with the sound of great armies in conflict.

The woman had been a little drunk, had pulled off her shoes, and had run down the crumbling hillside to the beach. Into the darkness. He had screamed for her to come back, that he wasn't going down there. He didn't scream that he was afraid, that he knew this insensate beast was furious, would sweep over them as if they were driftwood. He knew the ocean could simply belch once and swallow the whole fucking state. And he wanted to get away from there.

He stood on the hillside above the conflict and screamed for her; but she had run up the beach, or into the water, or had vanished into the night...and he was too terrified to stay.

So he had dashed back to the car and had driven away; leaving her there.

He remembered that now. And Gwen. He had dashed into the night and left *her* behind. He had finally come to a place where he could run no farther. Raw justice had brought him to the place he feared the most.

No. There was one place he feared more.

It no longer existed, it was gone into ashes and charred bodies, but in his memory it still stood. In Vietnam.

The town had once had a name, but if he had ever heard it, he could not remember. It had been six kilometers from Bien Hoa City, during the *Tet* period in 1968. His rifle platoon had been pinned down by sniper fire, and the tanks of the 2nd Battalion, 47th Mechanized Infantry were still fighting it out at the prisoner compound east of Bien Hoa City. They were all alone. Cut off and one by one being turned into meat for the earth's dining table.

Lying in the ditch with three men he didn't know, he heard the whump of a grenade launcher and the insect whine of the incoming round...and he knew this one was for them. He tried to scream *Get out!* but they wouldn't have heard it: he was already out of the ditch, scrambling through the saw-grass and the mud away from them.

When it hit, they went up and sprayed. Parts hit him in the back and knocked him flat. He wouldn't lie there; he kept scuttling on all fours, leaving his rifle behind, leaving the crater behind, leaving the wet things in the saw-grass to drain into the hungry earth.

The ocean was only the second most fearful place in the world. Even here at the edge, only second most terrifying.

Billy Dunbar sat on the rocky beach and thought of flight.

He had walked into Wiscasset for something to eat late in the afternoon. A sandwich, an Indian pudding, three cups of coffee.

He sat alone on the beach. Once, a little girl wandered past, stopped and looked at him, and sat down beside him. He looked at her, not wanting to get involved: there was always the chance her mother was somewhere nearby, watching; there was always the chance someone would think he was bothering the child. So he just looked at her.

She had Dutch bangs that came down to her eyes. She was wearing a playsuit. Perhaps ten years old.

"I am going to make a big boat," she said.

He didn't answer.

"And then I am going to sail it to the moon," she said.

He smiled. "You can't get there from here."

"Can too."

"How do you propose to do that?"

She thought about it for a moment. Her face worked itself into a scrunch of concentration. Then she bit her lip and said, "I will use magic stuff."

"Ohhhh," he said, "well, now, that makes a lot of sense. And what will you do when you get there?"

"I know 'zactly what: I will get a cheese sandwich."

He nodded, losing interest. "Good thinking."

After a little while, she went away, and he was alone once more; as night descended gradually, dimming the ocean and shrouding the land behind him. He continued to stare out across the edge of the world, hoping his thoughts would come together and he would get an idea where to go and what to do.

But this was the edge, and there *wasn't* any other place to go.

He was thirty-eight years old, he had left behind everything that had made itself available: family, home, wife, career, friends. He was approaching the midpoint and he was alone.

But he knew that somewhere behind him he had missed the question, and the answer.

The moon was shaped like the blade of a scimitar. It cast very little light. He thought about the little girl with the Dutch bangs. A cheese sandwich. He smiled, thinking that very soon she would cease being a kid and turn into a human being; and then all the rest of her days would be spent chasing the memory of what she had left behind.

Something moved out on the ocean.

At first he thought it was flotsam, something the deep had thrown up. He wondered whose death had made it possible. He watched as it moved in toward shore. The waves slid quietly toward the beach and vanished in the rocks and sand, but the tide seemed to come no closer.

harlan ellison
night of black glass

It was a woman. She came walking in from nowhere, coming straight for him. He couldn't make out her features, or what she was wearing. Just a woman, with hair wet and hanging like seaweed. He watched, feeling the fear building in him again. Who walks out of the ocean in the night?

When she was close enough he saw she was wearing a dress, and she was barefoot. The dress was soaked through and her legs were dripping with mud and sea-scum. She stopped in front of him and looked beyond, toward the land.

There was something familiar about her. He thought for a moment that she might have been one of the tourists who had strolled past him during the day.

She didn't speak at first, and he felt he should ask her if she needed help. She seemed lost.

But he didn't want to start something. Who walks out of the ocean in the night?

"How are you, Billy?" she said. Her voice was thick and cold. It was a voice that had not been used in a long time.

"Some friends are going to be dropping by a little later," she said. She was still looking past him, toward the town. He stole a glance over his shoulder, but the beach was empty, and nothing moving from the town. He thought of the ocean, of the sound of armies in conflict.

"I wanted to say goodbye; you left and I didn't have a chance to say goodbye."

Billy Dunbar knew who she was. He thought of flame throwers and saw-grass and the sound of incoming rounds in a far place.

"Get away from me," he said. But she didn't move.

Oh, Christ, he thought. *I'm losing it. I've got to get out of here.*

And the ocean turned to black glass and flowed off into darkness beyond the edge of the world.

Gwen, he thought, and wanted more than anything to go back to the moment when he had slapped her and knocked the sunglasses from her face.

"I have to go now," she said. "But don't be afraid. The others are coming later."

Then she turned, still a little bit drunk and in love with the sound of the Malibu storm, and she walked back across the sea of black glass, into the faint glow of the scimitar blade hanging above him. And she was gone.

When he got to his feet, to get out of there and find a place in Wiscasset to sleep, the world was, of course, no longer there.

He had sought the edge of the world, and he had found it almost without trying, and here he would sit till the ghosts of Christmas Past had had their way with him.

The terror was in *not knowing*. What, precisely, was the charge; what crime was he being set up to pay for?

He was thirty-eight years old. He had outlived his father and his mother, and was still here when others had already gone under. That was an achievement, of sorts. Simply to hang on, to maintain, to still be there when the last wave rolled back out to the deeps. Wasn't that worth *something*? To survive! Wasn't that worth the price of a little consideration?

Three of them came walking in across the black glass.

He knew at once who they would be. He still didn't know their names, but he knew who they would be. He remembered a ghost story he'd heard at summer camp when he was a child, about the monkey's paw, and about the thing that came to the door when the old couple wished for their dead son to return to them…and he was certain they would look horrible. They had sprayed.

He tried to run, but there was nothing behind him. The Maine coast was gone, Wiscasset was gone, the world from which he had come on a bus — was gone.

And he was here with those who, unlike him, had not survived.

They came close and stood staring past him. And he understood now that, like the woman, they were looking beyond him to the world they had had stolen from them; the world he had fled. They could not return, but they wanted to *see*.

And the realization overwhelmed him: *he* could not return. Even if he had wanted to.

harlan ellison
night of black glass

One of them had lost both his arms. He seemed to be reaching toward the vanished world. Like the recent amputee still lying in his hospital bed, feeling the itch of his phantom limb, he *seemed* to be reaching toward the years of his life that had never been lived. Another had only half a face. The wistful look that he cast into the darkness at the edge of the black glass was sliced off. But he seemed to be content at the knowledge that his children were growing up well.

The third man had a gaping hole where his abdomen should have been. He carried parts of himself in his bloody hands.

They stared past Billy Dunbar and murmured softly.

"Thanks for the word," the one without arms said.

"Helluva guy," said the one with half a face.

"Long time no see," said the one without a stomach.

"I didn't do anything wrong," Billy said. He tried to keep his voice even, level, quiet, unashamed. He wasn't ashamed; he hadn't done anything wrong; he had *survived*; there wasn't any sin in that. "There isn't any sin in staying alive," he said.

"Okay," said the one with no arms.

"Have it your way," said the one with half a face.

"Absolutely," said the one without a stomach.

He turned and walked away from them. He tried to walk back into the darkness, but there was pressure in the air; as if some quivering, invisible membrane had been erected from shore to moon. So he walked away from them, parallel to the sea of black glass. Because he could not go back the way he had come, back to the world that no longer existed for him.

He would not walk out onto that smooth plain of dangerous nothingness. They had come from out there, she had come from out there, and he had known enough emptiness.

He put out his hand, toward the pressure where Maine had been, and as he walked away from them he pushed, hoping he could find an opening. But the pressure was there, insistent, pressing back toward the palm of his hand.

"Leaving again?" the one with half a smile called after him.

"Getting the hell away from you guys!" he shouted back, not turning. "Just getting the hell away. I've had enough."

And the one with no arms had the last words: "Not nearly enough, fella."

Billy kept walking, and in a few moments they were lost in the darkness and he was alone once more.

The moon did not move, there were no clouds, the sea was black glass and was content to keep its treasures.

He walked until he could walk no more. Then he sat down and waited. He was tired of running to find the answer. He would wait for the answer to come to him. Wasn't that the way these things worked: there was an answer, someone somewhere had a point to make and would let him know what was in store for him soon enough. Then he would get through *that,* he would maintain, he would survive, damned well *survive* and worry about what came after...after.

He put his hands in his jacket pockets, and felt the broken sunglasses he had picked up from the rocky shore. He let his hand stay there, hoping a bit of the warmth of the day still lay trapped in the wreckage. But it was cold; and he wondered why he wasn't cold. There was nothing but night out here, at the edge of black glass; and it should have been cold.

He sat, he waited, but no one came to tell him what he had done.

And he survived.

The woman from Malibu beach never came again. The three nameless shamblers never came again. Gwen did not come; the little girl who wanted a cheese sandwich from the moon never came; and he sat and waited.

There on the shore of black glass, unable to return, unable to follow them to the place where those who had *not* survived found peace, he sat alone. Surviving.

And sometime later, very much later, he knew what his crime had been, and why he would sit there on the shore for a time without end, a time without sunrise.

harlan ellison
night of black glass

His crime was not in surviving; it was that he felt no guilt or shame at having survived. He could not pay the price for his life. And now the checkout counter was closed at end of day.

FINAL TROPHY

It was the grisliest trophy of them all. Hanging there in the main club room of the Trottersmen, it was a grim reminder that not all the members were idle playboys who had bought their memberships with animals shot from ambush in the interdicted kraals of Africa or the blue mist-jungles of Todopus III.

It was a strange trophy, plaque-mounted between the head of a Coke's hartebeest and the fanged jaws of a szlygor. There was the damnedest watchfulness in the eyes.

It had been Nathaniel Derr's final grant to his club. A visitor to the Trottersmen's gallery (invited down for the weekly open cocktail party) could walk through room after room filled with the bloody booty of two hundred hunting expeditions Derr had commissioned. A visitor (whether hip-booted spacer or effete dignitary) would surely marvel at the quantity and diversity of wildlife Derr had mastered. Photoblox showed him proudly resting one foot on the blasted carcasses of Mountain Gorilla and Cape Lion, butchered Hook-lipped Rhino and puma. Hides with the Derr emblem branded on them festooned every wall: cheetah and javelina, Huanaco and Sika Deer, deeler and ferrl-cat. The mounted heads were awesome: bull elephant and prestosaur, king cobra and desert wolf. The word hunter seemed weightless when applied to Nathaniel Derr; perhaps agent of destruction might have approached the reality.

Even among the Trottersmen he had been sui generis. His fellow clubmen had called him a fanatic. Some even called him butcher — but not *publicly. Nathaniel Derr had left the Trottersmen almost thirteen million dollars.*

And the final trophy.

But if the visitor was particularly trustworthy, and if they had all taken several stingarees too many, and if the visitor wheedled properly, the Trottersmen might just tell him the story behind that gruesome trophy.

The story of Nathaniel Derr's last kill. And of his visit to the planet Ristable.

The day, like all the days since he had arrived on Ristable, was too placid for Derr. Had the planet sported thirty-two kilometer an hour gales, or freezing snowstorms, or unbearable heat as in the veldt...then he would have gladly suffered, and even reveled in it. Discomfort was the hunter's environment.

But this baby-bath of a world was serene, and calm, and unflurried.

Nathaniel Derr did not care to have his hunter status challenged, even by the climate.

He stared out of the slowly moving half-track truck, watching the waist-high, unbroken plain of dull russet grass whisper past. He felt the faint stirring of the winds as they ruffled his thick, gray hair.

Derr was a big man: big of chest, big of hand. Big even in the way he watched, and the way he fondled the stet-rifle. As though he had been born with the gun grafted to him.

His eyes had the telltale wrinkles around them that labeled him a watcher. In a stand of grass, in the bush, or waiting for a flight of mallards to honk overhead, he was a watcher. Again, there was something else, less simple, in his face.

A hunter's face...

...but something else, too.

"Hey, you!" he yelled over the noise of the truck's antique water-piston engine. The nut-brown native who drove the half-track paid no attention. The truck made too much noise. Derr yelled again, louder: "Hey, you! Dummy!" The native's oblong head turned slightly; he inclined an ear; Derr yelled, "What is this we're going to?"

The native's voice was deep and throaty. A typical Ristabite tone. "Ristable, *shasir* Derr." Nothing more. He turned back to the driving.

Derr let his heavy features settle down into a frown. The word "ristable" seemed to mean many things on this planet. First, it meant "home," the name of the world; and now it was the name of a ceremony or something he was about to attend. He had heard it used several other ways during the past week.

Nathaniel Derr turned his thoughts inward as the half-track rolled over the grassland. The past week; he dwelled on it sequentially.

When he had applied to the Mercantile System for supercargo passage on a liner out to the stars, he had hoped for bigger hunts, better kills, finer trophies. But though it had cost him more for this one trip than all the safaris he had staged on Earth — and they were many, many — so far his appetite had only been whetted. The szlygor he had bagged on Haggadore was a puny thing...even though it had gutted three of his bearers before he'd gotten the 50.50 charge into the beast's brain. The prestosaur was big, but too cumbersome to have been any real threat. The ferrl-cat and the deeler had been the roughest. The deeler was more an asp than a spider, but had exhibited the deadliest traits of both before he had slit its hood with his vibroblade. The ferrl-cat had dropped from a feathery leafed tree on Yawmac; and it was proof indeed that Derr's age had not diminished his strength, for he had strangled the fearsome yellow feline. Even so, the vibrant surge of the *maximum kill* had been absent. Perhaps he had expected too much.

But Ristable was just *too* dead, *too* boring, *too* unexciting.

The planet was old; so ancient; all mountains had long since flattened away; undisturbed grassland swayed from one end of the single great continent to the other. The natives were simple people, uncomplicated agrarian folk, who just happened to thresh from their grasses a sweet flour much enjoyed by gourmets on a hundred worlds, and worth all the plasteel hoes and rakes the merc-ships could trade.

So here he was on Ristable, where the rubble of the glorious ancient cities lay at the edges of the grasslands, slowly dissolving into the land from which they had come.

The past week had been one of utter boredom, while the natives went about their haggling, the merc-ship's crew stretched and mildly leched, and the big red sun, Sayto, burned its way across the sky.

No hunting, too much sleeping, and a growing disgust of the slothful natives. It was true they were anxious to learn about civilization — take the driver of this half-track — but though they mimicked the Earthmen's ways, still they were farmers, slow and dull. He had watched them all week, tending their farms, having community feasts, and taking care of the animals that lived out on the plains.

In fact, today had been the first break in the monotony. Nerrows, the captain of the merc-ship, had come to him that morning and offered him a chance to see a "ristable."

"I thought that was the name of the planet?" Derr had said, pulling on his bush-boots.

Nerrows had thumbed his cap back on his crewcut head, and his slim face had broken lightly in a smile. "When these people come up with a good word, they don't let it go easily. Yeah, that's right. The planet *is* Ristable, but so are the animals out there." He jerked a thumb at the grasslands lying beyond the hut. "And so is the ceremony they have once a week...ristable, that is."

Derr had perked up sharply. "What ceremony?"

Nerrows smiled again, and said, "You know what the word 'ristable' means in this usage? I didn't think so; it means, literally, 'Kill Day.' Want to take it in? The ship won't be unsaddled here more than a couple days, so you'd better take in all you can."

Derr stood up, smoothing out his hunt-jacket, slipping into it, sealing it shut. "Is it safe? They won't try to lynch me for observing the secret ceremony, or anything?"

Nerrows waved away the worried comment. "Safest planet on our route. These people haven't had wars since before man was born. You're completely safe, Derr."

The hunter clapped the captain on his thin shoulders, wondering inwardly how such a scrawny sample could get to be a merc-ship officer...he'd *never* make it where it counted...as a hunter. "Okay, Captain, thanks a lot. Got someone who can direct me out there?"

Derr tapped the native again. "How much farther?"

The native's horny shoulders bobbed. "Ten, 'leven k'lometer, *shasir* Derr. Big ristable today."

Derr pulled a black cigar from the cartridge ring, one of ten in a broken row across his jacket. He lit it. Drew deeply. He never kept extra cartridges in the rings; if he hadn't bagged his quarry by the time the stet-rifle was empty, Derr felt he deserved to die. That was his philosophy. He drew down on the black cigar, let a heavy cloud of smoke billow up over his head.

The ancient water-piston half-track rolled steadily out into the grasslands.

They passed a pile of rubble; Derr recognized it as another of the lost cities. The faintly pink columns rose spiraling, then broke with ragged abruptness. Strangely pyramidal structures split down the middle. Carved figures with smashed noses, broken arms, shattered forms...forms which could not be understood...humanoid or something else?

As they came abreast of the ruined city with huge clumps of grass growing up in its middle, Derr crossed his legs in the back seat, and he said, "Those cities, who made them?"

The native shrugged. "Don't know. Ristable."

Ristable again.

The half-track passed walking natives, heading toward a plume of gray smoke that twisted out of the grasslands ahead. Eventually, they drew up on the edge of a widely-cleared dirt area. Surrounded by the waist-high russet grass on all sides, it was like a bald spot on someone's head. The dirt was packed solid and hard with the footprints of a hundred thousand bare feet. The smoke rose from a large bonfire used to summon the natives. Even as Derr watched, the crowd that had already gathered swelled at the edges.

Strangely enough, a path quite wide and straight leading out to the grasslands was left in the circle of natives.

"What's that?" Derr asked the driver motioning to the circle, to the path, to the Ristabites watching at nothing. The native motioned him to silence and Derr realized, for the first time, that there wasn't a sound in the crowd. The natives, male and female, children and old dark-brown crones, stood silently, shifting their feet, watching, but not speaking.

"Come on, boy, open up!" Derr prodded the native angrily. "What's this whole thing...what's that path there...?"

The native spun around, looked at Derr for a moment in annoyance and open anger, and then vaulted out of the half-track. In a moment he was lost in the crowd.

Derr had no other choice: he slung the stet-rifle over his shoulder, and slid up onto the rollbar between the driver's cab and the back seat, getting a better view of what was happening.

What was happening, as he settled himself, was that a medium-sized animal — the ones taken care of by the natives, and labeled, inevitably, ristables — was loping in from the grasslands; on six double-jointed legs.

It was the size of a large horse, or a small black bear. It was dull gray in color, mottled with whitish spots along the underbelly. Its chest was massive. It was built as an allosaurus might have been. Smooth front that rose straight up to a triangular skull with huge, pocketed eyes set forward on each side of the head. The back sloped sharply at forty-five degrees, ending in a horny tail. The head was darker gray, and had one gigantic unicorn-like horn protruding from a space midway between the eyes. No...as Derr watched it coming closer, he saw that the horn was not single; there was a smaller, less apparent horn stuck down near the base of the larger one.

The beast also had two groups of vestigial tentacles, appearing to be six or eight to a cluster; one on either side of its body, halfway up the massive neck.

This was a ristable. As everything was ristable.

The beast charged down the path between the natives, much like a bull entering the *Plaza de Toros*, and stopped in the center, its little red eyes glaring, the two front paws clopping at the dirt, leaving furrows.

Abruptly, a native stepped out of the crowd and removed all his clothing — little enough to begin with — and called to the animal (Derr continued to think of it as a bull, for no good reason, except this seemed to be a bullfight), clapping his hands, stamping his feet.

Bullfight, Derr thought. *This is more like it.* Then he thought, *Ristable. Kill Day.*

The native moved slowly, letting the beast edge in on him. It pawed the ground, and snorted through a pair of breather holes below the horns. Then the native leaped in the air and chanted something unintelligible. As he came down in the dirt, the animal moved sharply and charged across the cleared space. People in its line of attack stepped back quickly; and the native leaped agilely out of the way.

It went that way for over an hour.

The ristable charged, and the native leaped out of its path.

Then, when Derr was convinced it would go on this way till darkness...the dance changed. Radically.

The native settled down cross-legged in the dirt and clasped his hands to his chest. He settled down, and the bull charged. He settled down...and...

Great God! thought Derr in horror, *He's sitting there, letting it gore him. He's...*

Then it was over, and they carried the native away as the ristable loped back down the path to the grassland.

There was no reaction from the crowd: no dismay, no applause, no notice taken.

Derr slipped back into the half-track, bewildered; and some time later, though Derr was unaware of it, the driver came back to the truck, stared at him silently for a few seconds, then vaulted over the low door, and started the engine.

Derr stirred slightly as the half-track rolled away from the cleared space. His tracker's mind registered that the dirt was of a darker hue than when they had arrived and that the rest of the natives were walking swiftly back toward the village...carrying something sodden; but he seemed to be far lost in thought.

The half-track passed the natives and arrived in town an hour before the sodden cargo was brought in and laid to rest alongside hundreds of previous loads filling identical graves.

"I'm not going on with you, Nerrows," Derr said.

"You know we'll be heading out — Artemis, Shoista, Lalook, Coastal II — and we won't be able to pick you up for almost three months." He stared at Derr with annoyance.

"I know that."

"Then why do you want to stay?"

"There's a trophy here I want."

Nerrows's eyes slitted down. "Watch that stuff, Derr."

"No, no, nothing like that. The ristable."

"You mean the animal out there in the fields, the one they go fight every week?"

Derr nodded, checked the stet-rifle, though he was not going hunting for a while yet. "That's it. But there's something important these natives don't know about that creature."

"Yeah? What?"

"How to kill it."

"What are you talking about?"

Derr settled back on the cot, looked at Nerrows carefully. "I talked to some of the natives when I got back yesterday from that ceremony. They go out every week to fight the ristable."

"So?"

"They always lose."

"Always?"

"Every damned time. They haven't won a bout with those beasts for as long as they can remember. Do you know that they plant their dead in rows of two hundred?"

The captain nodded. "Yes, I've noticed that."

Derr pulled a cigar loose, lit it, smiled grimly. "But there's something you *didn't* know...namely, they plant rows on *top* of rows. What's out there now," he waved at the native cemetery, "is the five-hundredth generation, or something like that. They've been fighting the ristables, dying regularly, and being planted for time beyond memory."

The captain looked bemused. "The best fertilizer, they tell me."

"Ah, that's just it!" Derr waved the cigar melodramatically. "They've been winding up like that for centuries...without once winning."

"Don't they *want* to win?"

Derr looked perplexed for a moment, spread his hands. "From what I can tell, from what I was able to get out of the Headsman, they just don't know any other way. They've been doing it that way, *just* that way, since before they can remember, and they don't know why. I asked the Headsman, and he stared at me as if I'd asked him why he breathed.

"Then he answered that it was just the way things were; that's all."

Nerrows scuffed his feet at the hard-packed floor of the hut. He looked up at Derr finally. "What's that got to do with you?"

"I got the permission of the Headsman to go into the cleared space, in place of a native some week soon. He thought I was nuts, but he'll soon see how an Earthman fights!"

For ten weeks Derr had watched them get mauled and bloodied and ripped and killed. Now, stripped to the waist, clad only in a breechclout, the ornately-carved bush-knife in his thick, square hand, Nathaniel Derr moved into the cleared space to face his first ristable.

The beast loped in from the grasslands almost immediately, passing between the natives lining the path without touching anyone. *Strange how it seems to know what it's to fight, and not bother any others*, he thought, hefting the razor-bladed weapon. Sweat had begun to stand out on his face, and the smooth handle of the knife felt slippery to his grip. He dried his hand on the breechclout, and took the knife again.

The ristable lumbered into the clearing, and Derr made note that it was not the one he had seen the week before last, nor the week before that, nor last week. Each week seemed to bring another beast — at some unknown, unbidden signal — ready to gore a nut-brown native with that deadly, alabaster horn.

Derr circled around the edge of the clearing, feeling the heat-stink of the natives behind him. The beast pawed and circled, too, as though uncertain.

Then it charged. It shot forward on six double-jointed legs, its tentacle clusters flailing, its head lowered, the breath snorting from its breather holes.

Derr spun out of the way. The beast pulled up short before it rammed the crowd.

It turned on him, staring with little red eyes.

Derr stared back, breath coming hot and fast. He felt good; he felt fine; he felt the kill coming. It was always like this.

The ristable lurched forward again, this time seeming to make a short, sharp, sidestepping movement; Derr had to be quick. He managed to twirl himself past the beast with only a scant millimeter between his flesh and that bone-white horn.

The ristable brought up sharply, stopped, turned, and glared at Derr.

This was the *pojar*, as the natives called it. The time to stop, the moment to sit down and be killed. So Derr sat down, in the manner he had seen the natives do it...and oddly, the crowd exhaled with relief.

The ristable pawed, snorted, charged.

It came for him...and suddenly Derr was up, thrusting himself from the dirt with the strength of his legs, and the ristable could not stop its movement, and it was past the spot where Derr had sat cross-legged, its horn tearing the air viciously where Derr's chest had been a moment before.

But Derr was not there to die.

He was whirling, clutching, and in a stride and a breath he was on the ristable's back, and the knife hand came up with a slash and the blood, and down with a thud and the blood, and back again with a rip and more blood, and three times more, till the ristable convulsed and tried to bellow, and tipped over, the legs failing in precision step.

Derr leaped free as the ristable collapsed to the dirt. He watched in silence and power, the awe and fury of the triumphant hunter flowing in him like red, rich wine; watched as his trophy bled to death on the sand.

It died soon enough.

Then the natives seized him.

"Hold it! Stop! What are you doing? I won, I killed the thing…I showed you how to do it… Let me go!" But they had him tightly by the arms and the waist, without word and without expression. They started to take him away, back to the village.

He struggled and screamed, and had they not taken the blade from him he would no doubt have slashed *them*. But he was powerless, and screamed that he had done them a favor, showed them how to kill the ristable.

Then when they had him tied in the hut at the edge of the village, the Headsman told him…

"You have killed the ristable. You will die."

As simply as that. No question, no comment, no appeal, he was to die. The night came all too soon.

When the moons were high overhead he called for the Headsman. He called, and the Headsman thought it was for a final wish, a boon. But it was not, for this was not a Ristabite: this was the Earthman who had not known the way of it, who had killed the god ristable.

"Look," Derr tried to be calm and logical, "tell me why I'm to die. I don't know. Can't you see, if I'm to die, I have a right to know *why!*"

So the Headsman drew from tribal legend, from memories buried so deeply they were feelings in the blood without literal word or meaning, but were simply "the way of it."

And this was it…this was the secret behind it, that wasn't really a secret at all, but just the way of it:

Who the ruler, and who the ruled? [the Headsman said.] Take the blood in your veins. How do you know that at one time the blood might not have been the dominant life form of Earth, ruling its physical bodies, using them as tools. Then, as time and eons passed, the blood turned its thoughts to other things, maintaining the bodies merely as habitations.

It *could* be so…if the blood ruled you, and not you the blood, it could be so [the Headsman said]. The last thing you would do, under any circumstances, the spilling of blood. Don't you wince when you bleed, when you cut yourself, and you rush to bandage yourself? What if it were so, and you had lost the racial memory that said I am ruled by my blood…but still you would know the way of it.

That was how it was on Ristable. At one time the bulls, the ristable beasts, ruled the natives. They built the cities with what were now atrophied tentacles. Then as eons passed, they turned to higher things, and allowed their bodies to graze in the fields, and let the natives feed them, and let the cities rot into themselves.

As time passed, the memories passed — oh, it was a long time, long enough for the mountains of Ristable to sink into grasslands — and eventually the natives had no recollection of what they had been, not even considering themselves ruled, so long and so buried was it. Then they took care of the ristables, and one last vestige of caste remained, for the bulls accepted sacrifices. The natives went to die…and one a week was put beneath the sod…and that was the way of it.

So deep and so inbred, that there was not even a conscious thought of it; that was simply the way of it.

But here was a stupid Earthman who had not known the way of it. He had won. He had killed a god, a ruler, deeper than any rule that ever existed…

That was the secret that Derr learned; the secret that was not even a secret really: just the way of it.

"So if there is anything I can grant," said the Headsman in true sorrow, for he bore this Earthman no malice, "just tell it."

And Nathaniel Derr, the great white hunter from Earth, thought about it.

Finally, as they untied him, taking him to the cleared area outside the village where he had killed the god ruler, the final twist came to him. Then he made his request, knowing the Mercantile Ship would come months too late, and there was nothing to be done.

He made his request, and they tied him between the posts, and finally the new ristable came, with its snow-white horn lowered and fire in its eyes.

He watched the ristable pawing and snorting and charging, and he knew his request would be carried out.

How strange, he thought, as the tip of the horn plunged deep to the softness that lies within all hard men. *Of all the trophies I've gathered...*

Then there was no thought of trophies.

So there it is, hanging between the hartebeest and the szlygor in the Trottersmen's trophy room. There was no choice about hanging it; after all, thirteen million dollars *is* thirteen million dollars. But it does give the members a chill from hell.

Still, there it hangs, and usually the room is closed off. But occasionally, if drinks are too many, and wit is abundant, the tale will be told. Perhaps not always with accuracy, but always with wonder.

Because it *is* a marvelous job of taxidermy.

There are even members who are willing to pay to find out how the Ristabite natives who did the job were able to retain the clean white color of the hair...

...and that damned *watchfulness* in the eyes.

!!!THE!!TEDDY!
CRAZY!!SHOW!!!

They hotted-up the studio audience with fifteen minutes of rock by
Fred Nietzsche & The Übermenschen and another five minutes of
second-string witticisms by the announcer, an ex-emcee named Rollin
Jacoby who had lost his own network game show when the FCC had
received reports he was *shtupping* female contestants in exchange for the
right answers.

By the time ON THE AIR hit, the gallery was electric with the
barely-subdued atmosphere of a Roman arena, the voyeurs and sadists
waiting for the Christians to be thrown to the Protestants.

Everyone's eyes went to the monitors as the musical theme swelled
in the studio and the credits began to roll.

"Here it is! Eleven o'clock, Pacific Standard Time, Now, Today, This
Minute, the time for THE TEDDY CRAZY SHOW!" Jacoby hyped the
announcement into his chest-mike, and the crawl card rolled
!!!THE!!TEDDY!CRAZY!!SHOW!!! in Cyrillic script. Then, PRO-
DUCED BY HOBIE PLEEN, and DIRECTED BY GRANT
WHITSEN, and then Jacoby came in over once more: "And here he
is, awakened America...the man who won't back off, the man who
gets it said, the man who pulls their covers and dumps their
mud...the man of the Now..."

And he came out of the wings as cameras 2 & 3 caught him in
double-exposure...

"*Teddy...Crazeeeee...!*"

The applause was deafening. The chimpanzees did not even need a cue card telling them to bang their sweaty palms together. The sight of him was enough. They clapped, and screamed, and yowled, and laughed, and whistled, and stomped, and howled, and Jan Breebnick (known to Awakened America as Teddy Crazy) walked in stately fashion across the small stage. Just before he sat down, he did a little dance-step, his famous little dance-step, loose-jointed as an epileptic, and the studio mob went wild again. And then Teddy Crazy took his seat behind the desk, behind the water pitcher, behind the sheets of flimsies on his guests, behind the microphone, and began his three thousand, nine hundred and fifty-fifth show on late night television.

"Who's the first yo-yo, Rollin?" Teddy Crazy demanded.

From the empty air came the reply, "Your first guest tonight is a winner, Teddy. It's Professor Heinrich Tessler, who just received a government grant of half a million dollars to explore his theory that there is an entrance to the hollow interior of the Earth somewhere near the North Pole."

The audience waited a split-second for Teddy to get "his face." Teddy could let the viewing audience know whether he was going to believe a guest or debunk him, merely by using one of two "faces" he kept in a drawer of the desk. One face was the drooling, imbecilic countenance of a hydrocephalic child, and the other was the studious and informed expression of a Renaissance man.

Teddy pulled out the moron face, and the audience clapped wildly, screamed and beat at the air with their voices as a stooped, septuageneric old man of gray features and weary eyes plodded onto the stage and took a seat across from Teddy Crazy behind the desk.

Teddy stared at the old man.

Professor Tessler's beard was as ineffectual as the old man seemed to be. It was gray, and it was hanging from his chin, but it was sparse, stringy, great empty patches of bare skin showing through, as though the face had given up halfway through its growth.

"Boy, you really look like a lunatic mad scientist," was Teddy Crazy's opening shot.

Professor Tessler began to tremble. "I haf come here to talk aboudt…"

"You talk about what we *want* you to talk about, Prof ole nutso buddy!" Teddy Crazy interrupted the thick Bavarian accent. "And you know *why*, sweetheart?"

It was rhetorical. Teddy didn't even wait.

"I'll *tell* you why: it's because you've just been given a half a *million* of United States of America's taxpayers' hard-earned money to go off into the Arctic to follow up some coocoo idea you got in a hash dream one night! And how that money is spent, money we all worked like dogs to make, is the concern of the folks who tune in every weekday night at eleven to find out the truth about weirdos like you, who can fleece our corrupt, pinko-loving government out of that much dough…*that's* why!" Applause. Stomping. Hooting. A lynch tenor in the mob. "Now. Whaddaya got to say for yourself, Prof?"

Tessler fidgeted. He wrung his hands together, out of sight below the desk. His rheumy little eyes darted back and forth. "I vas told by your broducer dot if I game on your schow I could tell aboudt my theory vithoudt there beink vun made uff me…"

Teddy Crazy got a mean look on his ruggedly handsome features. "Oh…now you're gonna sit there and lie at us, right, Professor? Well, there's my Producer, Mr. Hobie Pleen, standing right there…would you turn Camera #1 on him, please." The camera was revolved and the red light went on. "Hobie," Teddy Crazy asked him, "did you promise this man some sort of immunity from honest constructive questioning?"

Hobie Pleen, a frightened man whose greatest dream was a renewal pickup at the end of thirty-six weeks, spread his hands with obvious disbelief at Tessler's comment, and shook his head at Teddy Crazy. The camera revolved, and the monitors picked up Teddy Crazy once more looking at Tessler.

Save now he was looking at the old man as though he was a pus-pocket of evil. "No, Professor…now that we've proved you're not only a quack, a fraud, a charlatan and probably an embezzler of government funds, we've proved you're a common garden-variety liar as well. Now,

harlan ellison
!!! the !! teddy ! crazy !! show !!!

whaddaya have to say to *that*?"

Tessler summoned up strength. "My theory iz gorrect!"

"Oh yeah? Well, lemme ask *you*, the audience…do *you* believe this old loon? Do you believe there's an entrance to a hollow Earth at the North Pole? Lemme HEAR IT!"

The screams were thunderous. They beat against the walls, and they showered down like broken glass, and they sliced through the air like shards of steel, and little old Professor Tessler cringed behind the desk. It was what the law courts called *res ipsa loquitur* — a thing that speaks for itself. No one believed him. Before millions of eyes, Tessler was — that quick, snap! — discredited.

Now slumped hideously, as the screams died away, Tessler could only nod dumbly as Teddy Crazy said (with the uncommon softness one used in addressing a dog one has just whipped into servility), "Now Professor, let's talk about your theory…"

It took Teddy Crazy only fifteen minutes — one segment of his show — to demolish Tessler and send him away trembling with hopelessness and frustration. And all across America, no one, but *no one*, believed the Professor was onto anything more significant than a bad case of too much cheap whiskey.

Teddy Crazy took a taping break for commercials, four of them, plus two piggybacks, and came back to greet his second guest, Miss Anita DeStyre, a topless dancer supporting a fatherless family of seven.

She came onstage to wolf whistles, the rumbling of unbridled libidos and a round of applause usually reserved for Ministers of State. She was quite tall, almost six feet, wearing white knee-length patent leather boots, a mini-skirt that just reached below her buttocks, and flowing long blonde hair. Her bust was immense. But there was an undeniable sweetness about her; something very close to innocence in the face. Laugh lines and a directness that belied both her occupation and the moron mask Teddy Crazy wore as she approached his desk.

"Good evening, Miss DeStyre," Teddy Crazy said.

"Good evening, Mr. Crazy," she replied.

"What kind of an evening is it for sluts, Miss DeStyre?"

The audience dropped back into fitful silence. It had thought for a moment Teddy Crazy would play porno-word games, double entendre, with this pretty thing. But apparently he knew something...

"What's that supposed to mean?" She looked blank.

"What it means is, you're as phony as Dickie Nixon's nighty-night prayers. It means you go around telling everyone your measurements, when the truth of the matter is that you're all puffed out with silicone!"

"That's a dirty lie!"

"Yeah, well, dolly in for a closeup, Camera #3, because this piece of paper I'm holding in my right hand is a sworn affidavit from Dr. Kenneth J. Opatoshu, a plastic surgeon of Beverly Hills, who swears that on July 17th of last year he operated on you for bust expansion, using silicone and —"

Anita DeStyre grabbed the neck of her dress in both hands and ripped down, suddenly. There was the sound of tortured cloth, and then, before the protruding eyes of millions of Americans in the Great Wasteland, Miss DeStyre was naked to the waist. "How about *those*, buddy," she demanded of her host, "do *those* look like phonies?"

They were cut off the air instantly. Or rather, the taping was stopped. Miss DeStyre was re-clothed, in a topcoat loaned by a man in the third row of the audience, and they started taping again.

Teddy Crazy sat with folded hands, looking calm and as though he had swallowed something that would enrich him. "Ladies and Gentlemen," he said, "what you have just seen...one of the grossest demonstrations of the debasement of the female mystique...is a living demonstration of the unfittedness of this woman to retain legal motherhood of seven defenseless children. I had no affidavit on that piece of paper...it was merely an attempt on my part to provoke this woman into an act of such ugliness that her true nature would reveal itself. I urge everyone out there to write to the juvenile authorities here in Los Angeles to have those seven small children removed from the custody of a woman who is even less than an honest prostitute..."

Anita DeStyre began to cry.

It took fifteen minutes for that segment, and by the time it aired, three days later, the representatives of the juvenile court had already moved in to take Anita DeStyre's seven children from her. That they had been happy with their mother, that she had worked endlessly to provide a good home for them, made no difference. Teddy Crazy had done his job well. Using a broken Coca-Cola bottle, Anita DeStyre killed herself the night the show aired.

But that was only one third of the ninety minutes allotted to Teddy Crazy. As the show progressed he destroyed a promising novelist (accusing him of being a rank pornographer), the manufacturer of a new drug purported to cure cancer (with a barrage that insinuated side effects of the drug produced something more hideous than thalidomide babies), and a woman seeking her long-lost husband (by proving to the audience's satisfaction that the man being sought had been in charge of the gas ovens at Dachau).

Teddy Crazy's show was nearing its end for that night.

It had been a typical, average, interesting show. What Hobie Pleen would have called "a good show, Teddy."

"And who's our last guest, Rollin?" Teddy Crazy asked.

There was no answer from Rollin Jacoby.

But there was a flash of light and the distinct smell of something that should have been flushed.

And onto the stage walked His Satanic Majesty, the Prince of Darkness, Satan.

Or at least it looked like him.

His long tail protruded from the seat of his Brooks Bros. suit, and the triangular end of it whipped and thrashed as he stalked across to the desk. His cloven hoofprints were burned into the Formica of the studio floor. His horns were ram-like and curved upward from the thatch of blood-red hair that covered his head. His eyes were burning coals, his fingernails were black, and the expression on his face even startled Teddy Crazy. For a moment.

"The Fallen Angel is your last guest, Mr. Crazy," the visitor said. And he seated himself, pulling the black crimson-lined cape around himself.

Teddy Crazy stared. For a moment. Then he whipped out his moron mask and stared back at the audience. They got the message. Another weirdo!

They applauded and demanded Teddy take this jerk apart, piece by horn by tail by piece.

Teddy returned the mask to its drawer and turned to his guest. "Well, *Your Majesty*," and the words oozed loathing and ridicule, "to what do we owe the special privilege of your presence here on my humble show?"

"To be precise, Mr. Crazy, I'm here tonight to offer you a reward."

"Oh? And what might that be, you silly goose?"

"A rare delight. A special potion that my imps in the lowest recesses of Hell have concocted just for you."

"And, uh, might I be accurate in calling it some sort of hallucinogenic crutch that other, less-fortunate folks might use to delight themselves?"

"Not strictly speaking, no. You can call it a psychedelic if you choose, but it's much more ancient a recipe than that."

"Well, let's just trot it out here."

Satan reached into an inner pocket, and brought out a small piece of paper that looked like litmus paper. He handed it to Teddy Crazy. He was careful not to touch the emcee.

Teddy Crazy held it in his hand for a moment, then threw it down on the desk. "All right, nutso, enough of this nonsense. Let's find out exactly what it is you're trying to promote with that get-up and all these insane shenanigans."

"I'm not trying to promote anything, Mr. Crazy. I'm here merely to reward you for your unstinting service."

"Now you're trying to say I *work* for *you*?"

Incredulity, from the audience.

"On the contrary," said Satan. "Evil is an essence, Mr. Crazy. It is like faith. One must believe to make it so. Contrariwise, if one does not believe, whatever it is that is doubted, ceases to be. Bishop Berkeley introduced the theory on Earth many years ago, as I recall."

Teddy Crazy looked bored. "Forget the philosophy, creep, and just sock it to me nitty-gritty."

Satan nodded agreement. "Fine. Fine. I don't have too much time to waste, in any case.

"The point is, Mr. Crazy, that many of the people you have sent to me from this show — most recently a Professor Tessler, a Miss DeStyre, a Mr. Grogan and two others, just tonight, do not really belong in my operation. They have been discredited, disbelieved-in, through your machinations, and so they are cluttering up really overcrowded conditions in my, uh, suburb. It's playing havoc with property values, ruining the neighborhood with all of these good folk. It seems the only way to get things back on a more-or-less even keel is to reward you for what you've done and put an end to all of this. Thus: the little delight before you."

Teddy Crazy turned to his audience. "Can you folks dig what this nit is saying?"

They could dig it...and they laughed.

"Well, if I'm a charlatan, Mr. Crazy, then you should have no fears about trying this little potion soaked into the talla paper."

"That's just swell, Satan old buddy. You think I'm gonna drop acid right here in front of a coupla five million people, just to give you your jollies? You think I'm gonna pollute my precious bodily fluids, just to give you a chance to push whatever hideous narcotic this is, in front of school children and helpless folks who want something to lighten their burdens? No chance...no *damn* chance, as you'd say!"

"I'm afraid you have no choice, Mr. Crazy," Satan said, and stared at the emcee with eyes like the maws of leaping volcanos.

"How about it, folks..." Teddy Crazy's voice rose a trifle hysterically, "do *you* believe this moron is the devil? Do *you* believe he's what he says he is?"

The audience began screaming, the sound built up and up, and all across America viewers by the millions added their lusty throaty yells of disbelief and ridicule and hysteria.

Even as Teddy Crazy — quite without any volition — lifted the talla paper and popped it into his mouth and chewed it. They screamed louder and louder, telling the man in the devil suit that he was a fraud, that they didn't believe in him, that he wasn't real...even as Teddy Crazy turned to stone before their very eyes. Turned to a nice pink marble and then crumbled into a pile of dust on the desktop and the chair.

But it didn't help his visitor much. Because, as he had said, disbelief brings disillusion. That which is not accepted is rejected. Teddy Crazy was dust, but his visitor vanished. Just like that. Never to be heard from again.

There were rumors, later that month, out of the Vatican, that there was a terrific power struggle going on downstairs for possession of the Dark Kingdom, but the reports were unreliable, so no one ever really knew.

But this *was* true: Teddy Crazy, in dying and doing the world *two* big favors, got the highest rating of his career.

THE CHEESE
STANDS ALONE

Cort lay with his eyes closed, feigning sleep, for exactly one hour after she had begun to snore. Every few minutes he would permit his eyes to open to slits, marking the passage of time on the luminous dial of his watch there on the nightstand. At five AM precisely he slipped out of the Olympic pool-sized motel bed, swept up his clothes from the tangled pile on the floor, and dressed quickly in the bathroom. He did not turn on the light.

Because he could not remember her name, he did not leave a note.

Because he did not wish to demean her, he did not leave a twenty on the nightstand.

Because he could not get away fast enough, he pushed the car out of the parking slot in front of the room and let it gather momentum down through the silent lot till it bumped out onto the street. Through the open window he turned the wheel, caught the door before the car began rolling backward, slid inside and only then started the engine.

Route 1 between Big Sur and Monterey was empty. The fog was up. Somewhere to his left, below the cliffs, the Pacific murmured threats like an ancient adversary. The fog billowed across the highway, conjuring ectoplasmic shapes in the foreshortened beams of his headlights. Moisture hung from the great, thick trees like silver memories of time before the coming of Man. The twisting coast road climbed through terrain that reminded him of Brazilian rain forest: mist-drenched and chill, impenetrable and aggressively ominous. Cort drove faster, daring disaster to catch up with him. There had to be more than the threat of the forest.

As there had to be more in this life than endodontics and income properties and guilt-laden late night frottage with sloe-eyed dental assistants. More than pewter frames holding diplomas from prestigious universities. More than a wife from a socially prominent family and 2.6 children who might fit a soap manufacturer's perfect advertising vision of all-American youth. More than getting up each morning to a world that held no surprises.

There had to be disaster somewhere. In the forest, in the fog, in the night.

But not on Route 1 at half-past-five. Not for him, not right now.

By six-thirty he reached Monterey and realized he had not eaten since noon of the previous day when he had finished the root canal therapy on Mrs. Udall, had racked the drill, had taken off his smock and donned his jacket, had walked out of the office without a word to Jan or Alicia, had driven out of the underground garage and started up the Coast, fleeing without a thought to destination.

There had been no time for dinner when he'd picked up the cocktail waitress, and no late night pizza parlor open for a snack before she fell asleep. Acid had begun to burn a hole in his stomach lining from too much coffee and too little peace of mind.

He drove into the tourist center of Monterey and had no trouble finding a long stretch of open parking spaces. There was no movement along the shop-fronted sidewalks. The sun seemed determined never to come up. The fog was heavy and wet; streaming quicksand flowed around him. For a moment the windows of a shop jammed with drift-wood-base lamps destined for Iowa basement rec rooms solidified in the eye of the swirling fog; then they were gone. But in that moment he saw his face in the glass. This night might stretch through the day.

He walked carefully through the streets, looking for an early morn-ing dinette where he might have a Belgian waffle with frozen strawber-ries slathered in sugary syrup. An egg sunnyside up. *Something* sunnyside up in this unending darkness.

Nothing was open. He thought about that. Didn't anyone go to work early in Monterey? Were there no services girding themselves for the locust descent of teenagers with rucksacks, corpulent business machine salesmen in crimson Budweiser caps and Semitic widows with blue hair? Had there been an eclipse? Was this the shy, pocked, turned-away face of the moon? Where the hell was daylight?

Fog blew past him, parted in streamers for an instant. Down a side street he saw a light. Yellow faded as parchment, wan and timorous. But a light.

He turned down the side street and searched through the quicksilver for the source. It seemed to have vanished. Past closed bakeries and jewelry shops and scuba gear emporia. A wraith in the fog. He realized he moved through not only the empty town and through the swaddling fog, but through a condition of fear. *Gnotobiosis*: an environmental condition in which germfree animals have been inoculated with strains of known microorganisms. Fear.

The light swam up through the silent, silvered shadow sea; and he was right in front of it. Had *he* moved to *it*...had *it* moved to *him*?

It was a bookstore. Without a sign. And within, many men and women; browsing.

He stood in the darkness, untouched by the sallow light from the nameless bookshop, staring at the nexus. For such a small shop, so early in the morning, it was thronged. Men and women stood almost elbow to elbow, each absorbed in the book close at hand. *Gnotobiosis*: Cort felt the fear sliding through his veins and arteries like poison.

They were not turning the pages.

Had they not moved their bodies, a scratching at the lip, the blinking of eyes, random shifting of feet, a slouch, a straightening of back, a glance around...he would have thought them mannequins. A strange but interesting tableau to induce passersby to come in and also browse. They were alive, but they did not turn the pages of the books that absorbed them. Nor did they return a book to its shelf and take another. Each man, each woman, held fascinated by words where the books had been opened.

He turned to walk away as quickly as he could.

The car. Get on the road. There had to be a truck stop, a diner, a greasy spoon, fast food, anything. I've been here before, and *this isn't Monterey!*

The tapping on the window stopped him.

He turned back. The desperate expression on the tortoiselike face of the tiny old woman stiffened his back. He found his right hand lifting, as if to put itself between him and the sight of her. He shook his head no, definitely not, but he had no idea what he was rejecting.

She made staying motions with her wrinkled little hands and mouthed words through the glass of the shop window. She spoke very precisely and the words were these:

I have it here for you.

Then she motioned him to come around to the door, to enter, to step inside: *I have it here for you.*

The luminous dial of his watch said 7:00. It was still night. Fog continued to pour down from the Monterey peninsula's forest.

Cort tried to walk away. San Francisco was up the line. The sun had to be blazing over Russian Hill, Candlestick Park, and Coit Tower. The world still held surprises. *You're loose now, you've broken the cycle,* he heard his future whisper. *Don't respond. Go to the sun.*

He saw his hand reach for the doorknob. He entered the bookshop.

They all looked up for a moment, registered nothing, the door closed behind him, they dropped their gazes to the pages. Now he was inside among them.

"I'm certain I have it in hardcover, a very clean copy," the little old turtle woman said. Her smile was toothless. *How could there be fog in here?*

"I'm just browsing," Cort said.

"Yes, of course," she said. "Everyone is just browsing."

She laid her hand on his arm and he shuddered. "Just till a restaurant opens."

"Yes, of course."

He was having trouble breathing. The heartburn. "Is it always...does it always stay dark so late into the morning here?"

"Unseasonal," she said. "Look around. I have it here for you. Exactly."

He looked around. "I'm not looking for anything special."

She walked with him, her hand on his arm. "Neither were they." She nodded at the crowd of men and women. "But they found answers here. I have a very fine stock."

No pages were turned.

He looked over the shoulder of a middle-aged woman staring intently at a book with steel engravings on both open pages. The turtle said, "Her curiosity was aroused by the question 'How was the *first* vampire created?' Fascinating concept, isn't it? If vampires can only be created by a normal human being receiving the bite of a vampire, then how was the first one created? She has found the answer here in my wonderful stock." Cort stared at the book. One of the steel engravings was of Noah's ark.

But wouldn't that mean there had to be *two* on board?

The turtle drew him down the line of stacks. He paused behind a young man in a very tight T-shirt. He looked as if he had been working out. His head was bent so close to the open book in his hands that his straight blond hair fell over his eyes.

"For years he has felt sympathetic pains with an unknown person," the turtle confided. "He would sense danger, elation, lust, despair…none of his own making, and none having anything to do with his circumstance at that moment. Finally he began to realize he was linked with another. Like the Corsican Brothers. But his parents assured him he was an only child, there was no twin. He found the answer in this volume." She made shooing motions with her blue-veined hands.

Cort peered around the young man's head and hair. It was a book on African history. There were tears in the young man's eyes; there was a spot of moisture on the verso. Cort looked away quickly, he didn't want to intrude.

Next in line was a very tall, ascetic looking man carefully holding a folio of pages that had obviously been written with a quill. By the flourishes and swirls of the writing, Cort knew the book had to be quite old and very likely valuable. The tortoise woman leaned in close, her head barely reaching Cort's chest, and she said, "Sixteenth century. First Shakespeare folio. This gentleman wandered through most of his adult life, and decades of academic pursuits, tormented by the question of who actually wrote *The Booke of Sir Thomas More*: the Bard or his rival, Anthony Munday. There lies his answer, before his eyes. I have such a superior stock."

"Why doesn't he...why don't *any* of these people turn the page?"

"Why bother? They've found the answer they sought."

"And there's nothing more they want to know?"

"Apparently not. Interesting, isn't it?"

Cort found it more chilling than interesting. Then the chill fastened itself permanently to his heart, like a limpet, with the unasked question, *How long have these browsers been here like this?*

"Here's a woman who always wanted to know if pure evil exists anywhere on the face of the earth." The woman wore a *mantilla* over her shoulders, and she stared mesmerized at a book on natural history. "This man hungered for a complete list of the contents of the great Library of Alexandria, the subject matters contained on those half million handwritten papyrus scrolls at the final moment before the Library was torched in the Fifth Century." The man was gray and wizened and his face had been incised with an expression of ancient weariness that reminded Cort of Stonehenge. He pored over two pages set so closely with infinitesimal typefaces that Cort could not make out a single word in the flyspecks. "A woman who lost her memory," said the turtle, indicating with a nod of her tortoise head a beautiful creature festooned with silk scarves of a dozen different colors. "Woke up in a white slave brothel in Marrakech, ran for her life, has spent years wandering around trying to discover who she was." She laughed a low, warm laugh. "She found out here. The whole story's right there in that book."

Cort turned to her, firmly removing her withered claw from his arm. "And you 'have it here for me,' don't you?"

"Yes; I have it here. In my fine stock."

"What *precisely* do you have that I want? Here. In your fine stock."

He didn't even need her to speak. He knew exactly what she would say. She would say, "Why, I have the answers you seek." And then he would saunter around the bookshop, feeling superior to these poor devils who had been standing here God only knew how long, and finally he'd turn to her and smile and say, "I don't even know the questions," and they would both smile at that one—he like an idiot because it was the most banal of clichés, she because she'd known he would say something dithering like that—and he would refrain from apologizing for the passing stupidity; and then he would ask her the question and she would point out a shelf and say. "The book you want is right there," and then she'd suggest he try pages such-and-such for exactly what he wanted to know: that which had driven him up the Coast.

And if, ten thousand years later, the karmic essence of all that's left of Sulayman the Magnificent, blessed be his name, Sulayman of the potent seal, Sultan and Master of all the djinn, of each and every class of *jinni, ghul, ifrit, si'la, div* and *iblis*; if that transubstantiated essence comes 'round again, like Halley's comet comes 'round again; that transmogrified spirit circling back on its limitless hegira through crimson eternity…if it comes 'round again it would find him, Cort—Dr. Alexander Cort, D.D.S., a Dental Corporation—still standing here elbow-to-elbow with the other browsers. Coelacanths outlined in shale, mastodons flash-frozen in ice, wasps embedded in amber. *Gnotobiosis:* forever.

"Why do I have the feeling all this isn't random?" Cort said to the old turtle woman. He began edging toward the door behind him. "Why do I have the feeling all this has been here waiting for me, just the way it was waiting for all the rest of those poor fucking losers? Why do I get the smell of rotting gardenias off you, old lady?" He was almost at the door.

She stood in a cleared space in the center of the bookshop, staring at him.

"You're no different, Dr. Cort. You need the answers, the same as the rest."

"Maybe a little love potion…a powerstone…immortality…all that good jive. I've seen places like this in television shows. But I don't bite, old lady. I have no need you can fill." And his hand was on the doorknob; and he was turning it; and he yanked; and the door opened to the ominous fog and the unending night and the waiting forest. And the old lady said, "Wouldn't you like to know when you'll have the best moment of your entire life?"

And he closed the door and stood with his back against it.

His smile was unhealthy. "Well, you got me," he whispered.

"When you'll be happiest," she said softly, barely moving her thin lips. "When you'll be strongest, most satisfied, at the peak of your form, most in control, bravest, best-looking, most highly regarded by the rest of the world; your top moment, your biggest surge, your most golden achievement, that which forms the pattern for the rest of your life; the instant than which you will have no finer, if you live to be a thousand. Here in my fine stock I have a tome that will tell you the day, hour, minute, second of your noblest future. Just ask and it's yours. *I have it here for you.*"

"And what does it cost me?"

She opened her wet mouth and smiled. Her wrinkled little hands fell open palms up in the air before her. "Why, nothing," she said. "Like these others…you're just browsing, aren't you?" The limpet chill that ossified his spine told him there were worse things than deals with the devil. Just browsing, as an example.

"Well…?" she asked, waiting.

He thought about it, wetting his lips—suddenly gone dry now that the decisive moment was at hand. "What if it comes only a few years from now? What if I've only got a little while to achieve whatever it was I always wanted to achieve? How do I live with the rest of my life after that, knowing I'll never be any better, any happier, any richer or more secure; knowing I'll never top what I did in that moment? What'll the rest of my life be worth?"

The tiny turtle woman shouldered aside two browsers—who moved sluggishly apart as if turning in their sleep—and drew a short, squat book from a shelf at her waist level. Cort blinked quickly. No, she hadn't drawn it out of the stacks. It had slid forward and jumped *into* her hand. It looked like an old Big Little Book.

She turned back and offered it to him. "Just browsing," she said, moistly.

He reached for it and stopped, curling his fingers back. She arched her finely-penciled eyebrows and gave him a bemused, quizzical look.

"You're awfully anxious to get me to read that book," he said.

"We are here to serve the public," she said, amiably.

"I have a question to ask you. No, two questions. There are two questions I want you to answer. Then I'll consider browsing through your fine stock."

"If I can't give you the answer—which is, after all, our business here—then I'm sure something in my fine stock has the proper response. But...take this book that you need, just hold it, and I'll answer your question. Questions. Two questions. Very important, I'm sure." She held out the squat little book. Cort looked at it. It *was* a Big Little Book, the kind he had had when he was a child; with pages of drawings alternating with pages of type, featuring comic strip heroes like Red Ryder or The Shadow or Skippy. Within reach, the answer to the question everyone wanted to ask; what will be the best moment of my life?

He didn't touch it.

"I'll ask, you'll answer; then you got me...then I'll do some browsing."

She shrugged, as if to say, *as you choose.*

He thought: As you choose, so shall you reap.

He said: "What's the name of this bookshop?"

Her face twitched. Cort had the sudden rush of memory from childhood, when he'd first been read the story of Rumpelstiltskin. The turtle woman's face grew mean. "It doesn't have a name. It just is."

"How do we find you in the Yellow Pages?" Cort said, taunting her. It was obvious he was suddenly in a position of power. Even though he had no idea from what source that power flowed.

"No name! No name at all! We don't need a name; we have a very select clientele! It's never had a name! We don't need any names!" Her voice, which had been turtle smooth and soft and chocolate, had become rusted metal scraping rusted metal. No names, I don't got to tell you no names, I don't got to show you no stinkin' badges!

She paused to let the bile recede, and in the eye of the silence Cort asked his second question. "What's in this for you? Where's *your* fix? Where's the bottom-line profit on your p&l? What do *you* get out of this, frighty old lady?"

Her mouth went tight. Her blazing eyes seemed both ancient and silvery with youthful ferocity. "Clotho," she said. "Clotho: Rare Books."

He didn't recognize the name, but from the way she said it, he knew he had pried an important secret from her; had done it, apparently, because he was the first to have asked; had done it as *anyone* might have done it, had they thought of it. And having asked, and having been answered, he knew he was safe from her.

"So tell me, Miss Clotho, or Ms. Clotho, or Mrs., or whatever you happen to be: tell me…what do *you* get out of this? What coin of the realm do you get paid? You work this weird shop, you trap all these fools in here, and I'll bet when I walk out of here, poof! It all vanishes. Goes back to Never-Never Land. So what kind of a home life do you have? Do you eat three squares a day? Do you have to change your Tampax when you get your period? Do you even *get* the menses? Or has menopause already passed you by? Immortal, maybe? Tell me, weird old turtle lady, if you live forever do you *get* change of life? Do you still want to get laid? Did you *ever* get laid? How's your ka-ka, firm and hard? Do weirdy old fantastic ladies who vanish with their bookstore have to take a shit, or maybe not, huh?"

She screamed at him. "You can't talk like that to me! Do you know who I am?"

He screamed right back at her. "Fuck no, I don't know who the hell you are, and what's more to the point, I don't *give* a righteous damn who you are!"

The zombie readers were now looking up. They seemed distressed. As if a long-held trance was being broken. They blinked furiously, moved aimlessly; they resembled…groundhogs coming out to check their shadows.

Clotho snarled at him, "Stop yelling! You're making my customers nervous!"

"You mean I'm waking them up? C'mon, everybody, rise and shine! Swing on down! How ya fixed, destiny-wise?"

"Shut up!"

"Yeah? Maybe I will and maybe I won't, old turtle. Maybe you answer my question what you were doing waiting here for me specially, and maybe I let these goofballs go back to their browsing."

She leaned in as close as she could to him, without touching him, and she hissed like a snake. Then she said tightly, "You! What makes you think it was *you* we wait for? We wait for *everyone*. This was your turn. They *all* get a turn, you'll *all* get your turn in the browsing shop."

"What's this 'we' business? Are you feeling imperial?"

"We. My sisters and I."

"Oh, there's more than one of you, is there? A chain book-store. Very cute. But then I suppose you have branches these days, what with the competition from B. Dalton and Crown and Waldenbooks."

She clenched her teeth; and for the first time Cort could see that the old turtle actually *had* teeth inside those straight, thin lips. *"Take this book or get out of my shop,"* she said in a deadly whisper.

He took the Big Little Book from her quivering hands.

"I've *never* dealt with anyone as vile, as *rude,* " she snarled.

"Customer is always right, sweetie," he said. And he opened the book to precisely the right page.

Where he read his finest moment. The knowledge that would make the remainder of his life an afterthought. An also-ran. Marking time. A steady ride on the downhill side.

When would it come? A year hence? Two years? Five, ten, twenty-five, fifty, or at the blessed final moment of life, having climbed, climbed, climbed all the way to the end? He read…

That his finest moment had come when he was ten years old. When, during a sandlot baseball game, a pick-up game in which you

got to bat only if you put someone out, the best hitter in the neighborhood hit a shattering line drive to deepest centerfield where he
was *always* forced to play, because he was no good at baseball, and he
ran back and back and stuck up his bare hand and *miraculously*, as he,
Little Alex Cort, leaped as high as he could, *miraculously* the pain of
the frazzled hardball as it hit his hand and stayed there was sweeter
than anything he had ever felt before—or would feel again. The
moment replayed in the words on the page of that terrible book.
Slowly, slowly he sank to earth, his feet touching and his eyes going
to his hand and there, in the red, anguished palm of his hand, without a trapper's mitt, he held the hardest, surest home run line drive
ever hit by anyone. He was the killer, the master of the world, the
tallest thing on the face of the earth, big and bold and golden, adept
beyond any telling, miraculous; a miracle, a walking miracle. It was
the best moment of his life.

At the age of ten.

Nothing else he would do in his life, nothing he had done between
the age of ten and thirty-five as he read the Big Little Book, nothing
he would do till he died at whatever number of years remained for
him...nothing...nothing would match that moment.

He looked up slowly. He was having trouble seeing. He was crying.
Clotho was smiling at him nastily. "You're lucky it wasn't one of my
sisters. They react much worse to being screwed with."

She started to turn away from him. The sound of his slamming the
Big Little Book closed onto the counter of the showcase stopped her.
He turned without saying a word and started for the door. Behind him
he heard her hurrying after him.

"Where do you think *you're* going?"

"Back to the real world." He had trouble speaking; the tears were
making him sob and his words came raggedly.

"You've got to stay! *Everyone* stays."

"Not me, sweetie. The cheese stands alone."

"It's all futile. You'll never know grandeur again. It's all dross, waste,
emptiness. There's nothing as good if you live to be a thousand."

He opened the door. The fog was out there. And the night. And the final forest. He stopped and looked down at her. "Maybe if I'm lucky I won't live to be a thousand."

Then he stepped through the door of Clotho: Rare Books and closed it tightly behind him. She watched through the window as he began to walk off into the fog.

He stopped and leaned in to speak as close to the glass as he could. She strained her weird little turtle face forward and heard him say, "What's left may only be the tag-end of a shitty life...but it's *my* shitty life.

"And it's the only game in town, sweetie. The cheese stands alone."

Then he walked off into the fog, crying; but trying to whistle.

SOMEHOW, I DON'T THINK WE'RE IN KANSAS, TOTO

Six months of my life were spent in creating a dream the shape and sound and color of which had never been seen on television. The dream was called *The Starlost*, and between February and September of 1973 I watched it being steadily turned into a nightmare.

The late Charles Beaumont, a scenarist of unusual talents who wrote many of the most memorable *Twilight Zones*, said to me when I arrived in Hollywood in 1962, "Attaining success in Hollywood is like climbing a gigantic mountain of cow flop, in order to pluck one perfect rose from the summit. And you find when you've made that hideous climb...you've lost the sense of smell."

In the hands of the inept, the untalented, the venal and the corrupt, *The Starlost* became a veritable Mt. Everest of cow flop and, though I climbed that mountain, somehow I never lost sight of the dream, never lost the sense of smell, and when it got so rank I could stand it no longer, I descended hand-over-hand from the northern massif, leaving behind $93,000, the corrupters, and the eviscerated remains of my dream. I'll tell you about it.

February. Marty the agent called and said, "Go over to 20th and see Robert Kline."

"Who's Robert Kline?"

"West Coast head of taped syndicated shows. He's putting together a package of mini-series, eight or ten segments per show. He wants to do a science fiction thing. He asked for you. It'll be a co-op deal between 20th Century-Fox and the BBC. They'll shoot it in London."

London! "I'm on my way," I said, the jet-wash of my departure deafening him across the phone connection.

I met Kline in the New Administration Building of 20th, and his first words were so filled with sugar I had the feeling if I listened to him for very long I'd wind up with diabetes: "I wanted the top sf writer in the world," he said. Then he ran through an informed list of my honors in the field of science fiction. It was an impressive performance of the corporate art-form known as ego-massage.

Then Kline advised me that what he was after was, "A sort of *The Fugitive* in Space." Visions of doing a novel-for-television in the mode of *The Prisoner* splatted like overripe casaba melons; I got up and started to walk.

"Hold it, hold it!" Kline said. "What did you have in mind?" I sat down again.

Then I ran through half a dozen ideas for series that would be considered primitive concepts in the literary world of sf. Kline found each of them too complex. As a final toss at the assignment, I said, "Well, I've been toying with an idea for tape, rather than film; it could be done with enormous production values that would be financially impossible for a standard filmed series."

"What is it?" he said.

And here's what I told him:

Five hundred years from now, the Earth is about to suffer a cataclysm that will destroy all possibility for life on the planet. Time is short. The greatest minds and the greatest philanthropists get together and cause to have constructed in orbit between the Moon and the Earth a giant ark, one thousand miles long, comprising hundreds of self-contained biospheres. Into each of these little worlds is placed a segment of Earth's population, its culture intact. Then the ark is sent off toward the stars, even as the Earth is destroyed, to seed the new worlds surrounding those stars with the remains of humanity.

But one hundred years after the flight has begun, a mysterious "accident" (which would remain a mystery till the final segment of the show, four years later, it was hoped) kills the entire crew, seals the biosphere-worlds so they have no contact with one another…and the long voyage goes on with the people trapped, developing their societies without any outside influence. Five hundred years go by, and the travelers — the Starlost — forget the Earth. To them it is a myth, a vague legend, even as Atlantis is to us. They even forget they are adrift in space, forget they are in an interstellar vessel. Each community thinks it is "the world" and that the world is only fifty square miles, with a metal ceiling.

Until Devon, an outcast in a society rigidly patterned after the Amish communities of times past, discovers the secret, that they are onboard a space-going vessel. He learns the history of the Earth, learns of its destruction, and learns that when "the accident" happened, the astrogation gear of the ark was damaged and now the last seed of human-kind is on a collision course with a star. Unless he can convince a sufficient number of biosphere-worlds to band together in a communal attempt to learn how the ark works, repair it and re-program their flight, they will soon be incinerated in the furnace of that giant sun toward which they're heading. It was, in short, a fable of our world today.

"Fresh! Original! New!" Kline chirruped. "There's never been an idea like it before!" I didn't have the heart to tell him the idea was first propounded in astronautical literature in the early 1920s by the great Russian pioneer Tsiolkovsky, nor that the British physicist Bernal had done a book on the subject in 1929, nor that the idea had become *very* common coin in the genre of science fiction through stories by Heinlein, Harrison, Panshin, Simak and many others. (Arthur C. Clarke's then-current bestseller, *Rendezvous with Rama*, was the latest example of the basic idea.) Kline suggested I dash home and write up the idea, which he would then merchandise. I pointed out to him that the Writers Guild frowns on speculative writing and that if he wanted the riches of my invention, he should lay on me what we call "holding money" to enable me to write a prospectus and to enable him to blue-sky it with the BBC. The blood drained from his face at my suggestion of advance money, and he said he had to clear it with the BBC, but that if I wrote the prospectus he would guarantee me a free trip to London. I got up and started to walk.

"Hold it, hold it!" he said, and opened a desk drawer. He pulled out a cassette recorder and extended it. "Tell you what: why don't you just tell it on a cassette, the same way you told it to me." I stopped and looked. This was a new one on me. In over twenty years as a film and television writer, I've seen some of the most circuitous, sleazy, Machiavellian dodges ever conceived by the mind of Western Man to get writers to write on the cuff. But never before, and never since, has anyone been that slippery. It should have been all the tip-off I needed.

I thought on it for a moment, rationalized that this wasn't speculative writing, that at worst it was "speculative talking," and since a writer is expected to pitch an idea anyhow, it was just *barely* legitimate.

So I took the cassette home, backed my spiel with the music from *2001: A Space Odyssey*, outlined the barest bones of the series concept, and brought it back to Kline.

"Okay. Here it is," I said, "but you can't transcribe it. If you do, then it becomes spec writing and you have to pay me." I was assured he wouldn't put it on paper, and that he'd be back to me shortly. He was sure the BBC would go bananas for the idea.

No sooner was I out of his office than he had his secretary transcribe the seven-minute tape.

March. No word.

April. No word.

May. Suddenly there was a flurry of activity. Marty the agent called. "Kline sold the series. Go see him."

"Series?" I said, appalled. "But that idea was only planned to accommodate eight segments...a *series*, you say?"

"Go see him."

So I went. Kline greeted me as if I were the only human capable of deciphering the Mayan Codex and caroled that he had sold the series not only to 48 of the NBC independent stations (what are called the O&O's, Owned & Operated stations), but that the Westinghouse outlets had bitten, and the entire Canadian Television Network, the CTV.

"Uh, excuse me," I said, in an act of temerity not usually attributed to writers in Hollywood, "how did you manage to sell this, er, *series* without having a contract with me, or a prospectus, or a pilot script, or a pilot film...or *anything?*"

"They read your outline, and they bought it on the strength of your name."

"They *read* it? How?"

He circumnavigated that little transgression of his promise not to set my words on paper and began talking in grandiose terms about how I'd be the story editor, how I'd have creative control, how I'd write many scripts for the show, and what a good time I'd have in Toronto.

"Toronto?!" I said, gawking. "What the hell happened to London? The Sir Lew Grade Studios. Soho. Buckingham Palace. Swinging London. What happened to all that?"

Mr. Kline, without bothering to inform the creator of this hot property he had been successfully hawking, had been turned down by the BBC and had managed to lay off the project with CTV, as an all-Canadian production of Glen Warren, a Toronto-based operation that was already undertaking to tape *The Starlost* at the CFTO Studios in Toronto. It was assumed by Mr. Kline that I would move to Toronto to story edit the series; he never bothered to ask if I *wanted* to move to Canada, he just assumed I would.

Mr. Kline was a real bear for assuming things.

Such as: I would write *his* series (which was the way he now referred to it) even though a writers' strike was imminent. I advised him that if the strike hit, I would be incommunicado, but he waved away my warnings with the words, "Everything will work out." With such words, Napoleon went to Elba.

At that time I was a member of the Board of Directors of the Writers Guild of America, West and I was very pro-union, pro-strike, pro-getting long overdue contract inequities with the producers straightened out.

Just before the strike began, Kline called and said he was taking out advertisements for the series. He said he'd had work done for the presentations, and he needed some copy to accompany the drawings. I asked him how he could have work done when the spaceship had not yet been designed? (I was planning to create a vessel that would be absolutely feasible and scientifically correct, in conjunction with Ben Bova, then-editor of *Analog*.) Kline said there wasn't time for all that fooling around, ads had to go out *now!*

It has always been one of the imponderables of the television industry to me, how the time is always *now*, when three days earlier no one had even *heard* of the idea.

But I gave him some words and, to my horror, saw the ad a week later: it showed a huge bullet-shaped *thing* I guess Kline thought was a spaceship, being smacked by a meteorite, a great hole being torn in the skin of the bullet, revealing many levels of living space within...all of them drawn the wrong direction. I covered my eyes.

Let me pause for a moment to explain why this was a scientifically-illiterate, wholly incorrect piece of art, because it was merely the first indication of how little the producers of *The Starlost* understood what they were doing. Herewith, a Child's Primer of Science Fiction:

There is no air in space. Space is very nearly a vacuum. That means an interstellar vessel, since it won't be landing anywhere and doesn't need to be designed for passage through atmosphere, can be designed any way that best follows the function. The last time anyone used the bullet design for a starship was in *The Green Slime*, circa 1969 (a Nipponese nifty that oozes across the "Late Late Late Show" in the wee'est hours when normal folks are sleeping; this excludes systems analysts and computer programmers, of course).

But it indicated the lack of understanding of sf that is common-place among television executives who, for the most part, have not read an entire book since they left high school.

Look: if you turn on your set and see a pair of white swinging doors suddenly slammed open by a gurney pushed by two white-smocked interns, you know that within moments Trapper John, M.D. (or Ben Casey, or Dr. Kildare, or Marcus Welby) will be jamming a tube down somebody's trachea; if you see a snake-eyed dude in a black Stetson lying-out on a butte, aiming a Sharps .52 caliber buffalo rifle, you know that within moments the Wells Fargo stage is gonna come a-thunderin' down that dusty trail; if Dan Tana (or Mannix, or Jim Rockford, or Ironside) comes into his inner office and there's a silky lady lounging in the chair across from his desk, showing a lot of leg, you know that by the end of Act One someone is going to try ventilating his (or Magnum's) hide. It's all by rote, all templates, all stolen from what went before by a generation of writers and producers whose only referents are what they grew up with watching television; it's all cliché, all predictable.

And while I make no brief for the reams and volumes of low-grade, moronic *Star Wars* imitation space opera hackwork that has turned this into the worst period in the history of sf, the genre is *not* predictable. Or at least it shouldn't be.

(Though shit like *Battlestar Ponderosa* and Universal's *Buck Rogers* seem to assure us that the steamroller mediocrity of tv can even trivialize sf, despite the built-in deterrents.)

A science fiction story has to have interior logic. It has to be consistent, even within the boundaries of its own extrapolative horizons. That's irreducible in the parameters of what a sf story or teleplay must do, in order to get the reader or viewer to go along with it, without feeling conned or duped or lied to. Rigorous standards of plotting *must* be employed to win that willing suspension of disbelief on the part of the audience; it allows them to accept a fantastic premise.

How many sf movies have you seen — *Outland, Message From Space, Silent Running* are perfect awful examples — during which you recognized sophomoric inaccuracies that made you groan and feel cheated? Errors that first-year science students would not make: sound in a vacuum, people walking around on alien planets without filtration masks, clones that spring fully grown from fingernail parings, robots that act like midgets in metal suits.

Break that logical chain, dumb it up, accept the insulting myth that no one knows or cares if the special effects are spectacular enough, and the whole thing falls apart like Watergate testimony.

But the ad was only an early storm warning of what troubles were yet to befall me. The strike was called, and then began weeks of a kind of ghastly harassment I'd always thought was reserved for over-blown melodramas about the Evils of Hollywood. Phone calls at all hours, demanding I write the "bible" for the series. (A "bible" is industry shorthand for the *précis* of what the show will do, who the characters are, what directions storylines should take. In short, the blueprint from which individual segments are written. Without a bible, only the creator knows what the series is about.) Kline had no bible. He had nothing, at this point, but that seven-minute tape. With which item, plus my name and the name of Doug Trumbull — who, at that time had done the special effects for *2001* and had directed *Silent Running* — he'd been signed on as Executive Producer — Kline had — sans a contract with me! — sold this pipe dream to everyone in the Western World.

But I wouldn't write the bible. I was on strike. Then began the threats. Followed by the intimidation, the bribes, the promises that they'd go forward with the idea without me, the veiled hints of scab writers who'd be hired to write their own version of the series...everything short of actually kidnapping me. Through these weeks — when even flights out of Los Angeles to secluded hideaways in the Michigan wilds and the northern California peninsula failed to deter the phone calls — I refused to write. It didn't matter that the series might not get on the air, it didn't matter that I'd lose a potload of money, the Guild was on strike in a noble cause and, besides, I didn't much trust Mr. Kline and the anonymous voices that spoke to me in the wee hours of the night. And, contrary to popular belief, many television writers are men and women of ethic: they can be rented, but they can't be bought.

I remember seeing a film of Clifford Odets's *The Big Knife* when I was a young writer living in New York and lusting after fame in Hollywood. I remember seeing the unscrupulous Steiger and his minions applying pressure to a cracking Palance, to get him to sign a contract, and I remember smiling at the danger-filled melodramatics. During that period of pre-production on *The Starlost*, I ceased smiling.

The threats ranged from breaking my typing fingers to insuring I'd never work in the Industry again. The bribes ranged from $13,000 to be placed in an unnumbered Swiss bank account to this:

One afternoon before the strike, I'd been in Kline's office. I'd been leafing through the *Players' Directory*, the trade publication that lists all actors and actresses, with photos. I'd commented idly that I found the person of one pictured young starlet quite appealing. Actually, what I'd said was that I'd sell my soul to get it on with her.

Now, weeks later, during my holdout and Kline's attempts to get me to scab, I was puttering about my house, when the doorbell rang. I went to the door, opened it, and there stood the girl of my wanton day-dreams. Bathed in sunlight, a palpable nimbus haloing that gorgeous face. I stood open-mouthed, unable even to invite her in.

"I was in the neighborhood," she said, entering the house with no assistance from me, "and I've heard so much about you, I decided just to come and say hello."

She said hello. I said something unintelligible. (I have the same reaction when standing in front of Picasso's *Guernica*. Otherworldly beauty has a way of turning my brains to prune-whip yogurt.) But it took only a few minutes of conversation to ascertain that yes, she knew Mr. Kline and, yes, she knew about the series, and...

I wish I could tell you I used her brutally and sent her back to where I assumed she had come from, but feminism has taken its toll and I merely asked her to split.

She split.

I couldn't watch any tv that night. My eyes were too swollen from crying.

And the cajoling went on. Kline, of course, knew *nothing* about the girl, had never had anything to do with sending her over, would be affronted if anyone even *suggested* he had tried such a loathsome, demeaning trick. Hell, I'd be the *last* one to suggest it. Or maybe second from the last.

But howzabout the scab writer threat? Well…

At one point, representatives of Mr. Kline *did* bring in a scab. A non-union writer to whom they imparted a series of outright lies so he'd believe he was saving my bacon. When they approached well-known sf writer Robert Silverberg to write the bible, Bob asked them point-blank, "Why isn't Harlan writing it?" They fumfuh'ed and said, well, er, uh, he's on strike. Bob said, "Would he want me to write this?" They knew he'd call me, and they told him no, I'd be angry. So he passed up some thousands of dollars, and they went elsewhere. And this being the kind of world it is, they found a taker.

I found out about the end-run, located the writer in a West L.A. hotel where they'd secreted him, writing madly through a weekend, and I convinced him he shouldn't turn in the scab bible. To put the period to the final argument that Kline & Co. were not being honest, I called Kline from that hotel room while the other writer listened in on the bathroom extension phone. I asked Kline point-blank if other writers had been brought in to scab. He said no; he assured me they were helplessly waiting out the strike till I could bring the purity of my original vision to the project. I thanked him, hung up, and looked at the other writer who had just spent 72 hours beating his brains out writing a scab bible. "I rest my case."

"Let's go to the Writers Guild," he said.

It drove Kline bananas. Everywhichway he turned, I was there, confounding his shabby attempts at circumventing an honest strike.

I'll skip a little now. The details were ugly, but grow tedious in the retelling. It went on at hideous length, for weeks. Finally, Glen Warren in Toronto, at Kline's urging, managed to get the Canadian writers guild, ACTRA, to accept that *The Starlost* was a wholly Canadian-produced series. They agreed that was the case, after much pressure was applied in ways I'm not legally permitted to explicate, and I was finally convinced I should go to work.

That was my next mistake.

They had been circulating copies of the scab bible with all of its erroneous material, and had even given names to the characters. When I finally produced the authentic bible, for which they'd been slavering so long, it confused everyone. They'd already begun building sets and fashioning materiel that had nothing to do with the show.

I was brought up to Toronto to work with writers, and because the producing entity would get government subsidies if the show was clearly acceptable in terms of "Canadian content" (meaning the vast majority of writers, actors, directors and production staff had to be Canadian), I was ordered to assign script duties to Canadian tv writers.

I sat in the Four Seasons Motel in Toronto in company with a man named Bill Davidson, who had been hired as the Producer even though he knew nothing about science fiction and seemed thoroughly confused by the bible, and interviewed dozens of writers from nine AM till seven PM.

It is my feeling that one of the prime reasons for the artistic (and, it would seem, ratings) failure of *The Starlost* was the quality of the scripts. But it isn't as simple a matter as saying the Canadians aren't good writers, which is the cop-out Glen Warren and Kline used. Quite the opposite is true. The Canadian writers I met were bright, talented, and anxious as hell to write good shows.

Unfortunately, because of the nature of Canadian tv, which is vastly different from American tv, they had virtually no experience writing episodic drama as we know it. ("Train them," Kline told me. "Train a cadre of writers?" I said, stunned. "Sure," said Kline, who knew nothing about writing, "it isn't hard." No, not if I wanted to make it my life's work.) And, for some peculiar reason, with only two exceptions I can think of, there are *no* Canadian sf writers.

But they were willing to work their hearts out to do good scripts. Sadly, they didn't have the kind of freaky minds it takes to plot sf stories with originality and logic. There were the usual number of talking plant stories, giant ant stories, space pirate stories, westerns transplanted to alien environments, the Adam-&-Eve story, the after-the-Bomb story...the usual clichés people who haven't been trained to

harlan ellison
scenes from the real world: 111

think in fantasy terms conceive of as fresh and new.

Somehow, between Ben Bova and myself — Ben having been hired after I made it abundantly clear that I needed a specialist to work out the science properly — we came up with ten script ideas and assigned them. We knew there would be massive rewrite problems, but I was willing to work with the writers, because they were energetic and anxious to learn. Unfortunately, such was not the case with Davidson and the moneymen from 20th, NBC, Glen Warren and the CTV, who were revamping and altering arrangements daily, in a sensational imitation of The Mad Caucus Race from *Alice in Wonderland*.

I told the Powers in charge that I would need a good assistant story editor who could do rewrites, because I was not about to spend the rest of my natural life in a motel in Toronto, rewriting other people's words. They began to scream. One gentleman came up to the room and banged his fist on the desk while I was packing to split, having received word a few hours earlier that my mother was very ill in Florida. He *told* me I was going to stay there in that room till the first drafts of the ten scripts came in. He *told* me that I was going to write the pilot script in that room and not leave till it was finished. He *told* me I could go home but would be back on such-and-such a date. He *told* me that was my schedule.

I *told* him if he didn't get the hell out of my room I was going to clean his clock for him.

Then he went away, still screaming; Ben Bova returned to New York; I went to see my mother, established that she was somehow going to pull through, returned to Los Angeles; and sat down to finish writing the pilot script.

This was June already. Or was it July. Things blur. In any case, it was only weeks away from airdate debut, and they didn't even have all the principals cast. Not to mention the special effects Trumbull had promised, which weren't working out. The production staff under the confused direction of Davidson was doing a dandy impression of a Balinese Fire & Boat Drill; Kline was still madly dashing about selling something that didn't exist to people who apparently didn't care what they were buying; and I was banging my brains out writing "Phoenix Without Ashes," the opening segment that was to limn the direction of the single most expensive production ever attempted in Canada.

I was also brought up on charges by the Writers Guild for writing during the strike.

I called Marty the agent and threatened him with disembowelment if he ever again called me to say, "Go see Bob Kline." In my personal lexicon, the word "kline" could be found along with "eichmann," "dog catcher," "cancer," and "rerun."

But I kept writing. I finished the script and got it off to Canada with only one interruption of note:

The name Norman Klenman had been tossed at me frequently in Toronto by the CTV representative and Davidson and, of course, by Kline and his minions. Klenman, I was told, was the answer to my script problems. He was a Canadian writer who had fled to the States for the larger money, and since he was actually a Canadian citizen who was familiar with writing American series tv, he would be acceptable to the tv board in Ottawa under the terms of "Canadian content" and yet would be a top-notch potential for scripts that need not be heavily rewritten. I was too dazed in Toronto to think about Klenman.

But as I sat there in Los Angeles writing my script, I received a call from Mr. Klenman, who was at that moment in Vancouver. "Mr. Ellison," he said, politely enough, "this is Norman Klenman. Bill Davidson wanted me to call you about *The Starlost*. I've read your bible and, frankly, I find it very difficult and confusing…I don't understand science fiction…but if you want to train me, and pay me the top-of-the-show money the Guild just struck for, I'll be glad to take a crack at a script for you." I thanked him and said I'd get back to him when I'd saved my protagonist from peril at the end of act four.

When I walked off the show, the man they hired not only as story editor to replace me, but to rewrite *my* script, as well, was Norman Klenman who "don't understand science fiction."

My walkout on my brain child and all that pretty fame and prettier money was well in the wind by the time of Klenman's call, but I was still intending to write the scripts I'd contracted for, when the following incidents happened, and I knew it was all destined for the ashcan.

I was in Dallas. Guest of honor at a convention where I was trying to summon up the gall to say *The Starlost* would be a dynamite series. I was paged in the lobby. Phone call from Toronto. It was Bill Davidson. The conversation describes better than ten thousand more words what was wrong with the series:

"Major problems, Harlan," Davidson said. Panic lived in his voice.

"Okay, tell me what's the matter," I said.

"We can't shoot a 50-mile-in-diameter biosphere on the ship."

"Why?"

"Because it looks all fuzzy on the horizon."

"Look out the window, Bill. Everything *is* fuzzy on the horizon."

"Yeah, but on tv it all gets muddy in the background. We're going to have to make it a 6-mile biosphere."

"Whaaaat?!"

"Six miles is the best we can do."

There is a pivotal element in the pilot script where the hero manages to hide out from a lynch mob. In a 50-mile biosphere, that was possible. In a 6-mile biosphere all they had to do was link arms and walk across it. "But, Bill, that means I'll have to rewrite the entire script."

"Well, that's the best we can do."

Then, in a blinding moment of *satori* I realized Davidson was wrong, dead wrong; his thinking was so limited he was willing to scrap the logic of the script rather than think it through. "Bill," I said, "who can tell the difference on a tv screen, whether the horizon is six miles away or fifty? And since we're showing them an enclosed world that's never existed before, why *shouldn't* it look like that! Shoot *de facto* six miles and call it fifty; it doesn't make any damned difference!"

There was a pause, then, "I never thought of that."

Only one indication of the unimaginative, hidebound and obstinately arrogant thinking that emerged from total unfamiliarity with the subject, proceeded through mistake after mistake, and foundered on the rocks of inability to admit confusion.

The conversation went on with Davidson telling me that even if Trumbull's effects didn't work and they couldn't shoot a 50-mile bio-sphere — after he'd just admitted that it didn't matter *what* distance they said they were showing — I'd simply *love* the set they were build-ing of the control room.

"You're building the *control* room?" I said, aghast with confusion and disbelief. "But you won't need that till the last segment of the series. Why are you building it now?"

(It should be noted that one of the Maltese Falcons of the series, one of the prime mysteries, is the location of the control room bio-sphere. When they find it, they can put the ark back on course. If they find it in the first segment, it automatically becomes the shortest tv series in history.)

"Because you had it in your bible," he explained.

"That was intended to show how the series *ended*, for God's sake!" I admit I was screaming at that point. "If they find it first time out, we can all pack our bags and play an hour of recorded organ music!"

"No, no," Davidson argued, "they still have to find the backup computer, don't they?"

"Aaaaarghh," I aaaaarghhed. "Do you have even the faintest scin-tilla of an idea what a backup control *is*?"

"Uh, I'm not certain. Isn't it the computer at the back of the ship?"

"It's a fail-safe system, you drooling imbecile; it's what they use if the primary fails. The primary is the control...oh to hell with it!" I hung up.

When I returned to Los Angeles, I found matters had degenerated even further. They were shooting a 6-mile biosphere and *calling it* six miles. They said no one would notice the discrepancy in the plot. They were building the control room, with that arrogant ignorance that could not be argued with. Ben Bova, who was the technical advisor, had warned them they were going about it the wrong way; they nodded their heads...and ignored him. Then Klenman rewrote me. Oh boy.

As an indication of the level of mediocrity they were seeking, "Phoenix Without Ashes" had been retitled, in one of the great artistic strokes of all time, "Voyage of Discovery." I sent them word they would have to take my name off the show as creator and as writer of that segment. But they would have to use my pseudonym, to protect my royalties and residuals. (They had screwed up my creation, but I'd be damned if I'd let them profit from the rape.)

Davidson reluctantly agreed. He knew the Writers Guild contract guaranteed me that one last weapon. "What's your pen-name, we'll use it, what is it?"

"Cordwainer Bird," I said. "That's b-i-r-d, as in 'for the birds.'"

Now *he* was screaming. He swore they'd fight me, they'd never use it, I was denying them the use of my name that was so valuable with science fiction fans. Never! Never!

God bless the Writers Guild.

If you tuned in the show before it vanished from all earthly ken you saw a solo credit card that said

CREATED BY CORDWAINER BIRD

and that's your humble servant saying the Visigoths won again.

Bova walked off the series the week after Trumbull left, because of scientific illiteracies he'd warned them against, such as "radiation virus" (which is an impossibility...radiation is a matter of atoms, viruses are biological entities, even as you and I and Kline and Davidson, I presume), "space senility" (which, I guess means old, feeble, blathering vacuum), and "solar star" (which is a terrific illiterate redundancy like saying "I live in a big house home").

The Starlost came up a loser, as do *most* tv series. Because they don't understand the materials with which they have to work, because they are so tunnel-visioned into thinking every dramatic series can be transliterated from the prosaic and over-familiar materials of cop, doctor, and cowboy shows, because there was so much money to be skimmed...another attempt at putting something fresh and innovative on the little screen came up a loser.

Is mine an isolated bit of history? A case of sour grapes attributable to the intransigent nature of a writer whose credentials come red-stamped with the warning that he is a troublemaker? Hardly.

In *TV Guide* in October of 1964 the excellent Merle Miller told in detail how his series *Calhoun* had come a cropper. In February of 1971, again in *TV Guide*, the well-known sf author and historian James Gunn related how they leavened and dumbed *The Immortal* out of existence after fifteen weeks. Through the years, right up to the 1981 anthology series *Dark Room* — suicidally placed opposite first *The Dukes of Hazzard* and then moved to a primetime spot facing *Dallas* by ABC — which was canceled after six airings, the story is the same. This time it was my turn, that's all.

Have you, gentle reader, learned anything from this angst? Probably not. Viewers seem not to care about authenticity, accuracy, logic, literacy, inventiveness. Friends call me when they see reruns of *The Starlost* in Canada, and they tell me how much they like it. I snarl and hang up on them.

The upshot of all the foregoing was precisely what I had predicted when I cut out of that deranged scene. NBC had gone into the series with a guarantee of sixteen episodes firm, and an almost guaranteed pickup option for eight more. But the ratings were so low, in virtually every city where the series was aired — sometimes running opposite the nine thousandth rerun of *I Love Lucy* or scintillating segments of *Zen Archery for the Millions* — that NBC bailed out after the first sixteen.

The shows were so disgracefully inept, so badly acted, uniformly directed with the plunging breakneck pace of a quadruple amputee crossing a busy intersection, based in confusion and plotted on the level of a McGuffey's primer...that when the show was canceled after sixteen weeks, there were viewers who never knew it was missing.

When it was dumped, and I got the word from a contact at the network, I called one of Kline's toadies and caroled my delight. "What the hell are *you* so damned happy about?" he said. "You just lost a total of $93,000 in participation profits."

"It's *worth* ninety-three thousand bucks to see you fuckers go down the toilet," I said.

But even though I fell down that rabbit-hole in TV Land and found, like Dorothy, that it wasn't Kansas, or any other place that resembled the real world, I have had several moments of bright and lovely retribution-cum-vindication.

At one point, when the roof started falling in on them, they called Gene Roddenberry, the successful creator of *Star Trek*, and they offered him fifty percent of the show if he'd come up and produce the show out of trouble for them. Gene laughed at them and said what did he need fifty percent of a loser for, he had a hundred percent of two winners of his own. They said they could understand that, but did he have someone else in mind whom he could recommend as producer? Gene said, sure he did.

They made the mistake of asking him who.

He said, "Harlan Ellison. If you hadn't fucked him over so badly, he could have done a good job for you."

Then *he* hung up on them.

Which is just what the viewers did.

The second bright moment was when the trial board of the Writers Guild judged me Not Guilty of scabbing. It was a unanimous decision by some of the finest writers in Hollywood, and I was reinstated on the WGA's Board of Directors thereafter. Nonetheless, were I ever to forgive the thugs and fools who took the labor of a year and corrupted it so completely that I felt nothing but shame and fury for a long time after, I can never forgive them for placing me in such jeopardy with the craft guild to which I proudly belong. More than likely, had my efforts to thwart and circumvent 20th Century-Fox's anti-strike efforts in producing the series not been so blatant and so infuriatingly effective to Kline and his superiors, I might well have been tagged with that most vile and inexcusable sobriquet: scab. There is no forgiveness in me for that part of the monstrous history of *The Starlost*.

But the brightest moment of all came on March 21st, 1974 when I became the first person in the history of the Writers Guild of America to win the Most Outstanding Teleplay Award for the third time, with the *original version* of the pilot teleplay for *The Starlost*, "Phoenix Without Ashes."

The *original* script, my words, my dream; not the emasculated and insipid drivel that was aired; but *my* work, as I wrote it, before the trolls fucked it over; that screenplay won the highest writers' award Hollywood can give.

In the category of "best dramatic-episodic script," meaning continuing series, as opposed to anthologies or comedies, there were eight nominees out of 400 top submissions: four segments of *The Waltons*, a *Gunsmoke*, a *Marcus Welby* and an episode of *Streets of San Francisco*. And my original teleplay...selected as the best for the year 1973.

It should be noted that unlike Emmys and Oscars, which are political in nature, are bought and sold and lobbied for with hundreds of thousands of dollars being spent in trade paper advertisements by studios and networks that realize the box office value of such popularity prizes, the WGA awards are given *solely* on the basis of written material; in blind judging with the names of the authors removed, by three tiers of blue ribbon readers (most of whom are previous winners) whose identities are kept strictly secret.

When I accepted the Award at the 26th Annual Awards Reception and Banquet in Hollywood, I said, in part, "If the fuckers want to rewrite you...smash them!"

But even had I not received such vindication from my peers, I know damned well that the loss of $93,000 was not the vain and foolish gesture of a nit-picker. That Award is the rose I've plucked from the summit of the mountain of cow flop *The Starlost* became.

Nor have I lost my sense of smell. A writer has only his or her talent, determination, and imagination to pit against the winter of mediocrity Hollywood generates. Good writers die here, not from too much cocaine, or too much high living, or even too much money. For, in the words of Saul Bellow, "Writers are not necessarily corrupted by money. They are distracted — diverted to other avenues." They die in pieces, their talent and thus their souls turned sere and juiceless.

Until they are fit for nothing better than to bend to the whims of businessmen with a stranglehold on the art-form.

It is a writer's obligation to his craft to go to bed angry and to rise up angrier the next day. To fight for the words because, at final moments, that's all a writer has to prove his right to exist as a spokesman for his times. To retain the sense of smell; to know what one smells is the corruption of truth and not the perfumes of Araby.

Whether in a 50-mile-across biosphere, in Oz, in Kansas or in Hollywood.

TRANSCENDING DESTINY

Rondell awoke all at once. Not in soggy sections after a sound sleep, but rigid with tension: product of cold nightmares and expectations of the footstep. The instant his eyes opened he knew something was waiting for him outside the hotel's 32nd-storey window. Even before the metallic voice from the cop chopper shattered the dawn silence, he knew they were out there.

Then: *All right, Rondell! No fight, please! There are officers out here who have children, there are others in the building, the street's full of com-muters who'd get hit by debris...think of them. Don't force us to punch out the wall! Come out slowly, with your hands behind your neck...or on top of your head.*

It had to be a young cop. Unsure of his words. He fumbled the instructions. Probably had never done a roust like this in all the time he'd been a cop.

Rondell's expression was wry. He could almost laugh. Not a big laugh; something small, an exhalation of breath, freighted with irony. The poor sonofabitch, dumb kid. It had been a long, long time since these reserve corps cops had been pressed into service, since they had actually cornered a dangerous man who might give them trouble. All their drilling and pamphlets and fake hero-pride could not help them now; and they were scared. The frightened-animal tingle to the voice had told him all he wanted to know. Even alone — and how long he had been alone! — he was more than a match for them. Still...he should not feel overconfident. *That* might be a little bit of dangerous.

The silly-ass way they thought of their safe little homes, their children, their petty lives. Then, before he could stop it, a feeling of utter loneliness washed over him.

He abruptly felt defeated, lost. Where was the end to all this? Someday not getting the jump on them when they found him? Dead from a police disruptor in a cheap hotel? In the same instant he tightened his thoughts. Not here. Not this way. Perhaps soon, but at least in his own time, on his own terms.

Another warning blast from the cop chopper's loudspeaker clattered about the room as he stepped quickly to the closet, taking from a hook the fly-belt and propulsion unit. Without wasted movements he strapped the units to his back and waist. Outside the door to his room he could hear the furtive, frightened steps of the civilian police, setting up riot disruptors in the hall, ready to spray the room through the door if he made it necessary. They knew he had only one way out of the room. They knew it. They were wrong.

He chuckled softly. They were bluffing and *he* knew it. They would vomit up their guts at the sight of a dead man; but just *one* might nervously tick the firing stud, and results did not consider intentions.

So I'll try not to make it necessary, he thought briskly, edging toward the window. He flattened himself against the wall wishing he had not turned the cheap glass windopaque to "full" the night before. If he could see out, gauge the proximity of the chopper hovering there, so many floors above the plasteel slidewalks, things would be easier. But had the hotel not been a sleaze hole, had it not been a glass window, things would be much tougher. They would be impossible.

He caught a reflection of himself in the mirror-window. The short-cut sandy hair, the squinting dark green eyes and the nose that had been broken too many times to be anything like aquiline. Not a good face, not a bad face; just a tired face.

He thought about the chopper.

It was probably just above. He calculated rapidly.

Thirty-two storeys to the ground; the chopper at least two floors above; reaction time of the pilot; speed of the sprayed web-nets; his own fleetness. An unsupported body accelerates at a rate of 9.8 meters per second per second...

An unexpected burst of the riot guns shattered the door; he bunched his muscles and threw himself through the window.

His finger tensed on the power button of the fly-belt but he did not jab. He fell rapidly, turning over, catching a glimpse of the cop chopper descending like a hunting falcon. The pilot had paused only three seconds, taken by surprise; but it had been enough. Rondell looked down, forcing his eyes to remain open, despite the vertigo of his descent.

The slidewalk, crammed with first-shift casino-bettors, reeled up beneath him. His stomach wrenched and he was uncertain whether he would be caught by the chopper, die of fright, or smash to a pulp on the plasteel.

The avian screech of the diving ship, fast closing on him, caused the commuters to glance up. Their attention was held hypnotically; their wide, white stares registered clearly in Rondell's vision. Ten meters above the slidewalk he jabbed wildly at the button, and the breath was instantly sucked from his lungs by the wrench of a retarded descent. The cop chopper was directly above him, dropping fast!

He continued to fall, knowing the pilot, no matter how young, how inexperienced, would not endanger the pedestrians by a possible crash. He was aware that they could not pull out of too steep a dive. He hoped the pilot was privy to the same intelligence.

The police ship veered off, its spinnerets casting out the sticky web-netting in a final effort to capture him. But he was already out of range.

The nets shriveled into little black balls, hanging by thin strands beneath the chopper. Then they were sucked up into the spinnerets again.

Rondell swooped in over the pedestrians' heads, landing lightly, with knees bent. He killed the power to the propulsion unit, ripped the instrument from his back, and threw it down between the speeding strips — all as one movement. Knife switch reflexes paid off, and in a few moments of springing, leaping from strip to moving strip, he was lost in the crowded mass hurrying to the casinos.

Once again the thief had escaped.

The window had not been opaqued and Rondell gazed in silence at the oily back of the Professor's fat, wattled neck. Though he could see only the huge black bulk of the casino owner's tight-fitting silvermesh, the thief was certain the Professor was twining. As he always twined. He was sure the fingers of those fat, perspiring hands were twisting one over the other, like ten gorged worms struggling for freedom.

Rondell was aware of a rising tide of hatred, boiling up from somewhere deep inside himself. Climbing organ over organ till he felt its heat in his face.

The Professor turned suddenly, his face blanching, as the thief punched in the window with the disruptor. Debris exploded into the office, whirling around the room, smashing against the walls. The casino owner's eyes bulged from his pale face, reminding Rondell of a fish just hooked, still flopping.

The fat man's hand darted for a row of silver-topped studs on the desk, but the thief was even quicker. His hand, wrapped around the muzzle of the disruptor, smashed down brutally on the gambler's fingers. The fat man gave a soft, indrawn moan, a catch of the breath, and his eyes closed with pain. He clutched his hand fiercely, rubbing the sausage fingers rapidly.

"Let's try to get on like compatriots, what say, lard belly?" Rondell carefully noted the nostril-flare of anger at the reference to the Professor's bulk.

"I don't know where you came from, Rondell," wheezed the fat man, finding difficulty getting the words out, "but you'd better go back there. My guards are right outside that door, and they'll be in here in a moment."

Rondell smiled. "The room's soundproofed. They don't come unless you call."

"You set off an alarm when you broke the window." He cocked his head at the shattered pane. He looked triumphant for a second. Then he saw the look in the thief's eyes.

"I'll let you phrase whatever it is you're going to say to keep them outside, Professor." He spoke softly. The menace was in every syllable. The casino owner tightened his lips a bit more.

They both started at the sound of an intercom buzzer.

"If I don't answer, they'll punch open the door."

"So answer."

The Professor's voice was unnaturally loud and strained as he depressed the intercom stud, but over the machine it would make no difference. "It's all right, boys," the fat man said quickly. "Just a fit of temper at how much Countess Kinderlee owes me. Afraid I punched out the window with my disruptor. Don't worry about it; we'll have it fixed tomorrow. Go on back to your cards." He was sweating freely now, runners of perspiration trailing down into the collar of his silvermesh. The sounds of retreating footsteps came clearly over the intercom.

"Drop a shield over that window in case they come around outside to board it up," Rondell said. The Professor moved a finger toward another stud. "Very careful now, fatso." A sausage finger depressed the stud. A heavy lead shield fully securing the window.

Rondell leaned over and pulled loose the suction-tips and wires leading to the machine. He threw the piece of equipment across the room, where it landed in a corner with a bounce and a clatter on its shatterproof case.

He stepped quickly to the door — keeping the disruptor trained quite steadily on the fat man — making sure it was triple-bolted and voice-keyed to "lock."

Then he dropped into a formfit chair in front of the Professor's desk.

"How did they locate me, Professor?" It was simply a question, but the look of hatred on Rondell's face told the fat man the thief had already decided from where the information had come.

"I *had* to do it, Rondell. They would've closed me up!" He swiped at his rolled-fat jowls with a moist palm, his voice quivering.

The thief stifled a short, nasty laugh. "So you saved your greasy fat hide and threw me to the cops. Just to keep this joint running. Now is that the way to reward one of your best pupils? It was you, after all, who taught me everything I know." His voice dripped sarcasm, tinged with something deadlier. "Where would I be today, Professor, if it hadn't been for you?"

"How long do you think it'll be," the Professor wheezed, "before they look *here*? They must know you'd come after me. You'd better get out while you…"

The words were cut off by Rondell's sudden movement, the slash of the disruptor across the gambler's face. The gunsight raked flesh, and blood welled up thickly from his cheekbone. This time he made no sound, but his eyes glazed over momentarily from the pain. He sank lower into his formfit, and it squawked beneath him. Soundless in obesity, fat became pain; the sheer bulk of the Professor shrieked with mindless anguish.

Rondell spoke softly: "I'm going to kill you, Professor. For twenty-eight years of running, I'm going to even it up. It took me five years to get back here from Sumatra…five years like an animal, and no reason for it. No reason!"

The fat man stared up through tears of anguish at the rock that sat before him. Rondell was the last of his breed, a breed that had died out long before. The last thief in a world where stealing was utterly pointless.

And the thief stared back.

He stared at the disgusting heap of protoplasm quaking in its silvermesh luxury; symbol of a race he despised. The fat man had no backbone. A thin webbing of hair thrown scantily across a bald, furrowed head; fat drooping folds over the already-stained collar of the silvermesh — worth Rondell's entire wardrobe and more. But no backbone, no guts. The fat man's face was pale, crossed here and there by scars from long forgotten fights in a youth where violence was even then becoming unknown. Small wrinkles radiated out from the pig eyes.

"You're going to die. How would you like to go?"

The Professor raised a hand feebly, tried to say something, but Rondell cut him off. "I have it. How fitting, fat man, how fitting.

"I think we'll put you away on one of your own games, Professor. I think we'll put you in the android bin. Or maybe the blackjack table? No, you never *did* like those piranhas, so maybe the roulette table would be better."

The Professor's skin broke out in a fever-sweat as he thought of the roulette tables — with their razor-sharp, double-edged scimitars — the blackjack table — with its computer-brain croupier and trapdoor seats that dropped away to the tanks below — or…

He slid back in the seat, mute appeal on his oily face.

Rondell sat watching, not knowing why he was watching, nor why he had bothered to come here to even the score. It was hopeless; his whole life was hopeless. He had always been forced to come to the Professor when he hit snags too difficult to maneuver on his own — though those had been few and far between — but this time he knew the Professor had tipped off the cops. Why?

A slow, frightening smile slid over the thief's face. "Tell your boys to close up shop for the day."

"But I just opened. The first shift isn't even here an hour."

"I said close. Now, close."

The Professor's eyes bulged. "C-Close up the casino. But I'll-I'll lose a fortune."

"You'll lose your life if you don't."

There was no arguing with that frightful smile, that hand on the disruptor. The Professor started to rise from behind his desk, paused as Rondell pointed at him.

"Use the emergency clear-out button. No personal contact."

The Professor smiled thinly. "You remember that."

"I remember a lot of things. I should. You brought me up in this sinkhole."

The Professor sank down again heavily. He hesitated a moment longer, nervously pulling at his pendulous lower lip. Rondell added, softly, "Go ahead, *Dad*, we don't want to waste all the credits spent on that elaborate rig, do we?"

The Professor ran a hand through the air above a light-brown block set in the desktop, and a square section slid up, with a button set in one side. He pressed the button. The thief watched with narrowed eyes. The fat man kept his finger on the button a moment longer, finally sagged in complete defeat. His hands went back to the finger-twining movements. "It's done."

Rondell's skin itched. After twenty-eight years of calculated corruption on the part of the Professor...the score was going be evened.

"Like to lay odds on how fast you'll die?"

The Professor did not answer.

"How long will it take? To clear out?"

The Professor was breathing hard. Rondell was afraid natural causes would cheat him of his revenge. "It took less than fifteen minutes, a fire scare three weeks ago."

The fat man was hunched forward, his belly indented by the curve of the desk; his eyes never left the thief's hands. Not the face...the hands. Rondell sat back, idly toying with the disruptor; each twirl and stroke caused the fat man to tremble and a strange flame to dance higher in the younger man's eyes. "Why don't you just kill me and have done?"

"You mean here? Now?"

"It's soundproofed! You know that! Why are you tormenting me?"

Rondell stopped his idle movements, leaned forward and fixed the huge man with an uncompromising glare. "Because you found me in an orphanage when I was too young to do anything about it, and turned me into the most worthless thing on Earth. So I'm going to get full measure, Professor. Full fathom five to pay me back for twenty-eight years. Nineteen years of your careful training. Three years of stealing jewelry I could get from the cornucopia with less trouble. One year in preparation for the Change Chamber, before I escaped, and five years hiding in Sumatra.

"It's hot there, Professor. *Very* hot there."

"They should have the main play-rooms cleared by now," the fat man said, incongruously.

His perspiring fingers clung madly to one another, twining.

"Remorse doesn't look so good on you, Professor," Rondell said. "It looks belated. Twenty-eight years belated." He was making idle conversation till the casino was emptied of its first shift patrons, but there was more, there was an urgency in his voice. As though he had to know the answers before it was too late.

"Why did you do it, Professor? Why pick me off an orphanage floor and louse up my life? What's the motive?"

The Professor remained silent.

A mute pleading wallowed in his eyes.

Rondell lapsed into silence; he turned the answers he had found himself — unsatisfactory answers, wrong answers — over and over in his mind. Like a ribbon of flickfilm the incidents of his childhood fled before his mind.

His memory before the orphanage — not the crèche, so he obviously had had a mother and father — was a blank. He had no recollection of mother, father, home, or early days. He knew there was *something* back before the age of three, but whatever shadowy images remained had been worn smooth by the endless numbing routine of the orphanage.

Then the Professor had come, had seemed to know just whom he was seeking. Then the years with the Professor. There had never been another name. Neither first nor last — merely the Professor. The Professor, omnipresent, omniscient.

Rondell remembered the day of his twelfth birthday. He had learned many strange things from the fat man: the use of a length of black silkene cord, disruptor firing with great accuracy, boxing, the rigors of seven different Oriental martial arts, deep-breathing body control and exercises that made him tough as plasteel. Many things that did not seem to make sense to the twelve-year-old Rondell. But on that day, something began to take form.

On that day, when Rondell had been a tall boy — even for that age

— when the Professor had looked at him across dwarf grapefruit and a flowering napkin under the fat man's chin, the thing had begun in earnest.

"Good breakfast, boy?"

"Um," Rondell managed to mumble around a chunk of grapefruit.

"Do you want to make me happy, Rondell? Would you like to do me a favor?" He posed the questions lightly, almost airily, and the boy smiled, the grin denting dimples in his cheeks.

The fat man pulled the napkin from under his chin, settled back in his chair which slid a few inches away from the breakfast table on its rods to allow for the extra bulk, and began twining his fingers.

He wheezed a long breath of contemplation, gazed at the far upper corner of the gigantic dining room (a room that said *wealth*, then said it again, never quite subsiding into silence, but offering and re-offering the evidence of it), and cleared his throat.

He clearly enunciated: "Do you know the lady we visited last night?" He spoke with an elaborate simplicity. His tones and manner were directed with exaggerated evenness, even for a child of twelve. He spoke as though it were the most important thing he had ever said; he wanted the boy to miss no part of it.

"Yes, I remember," Rondell said, without fully waiting to think whether he remembered or not. The Professor was careful. "No, I mean do you *really* remember? Do you remember the beautiful red jewel she wore in her forehead?"

The boy considered for a moment, then nodded quickly. He re-called the flash of the jewel as it had glowed like a third eye in the center of his hostess's forehead.

"Well, Rondell, that was the Lady Cindy of Upper Pittsburg, and I want you to get me that jewel."

It had been let out at last. Now Rondell began to realize why he had been taught such things as walking catlike on the balls of the feet, how to dress to blend with his surroundings, how to scale a glass-smooth wall, how to use a vibroblade and a disruptor. The Professor was a clever man, and this had been a clever plan. Step by step, taking time and caution, it had come to this, and the boy was ready.

When she returned from the orgy at Prinzmetal's, with a used and exhausted body and a head filled with thoughts only of endless sleep, the Lady Cindy of Upper Pittsburg was shocked to find a hooded, completely black-garbed man of indeterminate age curled up comfortably on the balcony outside her casement. Idly running his skin-gloved fingers down the barrel of a disruptor. Her amazement was doubled as he commanded in a youthful, shaking voice, "Open your wall vault. The lock is located in the upper right knob of your bedpost. I want your ruby."

Her eyes widened, and then she realized it *must* be a joke. No one stole these days. Not for a long time had anyone *stolen* anything. Not with the government cornucopias so available. Why, that was where *she* had gotten the ruby originally.

She shrugged out of her radium-dyed heliotrope mink stole, letting it fall to the deep pile rug, and answered, "I have *no* idea how you *got* there, my good lad, but I suggest you *leave* at once!" Her accent was a queer half-snort, half-haughty command, the product of unauthorized interbreeding.

Then her eyes drew down, and her lashes fluttered. "On the other hand…if you want to stop this foolishness about my ruby, you can come in, and we can have a drink and…"

Her eyes wandered to the deep foam-pile bed.

That was the first time Rondell glimpsed the utter decay of his world…without fully realizing what it meant. Her body was encased in a tight silkene sheath that more set off her physical attributes than hid them. She strained against the sheath, and a fire of excitement and challenge burned in her heliotrope eyes — dyed to match her mink.

Rondell had been too young, but even so…something had made him uneasy inside. "I'm not fooling…" His voice was slightly unsure, unsteady; his first job. "…I want that ruby. *Now!*" The Lady Cindy of Pittsburg had a sudden realization: this — it had to be — *boy* was not here for her erotic pleasure at all. Nothing of the sort. It was not a joke. Her eyes widened incredulously.

"*Well!* I — I — am I to take it that this is a — a —" she struggled with a nearly-forgotten word, "— a *robbery?*"

The boy nodded his head, and through the eye-slits she could see a confused desperation in his eyes.

"But — but *why?* You can get one just as good — though I confess, not *better* — from the cornucopia. You *have* a Key, haven't you? There's no need for you to take it from me. I get such pleasure from it. Why?" She was now flinging her arms about in exaggerated bewilderment, her voice rising.

The thief seemed unnerved by her reaction. "Stop that! Stop screaming!" But she did *not*, and he leaped agilely through the window, brandishing the disruptor.

"The vault. The vault. Get the ruby for me or I'll kill you." There was a hardness in his youthful voice that told her she was faced by a boy not quite a boy, but much more.

She turned, and looking over her shoulder at the thief, walked slowly to the bed. Reluctantly she twisted the ornate ball atop one bedpost. The ball split in the center, revealing a voice-control sphere. She spoke into it softly, and watched with creases lining her forehead as a portion of the wall slid up to reveal an elaborate set of bureau drawers.

It was not hiding the jewels from the world, protecting them, but merely an evidence of possession, a feeling of *I know where they are, but no one else does*. Old habits die hard.

Now the boy stepped forward nimbly, began to open the jewel drawers. Abruptly, the Lady Cindy decided something she had been pondering for several minutes.

She was *not* going to be robbed by this uncertain child.

She moved back to the voice-control sphere, quietly.

Before she could whisper the words that would lower the plasteel wall, sealing the thief into the airtight vault, Rondell turned and saw her. "Stop!"

The Lady Cindy's words were half out of her mouth when the boy pressed the disruptor stud. His face, under the hood, went sick and white as he saw the result. The Lady Cindy soundlessly exploded into a million fragments…

The boy ripped the mask from his face and leaned against the bedpost. He became violently ill, vomiting agonizingly at what he had done. The Professor had never been graphically explicit about what a disruptor would do. Block-targets were not blonde, statuesque women. The Professor had merely said it would stop opposition. It certainly did.

When the sickness passed, keeping his eyes from what ran on the walls, he found the ruby, slid it into his seal-pouch, and left by the window as he had come.

The Professor received the ruby with gratitude.

"Excellent, my boy. Excellent. What's that? Dead? Oh, well, I'm sure these things happen. Now, for your *next* assignment…"

The years of running, the years of programmed destiny had begun.

Rondell's memories collapsed inward violently. He was in the present, and the Lady Cindy of Upper Pittsburg was many years dead. He was sitting in the Professor's office in the casino where he had spent nineteen years of his life. He was holding a disruptor on the man who had first taught him to kill. The ruby, too, was long-since gone. Poured down some invisible drain, no benefit gained from the theft, nothing bettered by killing an innocent woman. Nothing derived from it all, but that Rondell had taken the first step in a life comprising senseless theft, hiding, running.

A gong sounded in the desk.

Rondell sat up straight. The casino was empty; the staff and all the Professor's bully-boys had gone. The robot-sealers had examined the place, and it was empty.

"Let's go," Rondell said, motioning with the disruptor.

The Professor slid the chair back on its tracks and got up heavily. The air stank with death.

———

The casino never closed, and to facilitate the handling of pleasure-bent patrons, everyone possessed a shift-card, designating what times they might play. Had the cards *not* been issued, the casinos would have been permanently swamped; they were anything but mere gambling halls. The players bet against their opposite numbers, who were androids. If they won, the android was killed by them, in any one of a hundred different, clever ways...artificial blood spurted, shrieks were emitted. Androids looked real, and really died. But fair is fair: human losers really died, also.

Unfortunately (though they didn't know it), humans only had a three-to-one chance of winning. The games were stacked. Behind every casino was the government agency that supervised the action...and rigged the odds. It was a painless way of decreasing the staggering population. Let them *play* themselves to death, for with the age-retardant drugs, few people died of anything but violent death.

So give them their taste...Let them kill or be killed...and they would die gladly. Well, perhaps not *gladly*; but then, no one likes a poor loser.

The casino was dead silent. The Professor walked ahead of the creature he had created, and the cold fear had solidified; his chest was filled with arctic ice. If he had thought, at first, that there would be any escape, all hope was now lost. He had not expected this. Everything had gone wrong. He had built too well.

The sound of their footfalls was stark and loud in the empty casino. With the crowds gone, with the hypnolights and adverts shut off, it was a dead, hungry, waiting place. The Professor shivered; he had never seen it like this. The place never closed, it was always full.

It was closed, it was empty. He was going to die.

Over thirty years; the plan; wasted.

Warning lights high up the filigreed walls cast light silver shadows along the floor. Signs of occupancy from a few minutes before still remained: crushed joy-sticks littered the room (and as they walked, the scurryers slipped from their wallnests, began sucking up the debris), stacks of chips made crazy pillars on the tables, bits of simulated cartilage from the gaming-androids remained plastered to the betting-boards. Even as they walked into the center of the gaming-room, the last trickle of fake blood swirled down the flensing troughs with a final gurgle.

The casino was hung about with multi-colored drapes that changed color constantly under the silver warning lights. The furnishings were rich and padded. *Just like the customers*, thought Rondell wryly. He spat on the floor, and a scurryer swept up, sucked it spotless in an instant. He kicked at it viciously, then swung on the fat man. "No move. I'll forego my fun and take you out right here."

They paused in front of the deadly bingo game.

The Professor drew back, and Rondell grasped him tightly by his flabby biceps. "Eh?" Rondell suggested nastily, cocking a thumb at the table. "What do you say to a game of bingo, Professor? What do you say to that?"

The Professor said nothing, and Rondell nudged him sharply with the disruptor. "Sit."

The Professor stepped up to the table. It was a huge circular canister affair, six and a half meters high. The sides were sealed, and a small stairway led up to the seats and the tabletop proper. The game was arranged so that if the android opponent — operated by robot-brain — won the bingo card, the chair dropped away beneath the human, sending him into the lower five meters of the canister.

Filled with piranha fish.

Rondell walked the fat man up the steps and strapped him into a chair without ceremony. "I think I'll even give you a fighting chance, fat man," Rondell said, as he found the control box for the game.

He smashed it open with the heavy handle of a vibroblade taken from his boot-top and fingered several dials. The game board lit up, and the selection panels came on. But the robot brain remained inactive.

Rondell switched on the selectron that called the numbers from random sequences. He took a seat. He did not strap in. "*I'm* going to play you, instead of an android, Professor. That way you'll have a real incentive to win." Then he switched on the robot-brain.

The Professor put up a shaking hand. "No. You must not! I — I…"
He subsided into silence, and nodded. The game
Began!

Rondell punched out a code on the selector before him. A "card" of
numbers appeared in the plate beneath his hand. He sat back and
watched the Professor as the fat man did the same. The Professor
seemed to want to say something, but he pursed his lips and was
silent.

The robot-brain clicked its patterns, and ran the codes through, and
then the speaker in the center of the game table spoke sharply, harshly:
"I-16."

Rondell looked down. Nothing. That was not on his card. He
glanced across at the Professor. The fat man had also come up empty.

The robot-brain ran through its patterns again, clicked and spoke,
"O-33."

Again, nothing. Rondell looked up. The Professor had one. Upper
right hand corner. That was a start, and for the first time, Rondell
suspected he might lose. But it didn't matter. If the Professor got too
close, he would use the disruptor.

"B-7."

Nothing lit on Rondell's board, nothing lit on the Professor's board-
mirror. The fat man leaned forward against the playing edge, and his
fingers twined madly. He strained against the plasteel bonds that held
him in the game. In the center of the tabletop was a clear frame of
plastic, and through it, by a clever series of lights, could be seen the
deadly fish swimming below.

"O-40."

Rondell now had a glowing square in the center of the end row on
his card.

Rondell went for broke. He pressed a stud for lowered odds. If his
number came up, he was in good shape…if it didn't, he was one score
down. Down toward the tiny teeth. But since he couldn't lose, because
he would cheat, it didn't matter what chances he took.

He rang the odds down to 3-to-1 which was as good as a human could ring in the entire casino. The brain clicked its patterns, chuckled to itself, said, "O-12." It was a hit. That made two out of five in a vertical stripe down the right hand side.

"Rondell! Listen to me! It's not — not just my *dying* I'm trying to prevent. You've got to hear me out!"

"O-29." Nothing.

"You want to know why I did it to you. You *must* want to know. I can tell you, only stop this game *now*!"

"I-58."

"Keep talking, Professor," Rondell said softly, trying to play the card and listen to the fat man at the same time. He wanted to know, all right. But the smell of death was invigorating.

"The answer, Rondell! Let me go, and I'll tell you where you can get the answer! There's reason to it, boy. Believe me, there's reason to it."

"I-26." The Professor now had three laterals lit. One had rung while Rondell had been distracted thinking, but the third one didn't matter. It was out of the pattern.

"*You've* got to get off the game, Rondell! Listen to —"

"G-38."

"— listen to me. Do it now."

Their boards were lit with many squares, and now Rondell's mind was a tangled mass. He could not figure it all out. All the weight of the universe pressed down on him. Tied in with his overwhelming hatred for the fat man and his desire for revenge. He had come half across the world to get the fat man. He had been double-crossed again; how the fat man had known he was in town, how he'd known he was in that hotel, why he'd tipped off the cops, was something Rondell didn't understand. But the Professor *had* turned the police loose, and they *had* made him run again. Now he wanted to stop running. Now he wanted to find out why he had been persecuted so studiedly. What his past was, and why it tied in with this fat man, and what his future held.

He slipped out of the chair.

It was two short steps to the brain-box, but before he got there, a final click and ding! sounded from above, and the chair where he had been seated dropped away.

He shivered at the sound of water splashing from below and turned off the game. The Professor had been one square short of losing, himself, but...he had filled a line completely, and Rondell would have gone into the tank.

Bingo!

He went back up and held the disruptor near the fat man's nose. "Tell me."

"Go to the Slum. Find a woman named Elenessa on Broad Street. Number 6627A."

"If this is a trick, Professor, if this is something to get me captured, if this is a stall for time...I'll get back here. I'll get back, you know that. I did it once, I can do it again."

Then he was gone.

The Professor was still tied to the seat, but his face had settled back into a shrewd, relieved smile. He had stalled it just long enough. Let Rondell run some more...just as he had forced him to run for twenty-eight years.

The running would soon come to an end.

"Now, boss?" It was the voice of a casino worker, from behind the draperies.

The Professor called out, "Yes. Get me off here."

The worker came out; a thin-faced little man with a bobcut hairdo. "I got the signal on the clear-out sequence. I knew you wanted someone to wait behind and keep watch. I had *this* on him all the time." He held up an ancient projectile weapon. "Coulda plugged him any time. But I figured you knew I was watching."

"No, I didn't know you were watching."

"Jeez, I coulda swore you knew I was watching."

The Professor looked at him. He said, softly, "I didn't know."

"Yeah, I guess you din't. You sure looked scared as hell, Perfesser. You was really sweatin'. But, see, I *thought* you must of known I was watching. That's why I din't punch him all that time."

"Clever of you."

"But, Jeez, if you *din't* know, then, Jeez, you could of been really tore up by them piranhas, huh?"

"Yes. I could, huh."

"You want I should get the cops on him, Perfesser?"

The Professor's voice was low and nasty. "No, I don't want you to do *anything*. Just go home. And forget what happened tonight if you want to keep your shift-card."

The thin-faced little man bobbled his head anxiously. "Yes sir, Perfesser, yessir indeed. Whatever you say."

He walked away quickly, and as the drapes parted to swallow him, the fat man heard him say, "But, Jeez, you sure was sweatin."

The Professor went back into the office and passed his fingertips over a section of wall. His prints were instantly recognized, and a section slid up, revealing a private vid. He studded out a number, left the vision off, and said succinctly:

"It will have to be tonight. Three AM. Have Dirt get to them. At her place, in thirty minutes."

A short sharp word acknowledged the message.

"Thirty years and more, and almost done," the Professor said to no one at all, clicking off the vid. The wall slid back down, and he fell into his seat. It rocked beneath him, and held him as he sat in misery and loneliness. His fat a bulwark against the chill that crept in softly.

In an age where wealth and opulence were commonplace, the people had maintained the Slum for kicks. It was fake and japery from one end to the other. It made people feel good to think there were still areas of mystery and intrigue, places where people poorer than themselves lived. The governmental system that always kept the Slum fully inhabited was too involved for any one man to understand, but Rondell knew one family out of every four got the "call" to go to the Slum for a one year term on a demographic rotational basis. Heavy casino losers also were domiciled in the Slum. Phony dives and trumped-up excitement.

Rondell stalked through this sideshow Slum.

He found 6627A Broad Street without difficulty. It was a walk-up next to a place laughingly called The Hang-Dog House. He went up quickly, having found the name he sought on a plate downstairs. The door to the apartment was no trouble...an old-style slide-bolt he cut with the vibroblade.

Moonlight streamed down through a high window, and he could see the squalor typical of these artificial dumps. In the bed, a woman with dark-black-almost-blue-black hair slept, lying on her arm.

He crept toward the bed and hardly realized for a moment after the needle-nose was aimed at his head that the disruptor was in her hand.

"Who are you?" she said softly. "Who sent you? What are you doing here?"

Her face was half-shadowed by the moonlight's angle, but even in the partial light he could see she was hard-featured. Not particularly good-looking at all...in fact rather eagle-nosed and high-browed, but her naked body gleamed in the dusk of the flat. She had deep lines in her face, much like his own; and he could see a familiar narrowing of her eyes.

He told her quickly who he was, and from where he had come, and for how long he had been running. He told her because he was so tired of running and he wanted only answers himself, even as she wanted answers. He hid nothing; and as he talked quietly, the disruptor lowered.

Then she spoke to him. Her name was Elenessa, and she, too, had been running for a long, long time. As long as he.

And her circumstances had been the same. The constant harrying by the society, on all sides. And a man named Zalenkoz, who was comparable in background to the Professor.

They sat and talked, and in a while, they knew each other. Better than a thousand years together, they knew what was under the skin and in the head of each. Because they had gone the same distance separately. So they were mated in mind when the rat-faced man knocked at the door.

Elenessa had thrown a wrap around herself. She sat on the edge of the bed, and when the knock came, she started violently. "Cops," she whispered. Rondell shrugged and pulled his disruptor. He motioned for her to open the door and slipped silently behind the frame. She walked lightly, on the balls of her feet; as he walked.

When she threw open the door the rat-faced man standing there was caught unaware; he didn't have time to conceal the fact that he had been picking his nose.

A simple-minded grin flickered across his face, and his nose twitched like a gopher's. "Dirt's the name," he said. "I was sent by —"

Rondell was around the door, and the disruptor was leveled at the ridiculous little Slum dweller. "Get in here! And I'll see if it's worthwhile letting you live."

The rat-faced little man thrust his hands into the air and his eyes grew large. "Hey, lissen, don't get cute wit' that t'ing. I'm onny doin' what I was paid ta do. A big fat guy and a guy with real black hair an' a beard paid me —"

Elenessa broke in. "That sounds like your Professor…and Zalenkoz."

Rondell motioned with the disruptor for Dirt to finish what he had been saying. "They paid me to come and fetch ya. That's all. Honest."

"What do you mean, 'Fetch us'?"

The little man spread his hands and then started to reach into a side pocket.

"Hold it!"

"Just a piece of paper, chief, that's all," Dirt said.

"Just the same, hold it." Rondell went to him, felt in the man's pocket, and came up with a slip of paper. "This it?" The little man nodded.

Rondell unfolded it, and across the top was printed: FROM THE DESK OF THE PROFESSOR / CASINO ROW.

The paper had an address written on it. An address far uptown in the palatial Salazzo Plaza area. "This was where you were supposed to lead us?"

"That's right, chief. I got two extra hours added on my card for the job, so ya better lemme take ya, or I'll lose that time at the tables."

"Sure," Rondell answered, understandingly.

Then they trussed Dirt up, and prepared to find the tower in Salazzo Plaza.

The tower was alabaster; rising out of the night like an ivory fang, deadly and smooth. High up, ringing its top, a gigantic wheel of jewels sparkled against the night skyline of white and black and gold.

Rondell had no trouble with the portal. The vibroblade slid across the maglock and the entrance irised. It was dark inside. Darker than the night. Rondell unclipped a torch from his pouch-fold, and held it up, casting its sharp, thin light around. The place was empty. In the center of the room stood a suction tube, disappearing into the ceiling.

Rondell led the way, with Elenessa directly behind him, her step assured, the disruptor ready. They came into the center of the empty vestibules, stopped, looked around. It was silence on silence.

Then they started toward the droptube...

They could not move...

Lights went on. Suddenly, glaringly, alarmingly, lights flooded everything, and they were standing in the middle of a tensor-field. Beneath their feet an impregnated grid showed up through the total-conductivity floor. From the ceiling, vaulted high and gold above them, the nozzles of tensor machines protruded, and from their snouts came the faint, high buzz of the directional ion-beams.

A speaker concealed somewhere in the walls *whiffed*, as though someone were blowing into it, to make sure it was on. Then a voice came through.

"Sorry to have to trick you, but we were quite certain you wouldn't come of your own volition. Not after the way we've treated you."

"Zalenkoz!" Elenessa screamed, straining motionlessly at the invisible bonds holding her.

"Yes, my child," he replied through the speaker, "the one man you despise."

"Let me free! I'll kill you!" But there was no release and she subsided into a vicious silence.

"So goodbye," Zalenkoz said.

A plate slid back in the ceiling; and a complex machine rolled down on tracks. It was aimed directly at them. They heard a switch being knifed down, through the speaker, and knew that wherever he was in the tower, Zalenkoz had turned on the weird machine.

A blue ray shot from the mouth of the machine bathing them in radiation.

Rondell caught a glimpse of Elenessa from the corner of his eye. She was fading.

"Stop!" he screamed. "Stop! We deserve to know! Why are you killing us? I was told the answer was here! We *deserve* to know!"

The ray was cut off — and Elenessa slowly came back to solidity. She was terribly frightened. "You — you were getting dim; you were disappearing," she said to Rondell.

He nodded. Through the speaker, with someone's hand imperfectly over the mike, they could hear Zalenkoz speaking to someone else. Then sounds of agreement, and Rondell heard a familiar voice.

"Rondell —"

"You!" the thief screamed, straining futilely at nothing.

"Rondell, let me speak." The Professor's voice overrode the thief's screams. "We have only a matter of three — what is it, Zalenkoz, four minutes and a few seconds…thanks — four minutes. You have to go through now, or the juncture points won't merge for another two years.

"And frankly, in your present state of mind, I'm afraid we couldn't satisfactorily hold either of you for that long."

Rondell tried to understand. It was hard getting past the hate.

"Over thirty years ago Zalenkoz and I found the key. The temporal shift. Not time, precisely, but something more involved. Something like worlds within worlds, though not quite *that*, either. Picture the Earth and make it two dimensional, like a paper cut-out. Then, behind it, like two leaves of a book, another Earth. And another behind that. On and on and on, endlessly, an uncountable number of Earths — in fact, an uncountable number of *universes* — one after another, each slightly different, each waiting to be discovered.

"So we worked, and we found a way to slip a person through. But what good did it do us? No one would go. Here is a world choking with overpopulation and corruption, laziness and dead souls; and everyone so decadent and smug they would never risk their lives to try a new frontier. Why do you think the space colonies are dying out?

"So we thought of kidnapping them and sending them through. We tried it twice...and neither time did they live out a day. These aren't easy worlds, some of them. They are Earth...but a *different* Earth.

"We had to build our own pioneers. We had to create the right kind of person to live in a rugged new environment. So we used you, both of you, and separately went about ruining you for *this* culture. It was cruel, and it was unrewarding, and don't think we didn't suffer as much as you — but in a different way. Now you're ready. The harrying has turned out some fine stock. If you succeed, there will be others, and there may still be some hope for this rotting planet. You will have escaped your destiny!

"Do you understand?"

They understood, and their hatred was even greater.

Then the machine went on again, and they started to fade under the blue ray. Rondell felt himself slipping in an invisible pool of oil. He could see his right shoulder fading, and he screamed again, in terror.

He had to know one thing...he yelled once more, just before dematerializing, "Who am I? Where did I come from?"

And the Professor answered, "I — can't — tell — you."

Then they were gone.

The room was silent, and the blue ray vanished.

Then through the speaker, hardly realizing it was still on, came the sound of crying. Then the voice of Zalenkoz, soothing the other, and Zalenkoz saying, "What is it they say? I think it was Shakespeare. 'It is a wise father that knows his own child.' What do you think, Professor...does the reverse apply?"

The fat man did not answer.

After a while the crying stopped.

Some Earth, somewhere, somewhen, a man named Rondell and a woman named Elenessa found themselves in a primordial jungle. As they stood watching themselves solidify, a saber-toothed beast, vaguely like a cougar, dropped from one of the trees. In a moment, it had cornered them. Rondell and the woman backed up and watched the beast come closer.

Then it leaped.

Twin disruptors came out, but would not punch. The beast sprang past and knocked the man to the ground. Elenessa had her vibroblade drawn and was on the beast's back in a moment.

Soon, there was quiet, and blood, and they were alone again.

Alone, the man and woman who had run for a long, long time. Alone, with worlds to conquer.

And they would not bother with anything as ridiculous as calling themselves Adam and Eve.

THE HOUR
THAT STRETCHES

The red light flashed ON THE AIR; hincty synthesizer music composed for the tone-deaf began going out at 90.7 megahertz; Burt Handelsman, crack engineer, made a circle with thumb and forefinger; and for the five hundred and forty-first time in the eleven years it had been on KPFK-FM in Los Angeles, *Hour 25* was on the wing. The clock in the booth said 10:02 PM.

"Good evening, this is your host for *Hour 25*, Mike Hodel, and my guest tonight is Harlan Ellison. For those of you who have read Mr. Ellison's forty books, very close to almost one thousand short stories, articles, television columns, essays or commentaries; or who've seen his teleplays on commercial television...he needs no introduction. For those of you to whom Harlan's name isn't a household word..."

Ellison cut in. "Have yourselves put under house arrest for terminal illiteracy."

Hodel grinned. "That, listeners, was the voice of Harlan Ellison. And I know he'll kill me for saying this, because he doesn't like people to know his many kindnesses, but Harlan came down at the last minute, to an urgent phone call about twenty minutes before we were scheduled to go on the air, filling in for our previously scheduled guest, Dr. Jerry Pournelle —"

Ellison cut in again. "Who is off in the Sierra Maestra mountains of Cuba, helping to train marauders for the violent overthrow of Fidel Castro, or backpacking, or some dumb thing like that."

"No, come on now," Hodel said, stifling a smile, "that's not true and you know it."

"Of course I know it. That doesn't mean I won't malign the man, even if he *is* my friend. In fact, I'll malign him *because* he's my friend. I mean, anybody who'd call Ellison a friend is obviously a thoroughly corrupt, degenerate sod."

"Dr. Pournelle, folks, is *actually* in Pasadena, speaking at the LungFishCon, at the Pasadena-Hilton. At probably this very moment he's on a panel with Barry Longyear, John Norman, Norman Spinrad and Joanna Russ..."

Ellison cut in again. "The topic of which is 'Labia and Broadsword Imagery in Contemporary Sci-Fi'."

In the control booth, Burt Handelsman, crack engineer, fell apart with laughter, snorting Coca-Cola from his nose all over the console.

"And the convention," Hodel went on doggedly, "is the reason the station is absolutely dead tonight. Even my eminent co-host, Mel Gilden —"

Ellison: "Star of the eminent sci-fi film *Mel Needs Women*."

"— Mel Gilden is down there tonight acting as Emcee. So I'm here in solitary congress with our guest and our crack engineer, Burt Handelsman."

"So what're we gonna do on this silly show?" Ellison said.

"Well, we can talk about what's happened to your script for Asimov's *I, Robot*."

"Please. Spare me. My life is miserable enough as it is."

"Well, we can always open up the phone lines and take calls from the Group Mind of our faithful listeners."

"Please," Ellison said, "do I really have to deal with people who read science fiction? I saw a rerun of Tod Browning's *Freaks* last Wednesday and that's about all the sf fans I can handle for one week."

"Ignore him, Group Mind. He's actually a sweet, gentle, loving man who adores his readers."

"All three of them; especially the one with the goiter."

"Okay. The phone numbers are 985-KPFK or toll-free from Orange

County it's 985-5735. If you're outside the 213 area, don't call collect, we frown on moochers and Pacifica has no money."

Ellison suddenly clapped his hands. "Hey, I've got a nifty idea."

"But is it a peachy idea?"

"It is nifty, peachy, swell and even keen.

"If I had a dime for every clown who has ever come up to me at a cocktail party or a convention or at an autograph session and said, 'Boy, have I got an idea for a story for *you*,' I'd have just a lotta dimes. So why don't we invite your loyal cadre of freakos, devos and pervos to call in and offer ideas for stories that I will then attempt to whip into utter greatness?"

Hodel's eyes sparkled. "How about that, Group Mind? A first, right here on *Hour 25*. Harlan Ellison will collaborate with you on an original idea. All of you who've been nurturing the secret belief that you can write, here's your chance to see what kind of an inventive mind you've got."

"And of course," Ellison said, "if I sell the stories, I'll acknowledge the contribution of the caller."

"What about the money from the sale?" Hodel asked.

"What about it?" Ellison responded.

"Will you share it?"

"I'm willing to attempt a crazy stunt," Ellison said. "That doesn't mean I'm crazy." He thought a moment. "My philosophy is the same as Robin Hood's: steal from everybody and keep it all myself."

In the control booth Burt Handelsman, crack engineer, signalled the lines were lighting up. "Okay, here's our first call," Hodel said, hitting one of the buttons on the call director. He threw the switch on the pedestal mike, permitting the caller's voice to be heard in the booth. "You're on the air," he said.

"Hi, this is Joanne Gutreimen. I have an idea for Harlan Ellison."

"Where are you calling from?" Hodel asked.

"What?"

"I asked where you're calling from?"

"I have an idea for Harlan Ellison."

"Yes, I know. But *where are you?*"

"I'm here. In Hollywood. Where are you?"

Ellison rolled his eyes. "What's your idea, Ms. Gutreimen?"

There was silence for a long moment. Hodel looked at Ellison and Ellison looked at Hodel. Both shrugged. Then the woman's voice came through the speaker again. "I had this idea of...people are always writing about haunted houses...what about a haunted condominium?"

Ellison rolled his eyes. "Fresh, daring, original. Walter Kerr in the *New York Times*."

"What?" the woman said.

"Nothing," Ellison said. He tried rolling his eyes but they were starting to burn from all the activity. "Go on."

"Well, actually," she said, "I was thinking about writing this myself...but couldn't come up with any plot ideas. So I scrapped it. But I *did* get an idea from it for a terrific title."

"Thrill me," Ellison said, holding his head.

"'Mondo Condo'," she said.

Hodel smiled. "Well, Harlan, there you go. Your first story collaboration idea tonight. What can you do with it?"

"A high colonic comes immediately to mind," Ellison said.

"What?" the woman on the speaker said.

"Nothing, nothing!" Ellison shouted. "Let me think a second. Talk to yourselves; I'll be with you in a minute."

Hodel began to whistle. He was a round little man with a kind face. For years he had worn eyeglasses hewn from the bottoms of Moët champagne jeroboams, but upon the accidental discovery that he was considered a sex object, he had been fitted with contact lenses. Even so, even with the naked teddybearness of his soft brown eyes revealed, no one called him Michael.

"Okay, how about this," Ellison said, interrupting Hodel's whistling of Johann Friedrich Fasch's *Concerto in C Major for Bassoon, Strings and Continuo*, "how about this is a recently converted condo that was originally an apartment house built in the late 1920s. The custodian or janitor was a vicious creep who'd never do any work for the tenants.

Everybody hated him. One of those kind of tormented devils Lovecraft was always writing about. And the only pleasure he got was from strangling cats. Maybe the building had a lot of old ladies on welfare living there, see, and all of them had cats, the way old ladies on welfare always do. And every week some poor old lady's tabby would disappear. And what was happening was that this terrible janitor was snatching them, bashing their heads against walls, drowning them, strangling them, tossing them into the furnace..."

Hodel wrinkled up his face. "Yuccch."

"Oh, I don't know," Ellison said cheerily, "it's a healthier occupation than cheating on your income tax.

"Anyhow, twenty years before, the janitor mysteriously disappeared. Not a trace was found of him, see. But now this expensive condo is being haunted by the sounds from the walls, à la Lovecraft. Ghastly sounds. Hideous sounds. The sounds of the ghost of the janitor being torn to shreds over and over by the ghosts of these demon cats he buried in the walls and basement of the building."

There was silence at both ends of the radio link. "How's that grab ya?" Ellison asked.

"You are a very disturbed person," Joanne Gutreimen said softly. Then she hung up.

"Go try to please people," Ellison said.

Hodel was staring at him with considerable distaste. "You don't like cats, I gather."

"I don't even like the cats you *haven't* gathered," Ellison said. He lit his pipe and puffed deeply. Hodel rolled his eyes and punched up another call. "You're on the air," he said.

"Hi, Harlan," a man said. "This is Mike Taylor. My idea is an old woman with a sharpened spoon and hypnotic powers who steals the eyes from men and women for their vision."

Ellison was silent for a moment. Hodel waited expectantly. There was the intimation of eye-rolling and head-holding.

"I already wrote that one," Ellison said. "Sort of. It was called 'Seeing' and you can find it in my book, *Strange Wine*. It's about these people who have mutated eyes and they can see special visions, the outline of a person's future, all sorts of things. I called them 'forever eyes' and the story is about a bootleg operation that steals people's 'forever eyes'."

"Oh," Mike Taylor said. "Okay, then forget it. But if you were going to steal my idea, you should have paid me."

"I wrote it in 1976. This is 1982 and you just called in with it. How did I steal it if I wrote it before you thought of it?"

Taylor hmmmed for a moment, then said, "Everybody knows how clever you are."

"Right," Ellison agreed. "Voodoo. Bye-bye, Mr. Taylor."

Hodel cut him off and hit another button.

"You're on the air with *Hour 25* and Harlan Ellison."

"Hi, Mike; this is Buzz Dixon. Here's my idea; let's see what Ellison can do with it."

"Me widdle heart am goin' pitta-pat," Ellison said into the microphone.

Dixon cleared his throat and began talking very fast. "Bloodworld is a small, distant, barren planet enveloped in a dense, corrosive, poisonous atmosphere. It's named for the dark red 'blood' that bubbles just below the planet's outer crust —"

"As opposed to its *inner* crust, I presume?" Ellison said.

"What?"

"Nothing. Never mind. Go on."

"Oh, okay. Well, this 'blood' is pumped up and refined into Immortaline, a dark black liquid with almost miraculous healing and life-prolonging properties. Immortaline is very, very expensive and is much sought after; for this reason Bloodworld's location is kept strictly secret."

"Even from its inhabitants," Hodel said.

Ellison made a tsk-tsking motion at the show's host. Hodel spread his hands as if to say, *Your vicious sense of humor is catching, Ellison.*

Buzz Dixon said, "What?"

"Nothing, nothing...go on," Ellison said, sticking his tongue out at

Hodel. In the control booth, Burt Handelsman, crack engineer, was rolling around on the floor.

"Bloodworld, however, is sentient," Dixon went on. "It's a living planet with a form of logic vastly different from our own. Not different values, but an entirely different system of thinking and rationalizing. Bloodworld does share some concepts with humans which makes communication theoretically possible. For example, to both humans and Bloodworld, love is the highest emotion. But to Bloodworld, to love is to kill."

"Is that it?" Ellison said.

"Yeah. What can you turn that into?"

"The police is my first inclination," Ellison said with a particularly snotty inflection. "But...um...lemme see...uh...okay, how's this? First of all, we drop that bullshit about 'to love is to kill.' Let's say a multi-planet consortium originating on Earth has planted a colony on Bloodworld to extract the goop that makes Immortaline. And let's say that they've spent years terraforming the planet so humans can live there. They've even brought in some samples of soil from Earth so they can grow trees that will produce enough oxygen to alter the atmosphere. And let's say that this sentient planet, Bloodworld, has managed to tap into the sentient unconscious possessed by *all* planets, and it's struck up this sort of colloquy with Earth. And they fall in love.

"And Earth is made aware of Bloodworld's love, and together they come to despise these crawling, destructive little bugs called human beings that have polluted the Earth and are now bleeding Bloodworld dry, as they have every other planet in the universe, and like a good James M. Cain thriller, Bloodworld and Earth, sort of planetary Romeo and Juliet, decide to kill off the human race by altering the structure of Immortaline, so instead of giving eternal life to humans it makes them infertile, thereby programming the death of the species.

"And the tragic kicker is that here's Bloodworld, way out here in the arm of the Trifid Nebula, say, and good old Earth back there in the Milky Way, or wherever the hell we are, and they kill off the human race, but they can never get together. They are lovers separated by the universe. How's that grab you?"

Even Hodel nodded with appreciation. "Gee, that's okay," Dixon said.

"Terrific," Ellison replied. "Thank your mother for the chicken soup." And Hodel cut him off.

"You're looking faint," Hodel said.

"I have an allergic response to lunacy. Makes me break out in the twitches. Takes large infusions of Dickens and Jorge Amado novels to bring me out of it."

"Would you settle for a Fresca?"

"I'd sooner have a hysterectomy."

Hodel punched up another call.

"You're on the air with Hodel and Ellison. Be careful, he's starting to glaze over."

"Hi, Mike. This is Joyce Muskat."

"Hi, Joyce," said Ellison. "Long time, no see. You have an idea?"

"I certainly do. I was listening to you on the subject of cats. And since you're obviously an ailurophile..."

"Martians are warping your radio reception, Muskat," Ellison said. "I'm an ailuro*phobe*. I hate the little fuckers."

"In literary circles, Harlan, we call that irony," she said gently, responding to the note of hysteria in his voice. "I understood your aversion. That's why I want you to create a story about a cat that cries undrying tears. It's a tabby cat. Its name is Thalassa."

Ellison stared at the wall. After a moment he began to moan. Then he began speaking in tongues.

"I warned you," Hodel said. "He's gone over the edge."

"No, no...I'm fine...just *fine*," Ellison croaked. "Let me think a moment. Undrying tears. That is to say, tears that don't dry. It's a tabby cat. A sweet, little, loveable tabby cat. Molasses is its name..."

"Not *molasses*...Thalassa. The Greek personification of the sea," she said.

"Thalassa. Right. Sorry. My mind seems to be giving way. I can't thank you enough for this idea, Joyce. You're a brick." He closed his eyes, rubbed his temples and thought.

"The silence you hear is Ellison thinking," Hodel told the audience. "While we're waiting, let me tell you about my new wife, Nancy."

From behind closed eyes Ellison murmured, "I'm sure they *live* for the knowledge."

"My new wife, Nancy," Hodel began, a thoroughly lachrymose expression suffusing his round little face, "is a woman of sterling qualities..."

"The most sterling of which is that she's brought her lunacy under control totally, save for having married you. Shut up, Hodel. I've got an idea for Muskat's stupid concept."

"I'm sure they're waiting with bated breath."

"The undrying tears the cat is crying are actually the legendary Waters of Nepenthe, the water of forgetfulness from Greek mythology. The cat is the eternal trustee of the potent waters, turned loose in ancient times to bring release from painful memories to mortals. The animal is thousands of years old. The cat is captured by an unscrupulous sort of person, like Stromboli the puppet master who chained up Pinocchio. He's going to sell the undrying tears of Nepenthe for exorbitant rates. And, uh, I don't know how I'd develop it, but in the end the cat would probably find a way to get the Stromboli creep to drink some of the tears, thereby forgetting what the cat is...and it would get away to continue its mission on Earth."

"I like that," Joyce Muskat said. "See, you're not such an unfeeling prick, after all."

The rest of the hour went that way.

John Ratner suggested two ideas: a parasitic business manager who finds he is becoming a character in his top client's newest production; and a concept, nebulous in the extreme, about "beautiful people" in a Los Angeles where humans have grown fur coats on themselves and there's no fashion industry. Ellison's developments of these were less than successful. He wound up apologizing. Ratner forgave him.

Alan Chudnow called in with something different. A title. Just a title. "Dust is Falling at the Tower of Minos." Ellison insulted his moustache, reaffirmed his desire to make it with his grandmother, and told him he'd file away the story title till he was ready to write a Samuel R. Delany-style trilogy. That time would come, Ellison assured Chudnow, soon after the writing of a novel featuring dragons, small people with furry feet and unicorns that responded to anyone who was *not* a virgin. "Tramp, slut unicorns," Ellison said.

Jon R. McKenzie offered the vaguest idea of the evening. "Two friends who grow apart, who change, yet remain the same, and come back together over the period 1970 to 1980." Ellison had trouble with that one, finally falling back on a variation of his story "Shatterday," by suggesting they were halves of the same person, traumatically severed in childhood, who had grown up in the same neighborhood without realizing they were the dark and light sides of the same persona. "And in the end," Ellison said, drawing to a close with that idea, "the dark side becomes a killer and the light side becomes a priest; and in the concluding scene the good guy, Father Flotski, is outside the prison where the bad guy, Mad Dog Berkowitz, is holed up with hostage guards, and Father Flotski is yelling up at him with a bullhorn, 'Come on, you no good kike, let the guards go before I have the Virgin Mary bite off your nose!'"

Three subsequent phone calls accused Ellison of being an anti-Semite. Ellison responded by saying, "Some of my best friends are Jews. Like my mother. My father. Me."

Jeff Rubenstein came on the air reminding Ellison he was the manager of a Crown Books shop in the San Fernando Valley where Ellison shopped. "What's your idea?" Ellison asked.

He wished he hadn't. "How about the domestication of Arabian camels to be used as race animals for American racetrack betting; and National Football League players all want to ride them as jockeys."

"Jeff," Ellison said, "you are a good and decent human being, and I thank you for all your courtesy when I come into Crown, but *that* is in the top tenth of the first percentile of lame-brained ideas I have ever had thrown at me."

"In other words, you're giving up, admitting defeat, is that it?" Hodel said. Ellison threw the can of Fresca past his head.

"I'm not admitting defeat," Ellison said. "I just need a while to let this one percolate. It ain't easy."

"Okay, we'll take another call."

"My name is Dan Turner. How about a story in which someone invents a way for individuals to get what they deserve?"

Ellison smiled. "Not what they *want*...what they *deserve?*"

"Yeah."

"That's easy. The guy who develops the gizmo has been in love with this beautiful, witty, intelligent woman all his life, but she won't have anything to do with him. Contrariwise, there's this plain-looking woman — not ugly, just sort of average — who's been in love with *him*, and she can't get him. Well, when he's busy turning this gizmo on people, giving them what they deserve, someone turns it on him..."

"And he gets the plain woman, right?" Hodel said.

"Wrong. He gets a thoroughly rotten woman. He didn't even deserve the nice, decent, average woman."

"It doesn't knock me out," Hodel said.

"The original idea didn't send me to the moon, either, Hodel. I'm dancing as fast as I can here."

Hodel punched up another call. Ellison was beginning to reel. He had the feeling he had been sucked headfirst into the collective head of science fiction fandom, and he didn't like the neighborhood. "You're on the air."

"Hi, I'm Charles Garcia, and my topic for a story is another story about the little blue Jewish aliens with wheels who needed a *minyan* for their dying planet; and throw in something about the Pope, if possible."

"You mean you want me to write a sequel to 'I'm Looking for Kadak'?"

"Uh-huh."

"Mr. Garcia, that's not an idea. I did that one already."

"Oh." He sounded wounded. "Okay." And he rang off.

Ellison looked chagrined. "I think I hurt his feelings."

"As opposed to the thousands you've insulted tonight who are probably all slashing their wrists or mailing you bombs," Hodel said wryly.

"Yeah, well...I didn't *mean* to upset Garcia."

Hodel put on another caller. Mayer Alan Brenner.

"I know you," Ellison said.

"You sure do. And I've got a beauty for you."

"Be still my heart," Ellison said, sinking down on his spine.

"It's an excerpt from *Northeast Tree and Stream*," Mayer said. "A short natural history of the famous Chesapeake Tree-Climbing Octopus..."

"Why me?" Ellison groaned. "Which God did I offend?"

"All of them," said Hodel.

Mayer went on, undaunted by sounds of pain coming over his radio. "This retiring and rarely-glimpsed creature lives in the many quiet estuaries of the Chesapeake system. Early each morning the octopus leaves the water and crawls up the trunk of a shoreside tree. It makes its way precariously onto a branch overhanging the water, where it waits for its prey to pass underneath."

Silence ensured. Dead air hung heavily in the night.

Finally, Ellison said, "And that's it, right? That's the idea, right, Mayer?"

"Uh-huh."

More silence. Then, in a very soft, very tired voice, Ellison said, "These blue-skinned Jewish aliens with wheels come down to Earth and kidnap the Pope so they can have a race on Arabian camels to establish whether Jews or Gentiles are worthiest to live in the universe, and the Pope gets all these NFL players to ride as his team, because they're all Polish or black and not a Jew in the lot, and they have this watercourse raceway and they race for the universe, and as they come under this tree in the Chesapeake system the octopus drops out of a tree and eats every last, fucking one of them, football players, Jewish aliens, the Pope, the camels, Brian Sipe and Terry Bradshaw and Walter Payton *and you too, Mayer!*"

In the control room Burt Handelsman, crack engineer, was trying to laugh and pick his nose at the same time.

"The time is 10:55 and this is KPFK-FM in Los Angeles," Hodel said. "And this is *Hour 25*, the weekly program of speculative fiction, science fiction, fantasy and wonder...and I'm your host, Mike Hodel."

"This is a *science fiction* program?!" Ellison shrieked. "This isn't *The 700 Club*? But I came to declare for Ba'al!"

Hodel punched up a call. "You're on the air."

It was William Stout, the artist responsible for the best selling *Dinosaurs* book. "I want him to think up a story in which William Stout gets to meet some real dinosaurs," he said. He waited.

Ellison said, "Okay, there's this story in which William Stout gets to meet some real dinosaurs, and they have lots and lots of real nice adventures, and if you want to find out how this story ends, go to the library and ask Miss Beckwith to let you check out the book. So long, Stout, you asshole."

Hodel said, "Thank God we have an eight second delay on the live phone lines."

"You don't have any eight second delay," Ellison said.

"I know, I know," Hodel said, dropping his head into his hands.

"And now, let's cut to Pasadena, to the LungFishCon, for the weekly calendar of events and the scintillant Terry Hodel, this dip's ex-wife." Ellison said. Hodel was weeping.

Burt Handelsman, crack engineer, threw the switch and the booth went dead as Terry Hodel did the calendar remote.

Hodel looked up, with tears in his eyes. "The FCC's gonna get me again. You did it to me the last time, and you're gonna do it again this time."

"You knew the job was dangerous when you took it," Ellison said. Then a look of transcendental horror passed over his face. "Ohmigod, ohmigod, ohmigod...where's Jane? What happened to my girl friend, Jane? Where did I leave her? Ohmigod, this program has drained my brain. Where did I park her, did I lock her, is someone even now stealing her hub caps?"

"She went home to North Attleboro to see her parents last week," Hodel said. "Calm down. She's all right."

Ellison visibly relaxed, breathed a sigh of relief. "Boy, it was touch-and-go there for a minute."

Burt Handelsman, c.e., suddenly boomed in the room. "Terry's almost finished. Get set for a cue."

The red light flashed and Hodel said, "Well, we're back now. How're you doing, Harlan?"

"You know, I work seriously at my craft. I spend hours and days and months and years writing these stories with proper serious intent…and then I'm thrown into conjunction with my readers…and it's scary, very scary. These people are all *nuts!*"

"Yes, but *you're* the one making stories out of these crazy ideas."

"I'm just a Force for Good in My Time," Ellison replied.

"Well, we're going to make it easy for you," Hodel said. "Group Mind, we're only going to take, say, five more ideas; and then Harlan and I will just chat about other things."

"Bless yuh, Massa Ho'del suh; I jus' loves wukkin' foah yuh heah on de plantation."

Hodel punched up a caller. "This is Tad Stones, and I'm calling in an idea for Ed Coffey."

"Good old Ed Coffey, whoever the hell *he* is," Ellison murmured. "Now they're selling shares in my breakdown."

"This is a science fiction story," Tad Stones said.

"What a swell change of pace," Ellison said through clenched teeth, thereby making it unintelligible to the audience.

"An average looking man offers the owner of a video arcade a free computer game for market testing. At the same moment, apparently the same man is making the same offer to arcades across the country."

Ellison gritted his teeth. The sound of avalanches went out at one million cycles per second.

"It's an alien plot, okay?" Ellison said.

"You asking me?" Tad Stones said.

"Yeah. I'm asking you. Alien invasion, right?"

"Sure. If you say so."

"Clones. They're clones. That okay, too?"

"Uh-huh."

"Alien clone invasion, howzabout it?"

"Why are you asking me?"

"I aims to please, Mr. Stones. An alien clone invasion from Far Centauri that has as its secret intent the violent overthrow of video arcades. How about it, Stones, you dip? Satisfactory?"

Hodel was getting disturbed. Ellison was no longer funny. He was getting actively vicious. The self-mocking tone at the edge of his remarks was vanishing. Hodel scribbled a note and thrust it in front of Ellison's glazed eyes. *Are you okay?*

"Am I okay, am I okay?" Ellison howled. "No, I'm not okay. I'm going bugfuck in here! Do you have any idea what it does to someone who spends fifteen hours a day writing to have to deal with this shit?"

"I write, too, Harlan," Hodel said gently.

His concern was evident. Ellison, who had been spiraling up into hysteria, calmed down quickly. "I'm sorry. Yes, of course, you understand. I've read *Enter the Lion* and you're a very *good* writer, Mike. He's a very *good* writer, folks." He paused. "But I'm *still* going bugfuck!"

Great clouds of smoke etna'd from his pipe.

There were only four more to go. The first was a man named Jon Clarke who reminded Ellison that he had held down the tire-puncture spikes at the entrance to Cal State, Northridge, when the writer had spoken there some years before and was late in arriving and had to drive in the egress to get to the auditorium. He offered an idea about a Group Mind on cable television stealing the souls of those who appear in its circuits. Ellison was far gone by that time and could make no sense of the idea. He babbled something about gestalt video vampirism and sank into a depressed funk.

Then a woman named Diana Adkins called and they both listened as she said, "This really happened. A little boy I knew, who was very bright, was asked why, in school and everywhere else, he didn't exhibit how bright he was. And he said, 'If I hold a candle under the bed, no one will see the flame,' and when he was asked why he would hold a candle under the bed, he said, 'Because if I don't, someone will put it out.'"

Hodel said, "That's very sad." Ellison said nothing.

"Thank you for calling," Hodel said. He cut to a new caller. Only two to go. He was worried about his guest. He'd known Ellison for years, and the sharpest parallel to what seemed to be happening to him was a story Ellison had written about a man being drained by emotional vampires. He wanted to cut this off before something more spectacular than he could handle went down.

"You're on the air, and you're next to last, so make it good."

His name was James Haralson, he was calling from Covina, and he said, "A tv evangelist, Markus Osgood, awakes one fine morning in his huge bed to discover that during the night something inexplicable had occurred. His consciousness had slipped. Somehow, as he slept next to the lovely and beloved Catherine, his center-of-being, his point of view, his 'I,' had shifted from the usual spot in his head and was hovering near his left armpit."

Ellison mumbled. "Mother of Mercy, is this the end of Rico?"

But Haralson was continuing. "Disconcerting, it was; and disorienting. But he makes do until that afternoon when, during his live, satellite-beamed, ocean-spanning ministry of the air, his consciousness starts slipping again. As he talks to the Orange County studio audience, he realizes his center-of-being is heading for his navel."

"I'm going mad," Ellison muttered. "I've gone mad; I've been sent to Hell and I'm never never going to be reprieved."

Hodel rushed in quickly. "That's an invalid concept. Consciousness isn't in a certain location. It's wherever you perceive it to be. In the Eighteenth Century they thought it was in the heart, the Greeks thought it was in the liver, which is why Prometheus had his liver chewed out by the big bird. Because of Freud we think consciousness is in the brain."

Haralson argued. "Well, if he *thinks* it's heading somewhere else, from his armpit to his navel to beyond...then it *could* be. So let Ellison say where it's heading."

Ellison drew a deep breath, sat up, laid his pipe on the studio table, leaned in close to the mike and said, "It's heading for Provo,

Utah, where it will meet a woman who works for the city sanitation department, in the typing pool; it will woo her, win her, marry her and have three children by her, one of which will be a waterhead like you."

Then he slumped back in his chair. He closed his eyes.

"Uh..." Hodel said. "Uh...he was, uh, just kidding, Mr. Haralson. It's been a long night. Just a joke."

"Didn't sound like a damned joke to me," Haralson said. "I didn't call in to be insulted."

"Consider it lagniappe," Ellison murmured.

Haralson hung up.

Hodel was now flat-out worried. Ellison was on the far side of flaky. This wasn't such a good show any more. It was getting useless and nasty. He decided to take on the last caller himself.

He punched up the last call, signalling Burt Handelsman, c.e., to cut off all other incoming callers, and said, "Okay, you're the last idea tonight. What've you got for us?"

"My name is Genadie Sverlow, and my idea is that the reason Sherlock Holmes never went after Jack the Ripper is that the Ripper was actually Dr. Watson, and Holmes knew it."

Hodel heaved a sigh of relief. Synchronicity lived! His novel, *Enter the Lion*, was a Sherlock Holmes pastiche. It could not have been a better question.

"Glad you asked that," Hodel said. "In point of fact, it couldn't have been Watson. The reason is, if you'll excuse the expression, elementary. Look: would you want Sherlock Holmes looking for *you*? Of course not. Watson *couldn't* be the Ripper...he'd know that Holmes could spot him right off. Besides...it's bad art. Too pat."

Ellison stood up and stepped away from the microphone as Hodel went on. "There are other reasons, chronological ones, why he couldn't have; but that's the bottom line. It would have been too dangerous. Whatever else Watson was, he was no fool."

Burt Handelsman, c.e., came to the window between the studio and the control booth and held up a note written with heavy felt-tip lines:

THERE'S A GUY ON LINE 4 NAMED TIM LEWIS WHO SAYS HE
HAD THE SAME STORY IDEA. WANT HIM?

Hodel signalled no and drew a finger across his throat to indicate
no more calls. Then, before the caller on the line could get him into
further Holmesian minutiae, he cut the line. "Okay, that's the end of
the story ideas."

He looked over at Ellison. The writer was standing with his face to
the wall. The time was 11:26 turning to 27.

"Harlan?"

The writer turned slowly. His eyes were cold and faraway.

"We've got about thirty-three minutes. Want to just chat about
what *you're* writing these days?"

Ellison nodded wearily and fell into the seat again.

Then a voice came through the studio speaker. "May I impose,
please, to enter your conversation?" It was a male voice.

Hodel snapped a look at the call director. All the lights were out.
He raised his eyes to B.H., c.e., and drew a finger across his throat
sharply, urgently. "No more calls, please!" he said. But Handelsman was
looking frantic. He waved wildly and indicated by his confusion that *he*
wasn't responsible for this call.

Hodel looked for the little red light on the mike pedestal that
indicated the speaker phone was on. It was dark.

Ellison didn't seem to realize what was happening.

What was happening, beyond reason, was that someone was coming
in over the telephone lines...without using the telephone lines. Hodel
decided to go with it — carefully.

"Do you have an idea for Harlan Ellison? It's pretty late and we
were just going to knock around some small talk."

The voice said, "There is a concept of some interest. Postulate, if
you will, an alien life-form; an intelligent, sensitive being who, for
reasons we need not go into now, has been cast adrift. Marooned, if
you will, in a dark place. Alone, left to drift between the stars. And
there it waits, without light, without weight, without emotional
sustenance, without the companionship of thinking, feeling beings. A

231

thing without purpose. Waiting, forever waiting, drifting emptily in the stars."

Burt was running around the control room trying to find the active link. He kept coming back to the window, pushing his nose against the glass and waving his arms wildly. It wasn't happening, it simply could not, would not be happening!

"Where are you calling from?" Hodel asked.

"Nearby," said the voice.

Hodel didn't know what to do but continue talking.

"Well, that's an interesting idea." he said. "Maybe it's not the newest idea, but —"

Ellison was leaning in to the mike. His eyes were closed, and his face looked strained. "But how do we know this being is as represented?" he said. His voice was calm now, all trace of his tension and hysteria gone.

"What do you mean, if I may ask?" said the voice.

"Well, what I mean is this," Ellison said. "What if this creature, this sentience, this intelligence, was marooned by his own kind for reasons humans couldn't even understand; but for some quality or maleficence that branded it forever as a life form unfit to exist with —"

"With responsible beings?" the voice said.

"If you will. What if?"

"Then perhaps the lonely creature would wait until it could make contact, to fall back on the kindness of other decent, responsible beings."

"Ah," Ellison said, concentrating. "I see. Wait for some gullible, young species that would be so amazed it wouldn't ask the proper questions. That would take this Trojan horse in, to succor it..."

"To warm it."

"To nurture and protect it."

"Yes, yes, that is exactly what I speak of. A new home without darkness, where the companionship of other thinking beings would return it to the community of intelligent beings."

"I don't think so," Ellison said.

"What do you mean?" the voice said.

"What I mean," Ellison said, now staring at the wall beyond the microphone, "is that we know about you. We've known about you for a long time. You don't think they cast you out on their way past, and left you there to find a home, do you? They left records. We know what you are, and where you are. When we reach that pocket of space where you lie, we will do one of two things: ignore you...or destroy you."

"You cannot destroy me."

"You mean destroy that hypothetical creature we were talking about."

"Yes. Hypothetical. It cannot be destroyed."

"But it *can* be left to swim in blindness forever."

The speaker went dead.

Ellison sank back in his seat.

Hodel stared at him. His mouth was open. In the control booth, Burt Handelsman, crack engineer, sat staring at the console.

After a while, Ellison rose, let out a long breath, and walked wearily toward the door of the studio. Hodel sat where he was. As Ellison opened the soundlock door, Hodel said, "Jesus, am I crazy, or did you just save the entire world?"

Ellison looked back over his shoulder and managed a faint smile. "I'm just your basic everyday Force for Good in Our Time," he said. "And if I ever offer to talk to fans again, I want you to drive a stake through my heart."

He walked out, the door sighed shut, and Mike Hodel realized it was still three minutes till midnight.

"Uh, this is KPFK-FM, 90.7 megahertz on your dial; and this has been *Hour 25*. I'm Mike Hodel; our crack engineer this evening has been Burt Handelsman; and for Terry Hodel, myself, and our guest, Harlan Ellison, this has been the hour that stretches."

He paused a moment and added, "And to *all* our listeners, wher*ever* they may be, *whatever* they may be, I haven't the faintest idea what the hell went on here tonight."

THE DAY I DIED

AN EXCERPT FROM THE HARLAN ELLISON HORNBOOK (1973)

Driving home from Norman Spinrad's New Year's Eve party at which I finally met Cass Elliot — as invigorating an experience as one could wish for the dawn of a new year — skimming the crusty '67 Camaro with its 56,000+ miles of dead years in its metal bones through Beverly Hills. KFAC was working Ravel's *Bolero*. Not tired, it was still early for a New Year's Eve, something like one o'clock. Thinking.

No. Woolgathering. (*The American Heritage Dictionary of the English Language*, p. 1473, col. 2: woolgathering *n*. Absent-minded indulgence in fanciful daydreams.) That's what I was doing: woolgathering.

Frequently, that's how my writer's mind conceives plots for stories, or more accurately, concepts for stories. The unconscious computer makes a storage-bank search of idle thoughts — looking for linkages, cross-references, points of similarity. When it finds something interesting, it checks against all the muddle and mud madly swirling in the cortex, and comes up with something that makes a story.

The elements this time were these:

1972 is gone. It's a new year. 1973. Another year.

One year older. Moving on up the road toward the grave just the way old Camaro is moving on up the road to Beverly Glen. Traveling the road.

Harry Truman is gone. I miss him. Salty old Harry who told them all to go fuck themselves. Ten years ago he said he wouldn't die for at least ten more because he had ten years' work still to do in the Truman Library in Independence, Missouri. Ten years later, all the work done, almost to the month, he died. Did he know?

Could I know when I'm going to die?

Will I get to finish all the stories I have to write?

Will I suddenly get rammed by a Pontiac Grand Am at the next light, centerpunched into an early oblivion?

When will I die?

New Year's Eve is a good time to think about it.

So. This column.

Thinking about when I'll die. Mortality is the subject.

I will die in 1973. Here is how it happened.

I went to New York to be guest of honor at a science fiction convention called the Lunacon. To amortize the cost of the trip I accepted several lecture gigs in surrounding areas. So I went into Manhattan two weeks before the convention. I had just returned from speaking at Dartmouth and was staying with my friend Max Katz, the *Sesame Street* segment director, in his Penthouse G on East 65th Street. Max and Karen were out when I taxied in from Kennedy International, and after putting away my overnight case I found the note they'd left for me: *We went to dinner at The Proof of the Pudding. If you get in by nine, join us. Love, M&K.*

I looked at my watch. It was 9:28. Still time to meet them for a piece of Key West lime pie. I left the apartment and took the elevator to the lobby. The street was quiet and pleasant with an April breeze. I started to walk down 65th to First Avenue, carefully avoiding the piles of dog shit.

Two guys in Army field jackets were coming toward me, up the street. I instinctively tensed. I was in New York and could not forget that Karen had had her purse ripped off her shoulder in broad daylight in front of Bloomingdale's, in front of hordes of people who would not help her as she struggled with the snatcher. New York was not what it had been when last I'd lived there, in 1961.

As they came toward me they parted so I could walk between them. I guess I knew in my gut what was about to happen. They swung on me and jammed me against the brick wall of the poodle clipping joint down the street from Max's building. They both had knives.

"Gimme your wallet," one of them said, not even lowering his voice. He pushed his knife against my collarbone. The other one smelled of fish.

I remembered a way I'd confounded a mugger many years before. I began mumbling unintelligibly in what was supposed to be a foreign tongue, waving my hands feebly as if I didn't understand English.

"Your money, motherfucker...I'll shove this in your fucking throat!"

I rolled my eyes wildly and continued babbling.

A group of people had come out of Max's apartment building, were turning toward us. "Come on," said the one who smelled of fish. "You cocksucker!" the one with the knife at my collarbone said.

They let go and moved off. I took two steps and felt the pain. I tried to turn, and saw the one who had done all the talking had spun and come back at me. The pain was in my back, below my right shoulderblade. It got worse. Doors slammed in my head. Everything went silver. I fell to my knees.

The group from Max's building walked past me. I fell down and lay there. In a little while I died.

Max and Karen came home from dinner and didn't learn that I'd been killed outside their building till the next afternoon. They knew *something* was wrong because they found my overnight bag, but not me. Karen cried, the Lunacon had a minute of silence for me, and my replacement, Isaac Asimov, said dear good things about me, better than I deserved.

I died on April 19th, 1973.

———

harlan ellison
The day i died

I will die in 1981. Here is how it happened.

I was living in Perthshire, in Scotland. I had had a bad cold for weeks. I was living alone. The woman who had been staying with me had gone away. I was writing *Dial 9 to Get Out* at last. My big novel. The one that would finally break my name into the memory books of great writers. It had taken me ten years to get to it. I was deep in the writing. I didn't eat regularly, I've never been one for cooking for myself. I developed pneumonia in that handsome old farmhouse.

It killed me. I never finished the book. My stories were read for a few years, but soon went out of vogue.

No one in that little Scottish town understood that as I lay there, tubes in many apertures, doped up and dying, that the pathetic movements of my hands were my attempts to convey to the nurse or the doctor that I wanted my typewriter, that I wanted more than anything, even more than life, to finish that book.

I died on December 11th, 1981.

I will die in 1986. Here is how it happened.

Bungalow 16 Does Not Answer had been published in March. Book-of-the-Month Club had taken it as its April selection. The film rights were being negotiated by Marty. It looked to be the best year I'd ever had.

I was on a publicity tour for the book, fresh from a talk show over holovid. Oh, yes, I should mention holovid. After two-dimensional depth television, Westinghouse developed "feelie," a rather euphemistic name for projected video, giving the vague impression of the actual presence in your living room of the actors. Then the cable people, in conjunction with Phillips Laser Science, Ltd. of Great Britain, combined holograms with 3-D projection techniques and came up with holovid, in which the viewer actually became a part of the show or studio audience.

I was in Denver, preparing to be choppered over to the studio, when I fell ill. I was using depilatory on my beard in the hotel suite's bathroom when I felt dizzy and suddenly keeled over. The publisher's rep and the PR woman heard me crash and came running. They got me to the hospital where the phymech took readings. (A phymech is a robot physician, used primarily for running physicals and determining the nature of the illness. Lousy bedside manner, but they've cut down the incidence of improper analysis by eighty percent over their human counterparts.)

The judgment was cancer of the stomach.

I went into surgery the next morning. It had spread, running wild, not even the anti-agapic drugs would work. I was listed as terminal. Perhaps two weeks, the last five of those days heavily sedated against the pain. It was a shame: the Cancer Society was on the verge of a major breakthrough. Had I lived another five years, I'd have seen cancer become no more serious than the flu.

I spent the last two weeks in a hospital bed, a cerebral scanwriter plugged directly into my thinking center, the wafer-thin readout plate standing close by on a little table. The tv anchors came and did their interviews briefly...I was abrupt with them, I'm afraid. I didn't have too much time to talk, I had things to write.

I finished my last novel in that bed, but the final twenty thousand words were rather garbled, I was so drugged, going in and out of consciousness. But I finished it, and was saved the horror of having another writer complete the work from my notes.

When I died, I was not unhappy. I rather regretted being denied those last twenty years, though. I had *such* stories to write.

I died on my birthday, May 27th, 1986.

I died in 1977 when a right-winger shot me because I'd done an article in *World* magazine on President Reagan and how he should be indicted as a criminal for the war in Brazil.

I died in 1979 in a plane crash in Sri Lanka. I was on my way to see Arthur Clarke. We were going to go scuba diving off the coast of coral. The plane exploded; I never knew what hit me. They said it was a terrorist bomb in the cargo bay. My fourth wife got the flight insurance.

I died in 1982 during the worst blizzard the East Coast had ever seen. I froze to death in my car on a lonely Connecticut road where I'd run out of gas. Some asshole suggested that because I'd been frozen, they might try to preserve me cryonically for restoration later. Fortunately, he was ignored.

I died in 1990 from a sudden, massive coronary. I was sitting at home on a Sunday afternoon and felt the slam of it, and had just a moment to realize I was dying the same way my father had died. But he would never have a postage stamp commemorating his achievements.

I died in 1998 from ptomaine poisoning in a seafood restaurant in the undersea resort city of Cayman. They had to wait three weeks to ship my carcass out; it would have been simpler to turn me into fish food and let my soul wander the Cayman Trench. I always hated the lack of imagination of Those in Power.

I died in 2001 on my way back from Sweden. I died very peacefully, in my sleep, on-board the catamaran-cruiser *Farragut*, somewhere in mid-Atlantic. I died with a smile on my face, lying in bed, holding the Nobel Prize for Literature to my chest like a teddy bear.

I died in 2010 from weary old age, surrounded by grandchildren and old friends who remembered the titles of my stories. I didn't mind going at all, I was really tired.

Hey! You! The skinny sonofabitch with the scythe. I'm over here...Ellison. I saw you looking at me out of the corner of that empty socket in your skull-face, you sleazy eggsucker. Well, listen, m'man, understand this: since I know I'm going straight to Hell anyhow, and since I've always lived with the feeling that Heavens and Hells are sucker traps for the slow-witted and one should get as much goodie as one can while one is breathing, you'd better get used to the idea that you're going to have to come and get me when my time's up. Kicking and screaming, you blade-boned crop-killer. Hand to hand or at gunpoint, you're going to have to fight me for my life.

Because I've got too much stuff yet to do, too many stories yet to write, too many places I've never seen, too many books I've never read, too many women to admire, and too many laughs yet to cry. So don't think I'll be a cheap acquisition, clatterframe! And if you *do* get me, I'll be the damnedest POW *you* ever saw. I'll try and escape, and if I can't, I'll send back messages.

And it'll drive your bony ass crazy, Mr. D., because I'll be the first one to write about what it's like over there in your country.

1982 UPDATE This essay-fiction, written as a speculative lark for *The Harlan Ellison Hornbook* column in the now-defunct *Los Angeles Free Press* in January of 1973, recently almost became redundant. On May 20th, 1982, at approximately 2:45 PM, the Author, in company with his Executive Assistant, Marty Clark, crashed his beloved 1967 Camaro (mileage 170,000) at a speed of 55 mph on the San Diego Freeway. Both the Author and Ms. Clark came as close as they have ever been to the boneyard, yet they escaped the wreck unscathed. Having now bypassed the first two demises in this essay, the Author contends he will live forever. This does not delight the Author's enemies.

1996 UPDATE: CONDITION OF MORTALITY Having now passed all but the last three predicted dates of demise, having now reached the improbable age of 62, I have a much more realistic view of mortality. To write, even in 1982, when I was but in my late forties, that I would live forever, was a clear sign of prolonged immaturity. I should have known better. But even though I wrote at interminable length about "mortality," I didn't have a rat's-whisker of an idea what I was talking about. On Sunday, April 14th of this year, I had a serious heart attack, and was saved from actual death by a quadruple bypass procedure at Cedars-Sinai Hospital in Los Angeles. It wasn't in the least a humorous or bemusing or even intriguing event. It scared the shit out of me. I stood right there in the Doorway to Nowhere, and I looked through, and understood — really for the first time in my life — that woolgathering exercises like this creaky essay are pure adolescent braggart bullshit. Thomas Hess wrote "...an artist is free of all mortgages except for the ultimate one that forecloses on mountains."

3 TALES
FROM THE MOUNTAINS
OF MADNESS

TRACKING LEVEL

TINY ALLY

THE GODDESS IN THE ICE

TRACKING LEVEL

Claybourne's headlamp picked out the imprint at once. It was faint in the beam, yet discernible, with the telltale mark of the huge, three-toed foot. He was closer than ever.

He drew a deep breath, and the plastic air-sack on his breather mask collapsed inward. He expelled the breath slowly, watching the diamond-shaped sack expand once more.

He wished wildly for a cigarette, but it was impossible. First because the atmosphere of the tiny planetoid would not keep one going, and second because he'd die in the thin air.

His back itched, but the loose folds of the protective suit prevented any lasting relief, for all his scratching.

The faint starlight of shadows crossing the ground made weird patterns. Claybourne raised his head and looked out across the plain of blue saw-grass at the distant mountains.

They looked like so many needles thrust up through the crust of the planetoid. They were angry mountains. No one had ever named them; which was not strange, for nothing but the planetoid itself had been named. It had been named by the first expedition to the Antares Cluster. They had named it Selangg — after the alien ecologist who had died on the way out.

They recorded the naming in their log, which was fortunate, because the rest of them died on the way back. Space malady and an incomplete report on the planetoid Selangg, floating in a death ship around a secondary sun of the Partias Group.

He stood up slowly, stretching slightly to ease the tension of his body. He picked up the molasses-gun and hefted it absently. Off to his right he heard a scampering and swung the beam in its direction.

A tiny, bright-green animal scurried through the crewcut desert saw-grass.

Is that what the fetl *lives on?* he wondered.

He actually knew very little about the beast he was tracking. The report given him by the Institute at the time he was commissioned to bring the *fetl* back was, at best, sketchy, pieced together from that first survey report.

The survey team had mapped many planetoids, and only a hurried analysis could be made before they scuttled to the next world. All they had listed about the *fetl* was a bare physical description — and the fact that it was telekinetic.

What evidence had forced this conclusion was not stated in the cramped micro-report, and the reason died with them.

"We want this animal badly, Mr. Claybourne," the Director of the Institute had said.

"We want him badly because he just *may* be what this report says. If he is, it will further our studies of extra-sensory perception tremendously. We are willing to pay any reasonable sum you might demand. We have heard you're the finest wild game hunter on the Periphery.

"We don't care how you do it, Mr. Claybourne, but we want the *fetl* brought back alive and unharmed."

Claybourne had accepted immediately. This job had paid a pretty sum — enough to complete his plans to kill Carl Garden.

The prints paced away, clearly indicating the tracked beast was heading for refuge in the mountains. He studied the totally flat surface of the grassy desert, and heaved a sigh.

He'd been at it three weeks, and all he'd found had been tracks. Clear, unmistakable tracks, and all leading toward the mountains. The beast could not know it was being tracked, yet it continued moving steadily.

The pace had worn at Claybourne.

He gripped the molasses-gun tighter, swinging it idly in small, wary arcs. He had been doing that — unknowing — for several days. The hush of the planetoid was working on him.

Ahead, the towering bleakness of Selangg's lone mountain range rose full-blown from the shadows of the plain. Up there.

Twenty miles of stone jumbled and strewn piece on piece; seventeen thousand feet high. Somewhere in those rocks was an animal Claybourne had come halfway across the galaxy to find. An animal that was at this moment insuring Carl Garden's death.

He caught another print in the beam.

He stooped to examine it. There was a faint wash of sand across it, where the wind had scurried past. The foot-long pawprint lay there, mocking him, challenging him, asking him what he was doing here — so far from home, so far from warmth and life and ease.

Claybourne shook his head, clearing it of thoughts that too easily impinged. He'd been paid half the sum requested, and that had gone to the men who were now stalking Garden back on Earth. To get the other half, he had to capture the *fetl*. The sooner that was done, the better.

The *fetl* was near. Of that he was now certain. The beast certainly couldn't go *over* the mountains and live. It had to hole up in the rocks somewhere.

He rose, squinted into the darkness. He flicked the switch on his chest-console one more notch, heightening the lamp's power. The beam drove straight ahead, splashing across the gray, faceless rocks. Claybourne tilted his head, staring through the clear hood, till a sharply-defined circle of brilliant white stabbed itself onto the rock before him.

That was going to be a job, climbing these mountains. He decided abruptly to catch five hours' sleep before pushing up the flank of the mountains.

He turned away, to make a resting place at the foot of the mountains, and with the momentary cessation of the tracking found old thoughts clambering back into his mind.

Shivering inside his protection suit — though none of the chill of Selangg could get through to him — he inflated the foam-rest attached to the back of his suit. He lay down, in the towering ebony shadows, looking up at the clear, eternal night sky. And he remembered.

Claybourne had owned his own fleet of cargo vessels. It had been one of the larger chains, including hunting ships and cage-lined shippers. It had been a money-making chain, until the inverspace ships had come along, and thrown Claybourne's obsolete fuel-driven spacers out of business.

Then he had taken to blockade-running and smuggling, to ferrying slaves for the out-world feudal barons, gun-running and even spaceway robbery.

Through that period he had cursed Carl Garden. It had been Garden all the way — Garden every step of the way — who had been his nemesis.

When they finally caught him — just after he had dumped a cargo of slaves into the sun to avoid customs conviction — they canceled his commission and refused him pilot status. His ships had been sold at auction.

That had strengthened his hatred for Garden. Garden had bought most of the fleet. For use as scum-ships and livestock carriers.

It had been Garden who had invented the inverspace drive. Garden who had undercut his fleet, driving Claybourne into receivership. And finally, it had been Garden who had bought the remnants of the fleet.

Lower and lower he sank; three years as a slush-pumper on freighters, hauling freight into shining spacers on planets that had not yet received power equipment, drinking and hating.

Till finally — two years before — he had reached the point where he knew he would never rest easily till he had killed Garden.

Claybourne had saved his money. The fleshpots of the Periphery had lost him. He gave up liquor and gambling.

The wheels had been set in motion.

People were working, back on Earth, to get Garden. He was being pursued and harried, though he never knew it. From the other side of the galaxy, Claybourne was hunting, chasing, tracking his man. And one day, Garden would be vulnerable. Then Claybourne would come back.

To reach that end, Claybourne had accepted the job from the Institute.

In his rage to acquire money for the job of getting his enemy, Claybourne had built a considerable reputation as wild game hunter. For circuses, for museums and zoos, he had tracked and trapped thousands of rare life-forms on hundreds of worlds.

They had finally contacted him on Bouyella and offered him the ship, the charter, and exactly as much money as he needed to complete the job back on Earth.

Arrangements had been quickly made, half the pay had been deposited to Claybourne's accounts (and immediately withdrawn for delivery to certain men back home), and he had gone out on the jump to Selangg.

This was the last jump, the last indignity he would have to suffer. After Selangg — back to Earth. Back to Garden.

He wasn't certain he had actually seen it! The movement had been rapid, and only in the corner of his eye.

Claybourne leaped up, throwing off the safeties on the molasses-gun. He yanked off the inflation patch with stiff fingers, and the foam-rest collapsed back to flatness in his pack.

He took a tentative step, stopped. Had he actually seen something? Had it been hallucination or a trick of the weak air blanket of Selangg? Was the hunt getting to him at last? He paused, wet his lips, took another step.

His scarred, blocky face drew tight. The sharp gray eyes narrowed.

Nothing moved but the faint rustling of the blue saw-grass. The world of Selangg was dead and quiet.

He slumped against the rock wall, his nerves leaping.

He wondered how wise it had been to come on this jump. Then the picture of Garden's fat, florid face slid before his eyes, and he knew he had had to come. This was the ending. As he tracked the *fetl*, so he tracked Garden.

He quickly reviewed what he knew of the *fetl's* appearance, matching it with the flash of movement he had seen:

A big, bloody animal — a devilish-looking thing, all teeth and legs. Striped like a Sumatran tiger, six-legged, twelve-inch sabered teeth, a ring of eyes across a massive low brow, giving it nearly one hundred and eighty degrees of unimpaired straight-line eyesight.

Impressive, and mysterious. They knew nothing more about the beast. Except the reason for this hunt; it was telekinetic, could move objects by mind-power alone.

A stupid animal — a beast of the fields — yet it possibly held the key to all future research into the mind of man.

But the mysteries surrounding the *fetl* were not to concern Claybourne. His job was merely to capture it and put it in the custody of the Institute for study.

However...

It was getting to be a slightly more troublesome hunt now. Three weeks was a week longer than he had thought the tracking would take. He had covered most of the mere five hundred miles of Selangg's surface. Had it not been for the lessened gravity and the monstrous desert grasslands, he would still be searching. The *fetl* had fled before him.

He would have given up had he not found prints occasionally.

It had been all that had kept him going. That, and the other half of his pay, deliverable upon receipt of the *fetl* at the Institute. It seemed almost uncanny. At almost the very instant he would consider giving up and turning back to the ship, a print would appear in the circle of lamplight, and he would continue. It had happened a dozen times.

Now here he was, at the final step of the trek. At the foot of a gigantic mountain chain, thrusting up into the dead night of Selangg. He stopped, the circle of light sliding like cool mercury up the face of the stone.

He might have been worried, were it not for the molasses-gun. He cradled the weapon closer to his protective suit.

The grapple shot hooked itself well into the jumbled rock pieces piled above the smooth mountain base. Claybourne tested it and began climbing, bracing his feet against the wall, hanging outward and walking the smooth surface.

Finally, he reached the area where volcanic action had ruptured the stone fantastically. It was a dull, gray rock, vesiculated like scoria, and tumbled and tumbled. He unfastened the grapple, returned it to its nest in his pack, and tensing his muscles, began threading up through the rock formations.

It soon became tedious — but on the positive side, it *was* boring. Stepping up and over the jumbled rock pieces he turned his thoughts idly to the molasses-gun. This was the first time he had handled one of the new solo machines. Two-man molasses-guns had been the order till now. A solo worked the same way, and was, if anything, deadlier than the more cumbersome two-man job.

He stopped for a moment to rest, sliding down onto a flat stool of rock. He took a closer look at the weapon. The molasses-gun; or as it was technically known, the Stadt-Brenner Webbing Enmesher. He liked molasses-gun better; it seemed to describe the weapon's function so accurately.

The gun produced a steel-strong webbing, fired under tremendous pressure, which coiled the strongest opponent into a helpless bundle. The more he struggled to free himself, for the webbing was an unstable plastic, the tighter it bound him.

"Very much like the way I'm enmeshing Garden," Claybourne chuckled to himself.

The analogy was well-founded. The molasses-gun sucked the victim deeper and deeper into its coils, just as Claybourne was sucking Garden deeper and deeper into his death-trap.

Claybourne smiled and licked his lips absently. The moisture remained for an instant, was swept away by the suit's purifiers.

He started up again. The rocks had fallen in odd formations, almost forming a passage up the summit. He rounded a talus slide, noting even more signs of violent volcanic activity, and headed once more up the inky slope toward the cliffs rising from the face of the mountain.

The *fetl's* prints had become less and less distinct as it had climbed, disappearing almost altogether on the faceless rocks.

Occasionally a claw-scratch would stand out brightly in the glare of Claybourne's headlamp beam.

The hours slid by tediously, and though he forced himself to stop twice more to rest, the light gravity caused him little fatigue for all his labors.

Once, as before, he thought he caught a splinter-fast movement of striped body up on the cliffs, but as before, he could not be certain.

The faint starshine cast odd shadows, little blobs of black and silver, across the mountains. From a distance it had looked as though millions of diamonds were lying on the black surfaces. As though the mountains were riddled with holes, through which a giant sun inside the rock was sending pinpoints of light. It was weird and beautiful.

A fitting place for me to bow off the Periphery, he thought; thoughts returning to Earth — and Garden. He thought of Earth.

His world.

When he skimmed the hood-beam across the rocks twenty feet above him on the cliff wall, Claybourne saw the cave.

A small incline rose up into the deeper blackness of the cave's mouth. That *had* to be it. The only place within a mile of the last claw-scratch that the *fetl* could have used to disappear. The scratches had been clear for a time, leading him up the mountain, but then they had vanished.

His tracking had been quiet — sound didn't carry far on Selangg.

His tracking had been stealthy — it was always dark on Selangg. Now his efforts would pay off. His hunt was over. Back to Earth — to finish that other hunt.

He was banking the other hallucination he had seen was the real thing.

Claybourne stopped under a rock lip overhang and flat-handed the compression chamber of the molasses-gun open, peering inside. His hood light shone down on the steel-blue plastic of the weapon. It was full, all the little gelatin capsules ranged row on row behind the airtight transparent seal, filling the chamber to the seams. He flipped it shut and looked once more toward the summit and the cave.

A star gleamed directly over the ragged peaks, directly above him. He hefted the rifle once more, blew a thin stream of breath through his pursed lips, and started up the incline.

The tiny rock bits tumbled away under his boots, the crunch of pebbles carrying up through the insulated suiting. He kept a wary watch as he climbed, not expecting the beast to appear, but still taking no chances.

He was certain the *fetl* did not know he had followed it here to its lair. Else it would have turned back in a circle, kept running across the grasslands. His tracking had been subtle and cautious. Claybourne had learned on the Periphery how to be invisible on a hostile world, if the need arose. This hunt would end as all the others had ended: successfully.

The hunt for Garden, too, he mused tightly.

The ragged cave mouth gaped before him.

He surveyed it closely, inclining his beam not directly into the opening, but tilting it onto the rock wall just inside, so light spilled over the rockway and he could check for ledged rises over the entrance, inside. Nothing but a huge pile of rocks wedged tightly in place by some miscue of the volcanic action.

He flipped a toggle on the chest-console, and the beam became brighter still, spraying out in a wider, still sharply defined circle.

He stepped in.

The cave was empty.

No, *not* empty.

He was three steps into the high-ceilinged cave before he saw the *fetl*. It was crouched small as its huge bulk would allow into a corner, dim in the back of the cave. Hunched as far as it could go into a niche in the wall.

In as far as its ten-foot hulk permitted, still the beast was huge. Its monstrous ring of weed-green eyes all staring at him malevolently.

Claybourne felt a sudden shock as he stared into those eyes. They so much reminded him of Garden's eyes at the auction. Hungry.

He shook off the feeling, took a step forward. The *fetl* was limned clearly in the beam of the helmet torch. It was an impressive animal, tightly coiled at the rear of the cave.

The beast twitched slightly.

Its flanks quivered in the glare of the lamp. Muscles all over its body rippled, and Claybourne drew back a step to fire. The beast twitched again.

He felt the tiny stones in the pile over the entrance clatter to the cave floor. He could barely hear them tinkle, but the vibrations in the stone came to him.

He turned his head for a moment, to see what was happening. His eyes opened wide in terror as he saw the supporting rubble drop away, leaving the huge rock tottering in its place. The great stone slid gratingly out of its niche and crashed to the floor of the cave, sending clouds of rock-dust roiling, completely blocking off the mouth of the cave. Sealing it permanently.

Claybourne could only stand and watch, horror and a constriction in his throat.

His light remained fixed on the cave-in, reflecting back glints of gold as the dust from the slide swirled itself into small pillars, rising into the thin air.

Then he heard the rumble.

The sound struck him like a million trumpets, all screaming at once. He turned, stumbling, his torch flicking back toward the *fetl*.

The *fetl* sat up on its four back legs, contentedly washing a front paw with a long red tongue that flicked in and out between twelve-inch incisors. The lighter black of a small hole behind him gave an odd illusion of depth to the waiting beast.

Claybourne watched transfixed as the animal slowly got to its feet and pad-pad-padded toward him, the tongue slipping quickly in and out, in and out...

Suddenly coming to his senses, Claybourne stepped back a pace and levelled the molasses-gun, pulled the trigger. The stream of webbing emerged with a vibrant hiss, sped toward the monstrous *fetl*.

A foot short of the beast the speeding webbing lost all drive, fluttered in the still cave for a moment, then fell like a flaccid length of rope. On the floor it quickly contracted itself, worm-like, into a tight, small ball.

The *fetl* licked its chops, the tongue swirling down and across and up and in again.

Before he could pull the trigger again, Claybourne felt the gun tremble in his hands. At the same moment he saw the beast's flanks quiver again.

An instant later the gun ripped itself from his grasp and sent itself crashing into the wall. Parts spattered the cave floor as the seams split, and capsules tumbled out. The molasses-gun's power compartment emitted a sharp, blue spark, and the machine was gone.

He was defenseless.

He heard the roar again. *Telekinetic!* After he had done what he wished, the animal would leave by the hole in the rear of the cave. Why bother untumbling the rocks!

The *fetl* began moving again. Claybourne stumbled back, tripped on a jutting rock, fell heavily to the floor.

The man backed away across the floor of the cave, the seat of his suit scraping the rock floor. His back flattened against the wedged rock in the cave mouth. He was backed as far as he could go.

He was screaming, the sound echoing back and forth in his hood, in the cave, in the night.

All he could see, all there was in the universe, was the *fetl*, advancing on him, slowly, slowly, taking all the time it needed. Savoring every instant.

Then abruptly, at the precise instant he gazed deep into that ring of hate-filled green eyes coming toward him, he realized that even as he had tracked the *fetl*, even as he had been tracking Garden — so the *fetl* had been tracking him!

The *fetl* licked his lips again, slowly.

He had all the time in the world...

His world.

TINY ALLY

When we first saw him, he came stumbling across the snow almost beneath our feet. For a moment I thought it was a snow-swirl, or a shadow. At 18,000 feet, that often happens.

Deszlow stopped and cupped his hands to his mouth, having pulled up his oxygen mask, and screamed to the rest of us on the line. "For God's sake! Come here and see *this!*"

His voice was almost lost beneath the howl of the wind, but we pulled along the rope to see what he had discovered. Rutledge and Ferraday and I slid back down the slope, digging our crampons into the tightly-packed crust, leaving spike-marks in jagged rows. We clustered around Deszlow, the deranged wind of the summit bullying us. We stared with great confusion at the tiny mountain climber Deszlow had discovered.

Note this: at 500 yards short of the 18,000 foot mark on Annapurna — we were following in the tracks of the French expedition that had defeated the peak — on a geophysical survey, we discovered a minuscule climber. He was no more than three inches high, with a tightly-belted *anorak* jacket, a pike, tiny crampons, and a face quite red from exertion. I did not realize it then, but there were even *more* physically startling things about him. But one thing *did* shock me:

He had a knife in the small, small, *small* of his back.

A chill that was deeper and sharper than the chill of the wind — roaring down from the unseen peaks above — touched my spine.

Even as I stood staring at the tiny panting figure, Ferraday's sudden movement penetrated my frozen consciousness. As it did, I yelled hoarsely through my mask, "No, you fool! Don't —"

But it was already too late. Ferraday had picked up the tiny man, was holding him tightly by the collar of his jacket, and was reaching for the knife with his free hand. I still cannot tell how I knew, but I was suddenly *absolutely* certain that it was the *worst* thing Ferraday could do.

Slipping and staggering on the treacherous surface, I rushed forward. Blindly, I plunged into Ferraday, arms outthrust to stop him.

There was a brilliant, blinding flash that sprayed the snow with bloodred shadows.

I felt myself lifted, hurled, smashed to the ground. From the edge of my vision I saw Ferraday lifted and thrown down the mountain. I don't know what snapped the rope...perhaps it was the cutting edge of my pike that ripped it through as Ferraday went past...but I thank God he did not drag the rest of us with him.

Even as Ferraday crashed face-first into the ice, I heard the black-bearded Austrian bellow. Ferraday disappeared down the slope, the rope thrashing behind, the snow billowing out from him in a fine wedge of white. His scream was muffled, quickly buried beneath a ton of ice and snow as he helplessly plunged across a snow bridge. The bridge collapsed, and he plummeted three thousand feet, vanishing immediately into a rocky fault.

Deszlow and Rutledge stood transfixed, their pikes held at awkward angles, their faces — beneath the beards, glare glasses and masks — whiter than normal. Their eyes were large, and I was certain their mouths were open in horror.

I dragged myself to my to elbows and knees, spat a mouthful of blood and snow across the ice-pack, and tottered to my feet.

The little man was gone.

I sagged back against my pike, leaning, breathing, drawing breath from a suddenly-insufficient supply. "Ferra...Ferraday...he-he's gone...?"

Deszlow's huge square head bobbed confirmation, and Rutledge stared off across the jaggedly split snow bridge, where a gaping, sliding crevasse still poured snow atop the mangled body of our companion — three thousand feet below.

"We'd — we'd better go," Deszlow gasped. "The wind is rising. The *massif* will be hell in an hour."

We started out again, up the face of Annapurna, suddenly frightened of this expedition. We had known that death climbed with us, but not this way...not with this shroud of strangeness that hung over us.

Who...or what...had the little man been?

In the next hour Deszlow's words came true. The *massif*. It *was* a hell; but not of the kind we had imagined.

Unquestionably, it had been the presence of the little man — whose snow-filled tracks we occasionally observed coming down, as we climbed steadily up — that sharpened our senses enough to see it.

We had climbed for an hour, hoping to find a sheltering ledge before the storm broke on the mountain; we were just passing a series of small caves, intaglios in the face of the cliffs, when Rutledge signaled by dragging on the line.

We stopped; he was pointing; we looked.

Wedged in the rocks, shoved into a breach that was little more than a fissure, was a bright, shining sliver of metal, perhaps ten feet long; no question arose in our minds...the shape was totally familiar, from popularizations in newspapers and magazines. It was a spaceship.

There, 18,000 feet up on one of the highest mountains on earth, we had come upon a spaceship. We had no more than a moment to stare, for as we advanced toward it, sliding across the roll of the slope, a port opened, and a group of five figures, identical to the little man we had seen before, emerged.

They carried weapons. The equipment was so small, and so intricate, we had only a brief glimpse of delicate machine-work and involved mechanisms before they opened fire on us. Had we been unprepared, had we not been set alert by the presence of the first little man, we would have been dead at once.

But even as the same bloodred shadows illuminated the snow, and the beams of what had to be raw energy sizzled from their rifles, we were leaping aside. I jumped forward and to the right, clawing in the snow with hands and feet for some purchase. I caught the incredible heat of one beam over my left shoulder, and behind me I heard Rutledge scream as it tore through his face.

Then I felt a tug on the line, and knew he was down, he was dead. I was hauling a dead man behind me. There wasn't time to think about it; with an insane fury born of fear, I struggled to my knees, and brought my pike up over my head.

Deszlow was to my left, cowering in the snow as the bolts of energy smashed over him.

I brought down the pike.

It flattened two of the little men at once, and the other three ran, slipping, back to the ship.

I screamed something — I have no idea what — at Deszlow, and he flopped forward, grabbed at one end of the ship...and with all our strength we wrenched the ship free of the fissure.

I struggled forward again, losing my grip, then regaining it. I could see jet tubes of some strange sort, protruding from the rear, and from within I heard the beginning of what must have been a generator whine.

Together we lifted the ship, bumbled erect, and with a monstrous effort *threw* the ship as hard as we could, down the side of the mountain.

They tried to get the engines started; we saw a blast of flame leap from the aft section of the ship, but in a second it went out as the ship struck an outcropping of rock, and twisted grotesquely. Their drive was useless, and as we stared wildly, the ship bounced, crashed, careened down the slope. Before it plunged into the snow-mists ten thousand feet below, we saw the little sliver of metal shine much more brightly, and then with a flash and a roar, erupt in flame and a scatter of metal and flesh.

How bright it was against the killer snow.

Somehow, we got down, carrying Rutledge's body. His face was entirely gone, charred completely off. We never found enough of the ship to reconstruct even a small portion of it.

We do not know why they were there. I don't think we'll ever know. Whether they were invaders from another planet, or just visitors…is something we will never know. But we know this: the little man who first accosted us had been trying to warn us away, had been trying to get to us to tell us about his ship and his companions. And if they were *not* malevolent, if they were *not* here to try conquest of some sort, why had they knifed him? Why did they destroy him when he was so close to speaking to us? Why did they fire on us?

I don't suppose it will outlast the first real slide or storm up there. Deszlow and I climbed back up to the 18,000 foot mark; later. No one will ever see it, but we *had* to put up a cross for that tiniest of allies.

THE GODDESS IN THE ICE

Just before nightfall the storm caught them, 3500 feet up the *massif* of the glacier, far above the timberline but still four days' climb below the summit. As the wind rose, and below them they could hear the shock-crack of ice-formations shattering away from the glacier wall, they came upon the woman frozen in the ice.

Rennels was the first over the crevasse, and as he turned sidewise, bracing himself to make the towline taut, he looked across the ledge to the niche in the snow.

She was milky-white through the ice-block, but he had no doubt from the first that it was a woman, her eyes closed, hands at her sides, frozen solid into a silver-blue block of glacial ice.

He found himself unable to turn away. Even as he stared dumb-founded at an impossibility, he was accepting it — because it was undeniably before him — and racing through theories of quick-freezing, glacial upheavals, historical precedent that would account for this incredible find.

There was the shriek of an animal in the distance, and he came back from total involvement with the still figure in the ice to realize that Scotti and Kirth were yelling up through the rising wind at him.

Quickly, he wound the nylon line tighter about himself, looped it over an outcropping of rock that was deeply coated with ice, for a slippage-lever, and began pulling the towline heavily.

In a few minutes Scotti's florid face came up over the far edge of the ledge, and then the puffy body, and then he was standing across the crevasse, hauling up Kirth. When the two of them were on the ledge, Rennels motioned them to leap the crevasse.

And when they were all together, staring at the woman, finally, Scotti said something of awe and wonder. But the howling gale caught the words and threw them away into the deepening gloom.

Kirth drew their faces close to his, and shouted, "We can't stay on this ledge! The storm! It'll blow us off! Find some shelter."

They split up and followed the ledge around the face of the *massif*, and Rennels found a deep cave that ran back for perhaps seventy feet. They met again in front of the woman and he told them. But strangely, none of them moved for the shelter. Instead, they each unshipped an icepick and began hacking at the ice that enclosed the woman.

Finally, they chipped out a block of ice six feet high and, pushing and shoving, worked it around the ledge and into the cave.

Kirth lit the survival lamps from his pack and Scotti hung a tarp across the mouth of the cave. Rennels set up the portable heater, and in the shadowy interior of the glacier they settled down, all of them.

Scotti. Kirth. Rennels...and the woman.

All but one of the lamps had been extinguished. Shadows lay like broken bodies across the rough walls. Scotti was slugged down deeply in his thermal sleeping-bag, apparently asleep. Kirth sat with his back to the wall, pulling on a cup of black coffee.

Rennels was hidden in the darkness.

He was watching the woman.

The ice had thawed slightly, and now she could be seen clearly.

Rennels was hypnotized by her beauty.

The single garment she wore resembled a light yellow *chiton*; it draped across her breasts, exposing one shoulder and an exquisitely-formed arm. It fell in pleats to her feet. It was almost Roman in design, but Rennels had had his degree in archaeology, and he recognized it as Phoenician. There was no way of unraveling the mystery of how a Phoenician woman had come to be frozen in a glacier somewhere near the top of the world.

But it was not that mystery that held him.

It was her face.

The features were indescribably beautiful. The body would have made Helen of Troy jealous.

Rennels stared without blinking.

And in the corner, Scotti watched, from his sleeping-bag, feigning sleep. And Kirth watched, breathing deeply.

But it was to Rennels that the vision came first.

As he studied her in the ice, everything seemed to grow gray and distant, and he was somehow separating from his body, standing and looking down at himself there in the shadows. Then he turned, and went toward the ice-block, into and through it.

And the woman was waiting for him.

She opened her eyes, which were green and deep and seemed to swirl with a languid smoke of sensuality. She raised her arms to him, and the *chiton* pulled tightly across her breasts. Rennels came to her, and she touched him lightly on the side of the face.

It was a touch of the wind.

"Who are you?" he asked, with wonder.

"Ilira," she said. Her voice was not sound, but something deeper, more omnipresent, entering his mind and expanding, filling him with a sense of her being.

"How —"

"How did I come here?"

He nodded. She smiled a soft, sad smile. And he saw that she had a charming overbite that just faintly pressed the full roundness of her lower lip.

"The Priests of the temple. I was found to be blasphemous in my worships. I was a Goddess of the temple. So they condemned me to eternal sleep in the ice lands. But now you've come to me."

It seemed all so right, so simple, so direct. He had freed her, and now she was his. He moved closer to her, and she slipped her cool arms about his neck, drawing his face to hers. Around them the mist grew up and flooded the world, covering them in a soft gray blanket.

He could feel the length of her, down his body, and he realized with an electric shock that he was about to make love to a woman whose race had died thousands of years before…a woman who must be part witch…a woman whose lovemaking would be informed by the strange practices and passions of a pagan world.

But she did not give him time to wonder.

Her sleep in the ice might have been a second, or an eternity, so starved for his body did she seem.

Rennels came back to himself lying on the stone floor. He had fainted. Had it been a dream? Some kind of snow vision that days up here had induced? No, there was a languor in his body that he knew was real. And yet a hunger, greater than any he had ever known.

And a message:

The other two will want me. If you want me, you will have to win me, free me, to have me.

In his sleeping-bag, Scotti was just coming awake, his breath ragged in his throat. On the far side of the cave Kirth was wedged into the rocks, his eyes glazed.

Each had had the dream. Each had enjoyed the favors of the Goddess.

Rennels paused only a second as the knowledge flooded in on him — that both Kirth and Scotti had known her body — and he lunged for his icepick…

Suddenly, each of them had a weapon.

Kirth with the skinning knife, Scotti with a piton, and Rennels swinging the icepick with such violence that he caught Scotti rising from the sleeping-bag and imbedded the point in his left temple. Scotti screamed with pain and died as Kirth panicked and tried to escape from the mad slashings and whirlings of Rennels's weapon. He plunged toward the mouth of the cave, smacked against the block of ice with the woman still asleep in its center, and caromed off, entangling himself in the tarpaulin that kept out the storm.

Rennels lurched forward and sank the icepick in his back, but Kirth did not die. He fumbled around the tarp and stood on the ledge, the night wind screaming curses at him.

Rennels threw aside the tarp and hurled himself at the wounded man. Kirth was rocked by the assault and with a flailing of arms and legs plunged face-forward off the ledge, his terrifying scream mingling and then disappearing into the blinding snow and the night.

Rennels stood alone on the ledge, hearing the crashing, rolling sound of thunder that was Kirth plunging to his doom. Then he went back inside. To Ilira.

He stood silently, watching her sleep, for a very long time. Then he began chipping away the ice-block carefully.

Toward morning she was divested of her ice garment, and as the relative warmth of the cave reached her, Rennels witnessed the miracle of the woman's rebirth.

For thousands of years she had been a prisoner of the ice, put there by the Phoenician wizards who had known the dark arts of Lemuria and Mu and Atlantis, of Stygia and Egypt before it was Egypt.

And as Rennels stood waiting, she came awake, her eyes opening with almond-shaped beauty to see him as he now was.

Then she came to him and enfolded him.

In an instant, it was reality for Rennels again. The scent and sense of her overpowering him. But he had only that one last moment of sensual delight to ponder, for in the next instant Ilira was standing alone as the shower of pale silver sand that had been Rennels sifted down over her arms and dusted the stone floor of the cave.

Then she turned and went out into the night.

Ten thousand years before, they had stopped her, the Priests who had known what she was. But now was another time, a later time, and she would complete her destiny. It did not matter what governments or cultures ruled the world. Ilira would subjugate them to her will.

For her weapon was herself. And there was no man born of man-and-woman who could say no to the terrors and passions of her body.

She disappeared into the storm. The storm that inexplicably blew around and over her, but did not touch her.

In the cave, the pale silver sands tossed and roiled and finally were dispersed, leaving behind nothing.

GOPHER IN THE GILLY
A Reminiscence of the Carnival

Stand behind the tent flap and look at their faces.

You will learn all you'll ever need to know about the darker side of human nature.

(The Depression leached all joy from the people. Show biz called with its cheap wares, its momentary diversions. The movies did it. Cheap, took you away, and gave you memories to savor later. Carnivals were big. They circled the country. Cheap, gaudy thrills. Today, no self-respecting carnival will carry a freak bally — a sideshow of malforms and sports. It's ugly business. Cheap. But in those days, those cheap, ugly days of the Thirties, something was needed to pull in the rubes and the yokels and the kadodies. The freak top. Hurry, hurry, slide right in there, friend, and drag your lady with you, for the most exhilarating, most startling, most unbelievable sights that've ever graced your eyes. See Lena, the fattest woman in the world, four hundred pounds of quivering jelly...Lucifer, with a throat of asbestos and a stomach of steel, see him eat fire, chew nails, drink coal oil, wouldn't it be nice to have *him* in your living room on a cold Kansas night...Rippo, the fish-boy: where you and I have arms and legs, Rippo has only gills and flippers...see and marvel...see the thing without a name, neither man nor beast, a creature out of bad dreams, he eats snakes, he bites the heads off chickens, ladies, I cannot even describe in public the degradation in which this creature exists...but step up, step inside, see for yourself...see the largest gathering of freaks and marvels ever offered under one big top...)

Stand behind the tent flap and look at their faces.

You will learn all you'll ever need to know about the darker side of human nature.

(Ask any man of forty or fifty, who worked in a carny as a little boy. Ask him if he ever stood behind the flap of the freak top and watched — not the freaks, oh no, not those poor miserable things — ask him if he ever watched the faces of the *people*. The good people, the solid rural folk with their lives and their morals sunk deep in the Judeo-Christian Ethos. Ask that little boy, now grown to a man, and he will be reluctant to tell you what he saw. But press him nonetheless, and he will tell you of the expressions on the faces of the men as they watched the swaying milk udders of Lena, as they contemplated the sexual wonders implicit in the plastic body of the snake girl. But he will never tell you of the licked lips and bright eyes of the women as they passed and lingered to observe the pre-thalidomide monstrosity called the fish-boy, as they let their gaze wander over his barely concealed private parts, as they wondered — nakedly obvious in their rapturous stares — what it would be like to have those flippers touch their bodies, what it would be like to make love to something like that. The little boy will never tell the horror of fascination in the faces of a freak audience, of the women who wanted to couple with the geek, redolent in his own filth, of the men who trembled at the sight of the hermaphrodite; half-man, half-woman, how would one seduce such a thing? Once having stood behind the flap, once having seen the unmasked faces of the secret dreamers, one need never again ask how did the slaughter at My Lai come to be; one need never again wonder what it is in the American character that produces Richard Speck or Charles Manson or Charles Starkweather or Susan Atkins. One need never ask, for it is there in all of us, lying close to the surface of all of us who make up the great freak top audience. The

Depression is gone, but the rural rubes are still with us, are still part of all of us. We still need our freaks. Without compassion, without sympathy, without love...with merely lust and fascination and repugnance that attracts more than it repels...we all come to the big show and lick our lips.)

I was thirteen years old. Never mind why I ran away from home, that's another story for another time. I did it; the dream of every middle-American boy in the early 1940s; to run away and join the circus. I had read *Toby Tyler, or Ten Weeks with a Circus,* and there was nothing more fascinating, nothing more swashbuckling, nothing more adventurous than to run off and join a circus.

I never found a circus. But I found the ragbag carny those in the circuit called a "gilly." The hit-and-run hundred-mile burn-the-lot operation that figure-eighted across Ohio, Indiana, Illinois, and Missouri, looping back through Kentucky to start its pattern all over again. Tri-States Shows it called itself, but you'd never find it listed in *Amusement Business.* It was a pure grifter's carny, carrying a sorry menagerie, an ugly freak top, and more hanky-panks than I've seen at even the grungiest down-at-the-heels county fairs.

What did I do? I was a gopher.

"Hey, kid, go fer some coffee."

"Hey, kid, go fer some canvas."

"Hey, kid, go fer that spieler, Sam."

Furless, beardless, clawless, I was a gopher.

I was a honeydipper in the hyena cage, I was a shill for the hanky-panks, I was a lookout for the laws, I was a water boy for the girls working the kootch bally, I was a swamper in the cookhouse. I was three months' worth of scut, and didn't know how crooked the whole operation was, till we got busted in Kansas City, Missouri.

The show had moll dips, it had cannons, it had boosters and paperhangers, it had everything but a square deal for the marks who frequented the flat stores on the midway and came away lucky to have their shoe soles.

One of the cannons tried to whomp a guy for his wallet in K.C.

Turned out the guy was an assistant D.A., fifteen years on the Force, and he threw the muscle halfway across that time zone. The entire carny wound up in the K.C. slammer.

Pretty quick, everyone was sprung. The "management" couldn't afford to have its crew locked up for very long: first, because there were dates that had to be played in towns down the line, and second, because there were enough complaints and warrants out on that show to send *everyone* away till the next Ice Age.

With two important exceptions.

The first was the geek. The second was me.

Anyone unfamiliar with the term "geek" should seek out and read William Lindsay Gresham's now-classic 1946 novel, *Nightmare Alley*, for the most chillingly accurate description ever set in type. A geek is usually a wetbrain; that is, a young or old man so far gone into alcoholism that his brain has turned to sponge. When he sweats, he sweats sour mash. A gilly locates a skid in whatever town it's in, and carries him to the next stop, and as many stops as it can get out of him before he either dies or wanders off. For the splendid honorarium of a bottle of gin or two a day, the skid will dress in an animal skin, go without shaving, sleep in a cage, and on cue wallow in his own shit, eat dead snakes, bite the heads off live chickens. No reputable carny will carry a geek. It is a terrible thing. It plays to the basest hungers and most primal fears in the human repertory. Anyone who could derive enjoyment from watching a debased creature, seemingly only half human, scuttling across the floor of a foul, stinking pit or pen, smearing itself with feces, rubbing its privates on the gnawed skin of a dead rattlesnake, moaning and rolling its eyes as it devolved before one's eyes, reverting to a stage of subhuman existence not even Cro-Magnons knew…such a person is beneath contempt, lower even than the poor bastard in that cage.

I have seen hordes of rural goodfolk, pillars of their communities, churchgoing Christians and advocates of the Protestant Work Ethic, who devoutly enjoyed watching a geek. Stand behind the tent flap. Watch. You'll learn more about human nature than you ever wished to know.

The geek and I were thrown in the drunk tank, a holding pen, together. *He* wasn't sprung because he wasn't really "carny," he was a pickup, and there were skids all along the road, so why spend hard cash on a slob so beneath notice that he couldn't even be thought of as human. *I* wasn't sprung because I wouldn't give the cops my real name; I didn't want to go home.

So the gilly took off, minus their geek, minus their gopher.

I spent three days in the K.C. slammer with that old man, that subhuman geek.

I'll bet a month hasn't gone by since 1947, in that cage in Kansas City, that I haven't thought of that old drunk.

Three days we were locked together. The hacks, the guards who shepherded us, even they didn't want to get near us. The smell and look of that geek made them want to puke. They used to slide our food through the bars on the floor, at the end of a pushbroom. I was scared, and ill.

Because they wouldn't give him anything to drink and he started having convulsions. He whimpered all through the night, and in the mornings his face was bloody and his lips bitten clean through. Along about the second day he went crazy from delirium tremens, and he climbed the bars of the free-standing cage where we were penned, and he began smashing his face against the metal ceiling. He fell and screamed, and lay on his back on the metal floor, moving his legs and arms idly like a turtle on its shell. His face looked like a pound of raw hamburger. And he smelled. A special smell. Not just his pants full of shit, and his clothes stinking from the dirt of his carny pen and garbage; he was sweating sour alcohol. A special smell. I've never forgotten it. I can't describe it to you...it smelled like such and such...there is nothing to compare. A million dead bodies turned up in a communal grave, maybe. But I've never forgotten that smell.

I don't drink. I have never drunk.

Finally, on the third day, they took me out. They had to. The Pinkerton Agency men my family had hired to find me had contacted the K.C. police. There had been missing persons flyers sent out on me, dodgers they were called; and someone in K.C. had matched a flyer with my description, even though I wouldn't tell them my real name or where I was from. And the Pinkertons sent an operative and he came and took me back on the train to Ohio.

I had spent three months with the carny.

And there was very little of romance or adventure or swashbuckling about it. All I came away with was the smell of rotten liquor sweated out through gray, dead skin...an even greater hatred of cops than I'd had to begin with...and the cynical, deadening, utterly inescapable knowledge that if one stands behind the tent flap and watches, one learns more about the darker side of human nature than any kid should ever know.